Herod the Great

Michael Grant

HEROD
THE GREAT

Weidenfeld & Nicolson
5 Winsley Street London W1

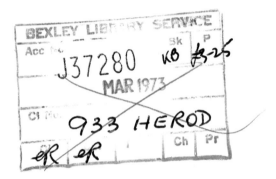

© Michael Grant Publications Ltd, 1971

ISBN 0 297 00393 3

Designed by Alan Bartram

Filmset by Keyspools Ltd, Golborne, Lancashire
Printed by C. Tinling & Co. Ltd, Prescot and London

Contents

List of maps
Acknowledgments
Sources of Illustrations
Introduction   11

I THE RISE OF HEROD
 1 Herod's background: Jews and Arabs   18
 2 Herod the King   37
 3 Herod takes over his kingdom   53
 4 Herod and the Jews   61
 5 Herod, Antony and Cleopatra   77

II HEROD'S GREATER JUDAEA
 6 Success with Augustus: tragedies at home   90
 7 Jews and non-Jews   106
 8 Generosity and splendour   121
 9 Expansion beyond the Jordan   137
10 The Temple   150
11 How Herod paid for it all   165
12 Marcus Agrippa and the Jews outside Judaea   175

III ANTI-CLIMAX
13 Changed plans for the succession   184
14 The second Arab war   189
15 The downfall of Herod's sons   195
16 Repression of the Jews: the last days of Herod   204

IV SUMMING UP
17 The aftermath   216
18 The achievement of Herod   225
19 Sources of information   235

Notes   240
Maps   250
Chronological table   259
Genealogical tables   262
Further reading   265
Index   267

Maps

1 The physical features of Judaea   250

2 Modern Israel showing frontiers before 1967 and
  territory occupied in 1967   251

3 The kingdoms of Israel (*c.* 937–721 BC) and Judah
  (*c.* 937–597 BC)   251

4 Judaea under the Hasmonaeans (Maccabees)   252

5 Judaea after Pompey's settlement (63 BC)   252

6 Rome's Syrian frontier and beyond in the time of Herod
  the Great   253

7 Judaea in the reign of Herod the Great   254

8 Israel in the reign of Solomon   255

9 Jerusalem   256

10 Herod's Temple at Jerusalem   257

11 Italy, Greece and Asia Minor   257

12 Judaea under Herod's sons   258

Acknowledgments

Acknowledgments are owed to the following for permission to quote: Cambridge and Oxford University Presses, the New English Bible; The Clarendon Press, Oxford, A. H. M. Jones, *The Herods of Judaea*; Hodder and Stoughton, London, and the Abingdon Press, Nashville, Tennessee, Stewart Perowne, *The Life and Times of Herod the Great*; The Loeb Classical Library, Josephus, trans. R. Marcus, *Jewish Antiquities*; John Murray, Lord Byron, *Herod's Lament for Mariamme*; Dr Conor Cruise O'Brien, *King Herod Explains*; Penguin Books, Josephus, trans. G. A. Williamson, *The Jewish War*.

Sources of Illustrations

Alinari, 163; Bibliothèque Nationale, 29, 209, 218; W. Braun, 112; British Museum, 40, 43, 47, 51, 57, 59, 71, 78, 84b and c, 96, 138, 146, 152, 155b, 158, 162, 178, 194, 197, 198, 201b and c, 205, 216, 220; Courtauld Institute of Art, 239; J. Freeman, 40, 43, 47, 51, 57, 59, 71, 78, 84b and c, 96, 138, 146, 152, 155b, 158, 162, 178, 194, 197, 198, 201b and c, 205, 216, 220; German Archaeological Institute, Rome, 176; Gimpel Fils, 140a and b, 141; Michael Grant, 26, 28, 84a, 143, 175, 192; David Harris, 10, 27, 32, 42, 67, 68, 70, 100, 102, 108, 110, 111, 113, 124, 159, 160, 168, 169, 213; Holyland Hotel, Jerusalem, 126, 128; Iranian Tourist Office, 55, 56; Israel Department of Antiquities and Museums, 27, 39, 65, 69, 70, 72, 150, 157, 165, 171, 172, 179, 201a, 207, 223; Israel Government Tourist Office, 22, 53, 63, 129, 134; Jordan Ministry of Tourism and Antiquities, 25, 139, 193a, 208; Mansell Collection, 229, 230; Middle East Archive, 15, 19, 58, 79, 107, 109, 132, 151, 155a, 156, 161, 219; Museo di S. Marco, Florence, 227; Museo di S. Stefano, Bologna, 226; Museum of Fine Arts, Boston, 91; National Parks Authority, Tel-Aviv, 193b; Palazzo dei Conservatori, Rome, 35; Paul Popper, 153, 196; Zev Radovan, 172; Rockefeller Museum, 177; Scala, frontispiece, 217, 225, 226, 227, 228, 233; Ronald Sheridan, 37, 74, 75, 119, 131, 154, 177; Staatsbibliothek, Berlin, 45; Uffizi, Florence, frontispiece; Vienna Kunsthistorisches Museum, endpaper; Yaacov Yannai, 24, 87, 190; Yigael Yadin, 93, 94, 133, 135, 136.

Frontispiece: The myth of Herod's Massacre of the Innocents at Bethlehem, to kill the future King of the Jews. By Lodovico Mazzolino of Ferrara (*c.* 1480–1528). Uffizi Gallery, Florence.

Endpaper: Massacre of the Innocents by Pieter Brueghel (*c.* 1530–69). Kunsthistorisches Museum, Vienna.

Introduction

The career of Herod, known as the Great, is an astonishing record of public adventures and successes, and of private melodramas and disasters. Yet it is difficult to think of any other man of the same degree of significance who is so little known outside specialist circles, and who is the subject of so many misunderstandings and confusions. This is partly because he stands at the confluence of the Jewish and Graeco-Roman civilisations, in a no-man's-land of cultural territory where it would be rash for any student to believe that he can tread with confidence. For Herod reached the height of his fame and power in the last part of the first century BC, when Augustus was on the imperial throne. Augustus had put an end to decades of disturbance and civil war throughout the vast Roman world, and then he overhauled and reorganised the entire complex machinery by which the empire was governed. He also re-drew and strengthened its long frontiers. But in these remote frontier areas he retained a special feature from his predecessors of the last years of the Republic, men such as Pompey and Caesar and Mark Antony. The empire, as a whole, consisted of Roman provinces under the control of Roman governors, but beyond the actual frontiers themselves there were also native kings who enjoyed the confidence of Rome and governed their territories as Roman 'clients', enjoying internal independence in return for loyal collaboration with imperial policy. Some of these client monarchs were men of remarkable gifts, and perhaps the most remarkable of all was Herod the Great. When Mark Antony had ruled the eastern Roman world, Herod was one of his most loyal collaborators, and after Octavian (the future Augustus) had defeated and superseded Antony, Herod was retained. His dominion was Judaea.

Looked at, then, with an imperial Roman eye, Herod is a peripheral figure; useful no doubt, indeed indispensable – and for a long time a model of what these dependent rulers ought to be – but none the less peripheral. To us, however, who derive so much of our tradition not only from Rome and Athens but also from Israel, he is by no means peripheral: he ruled at Jerusalem itself, the very centre of that other world. He and his career are therefore of fundamental importance to Jews and Christians alike. In his lifetime, and under his rule, Jewry developed apace, in ways and

Opposite: Qumran near the Dead Sea, site of the discovery of many scrolls which belonged to the monastic community of a Jewish sect.

directions that have often escaped notice owing to misconceptions about the policies of Herod himself. And the time when he reigned was precisely that most formative of all times for Christians, the era immediately preceding the birth of Jesus Christ himself. Indeed, it appears very likely that Herod was still alive at the time when Jesus was born. According to one of the most durable of all the world's stories, Herod learnt of his birth through wise men from the east who said that a King of the Jews had been born in Bethlehem. 'Then Herod, when he saw that he was mocked of the wise men, was exceeding wroth, and sent forth, and slew all the children that were in Bethlehem, and in all the coasts thereof, from two years old and under, according to the time which he had diligently enquired of the wise men' (Gospel according to Matthew, 1, 16).

The Massacre of the Innocents is all that most people have ever heard about Herod the Great, and the persistence of the story is demonstrated by a number of European works of art that are illustrated in this volume. As will become clear, however, when we come to this last phase of Herod's long life, the tale is not history but myth or folk-lore: a portentous symbol of the grip which one man's formidable personality exerted upon the imagination of his contemporaries.

And there were, and are, other sagas and legends about Herod. They are imaginative structures from which it is our duty to disentangle such historical realities as are recoverable. This, it is true, can only be attempted with a good deal of diffidence. It is painfully hard to find out anything at all for certain about people who lived two thousand years ago – especially if they were controversial figures. For one thing, the 'facts' about their lives were presented selectively, that is to say deceptively, in the first place; secondly, their survival down to our own times has been subject to another series of selective hazards. Thirdly, we ourselves, seeking to pull this material into shape, cannot avoid – however hard we try – imposing yet another dose of selectivity, that is to say introducing further mythical elements. Nevertheless, the attempt must be made. And for Herod the task is extremely well worth tackling, since he was such an extraordinary man, replete with features of perennial interest and relevance.

After Matthew's narration of the Massacre of the Innocents, the New Testament writers continue to pose problems for his biographers by choosing to employ the bare name of 'Herod' for three different men, one of whom was not, in fact, called Herod at all. As for the man who is the subject of this book, we find that his entire life-story, which had mostly run its course by the time Jesus was born, is dismissed in favour of the single folk-tale of the Massacre. Inevitably, this concentration on so grim a tale has done a good deal to ensure that Christians have not found Herod a suitable subject for study.

This tendency has been confirmed by Jewish disapproval not

only of Herod but of the writer of his surviving ancient biography. This was Josephus, about whom the salient facts are given at the end of this book. Here all that need be said is that he was a Jew, but that when, seventy years after Herod's death, the Jews rose against the Romans, he judged the Jewish cause to be hopeless, and after he had been captured by the Romans changed sides and became their open supporter. Naturally this career does not appeal to modern Jews and Israelis. Nor, incidentally, did it commend itself to the character-building natures of British educationalists of the nineteenth and early twentieth century. And they were further deterred by the sort of Greek he wrote – not at all the pure classical Attic which alone was considered suitable for study. Yet his abandonment was unfortunate, since whatever the flaws of his character or style he remains a very important writer.

The eclipse of Josephus has naturally exercised an adverse and cramping effect on modern investigations concerning Herod. Besides, Herod seems another collaborator — he too collaborated with Rome. However, the real problem raised by the career of Herod should be framed in rather different terms: how is it possible for a small country to reconcile its own special, peculiar way of life with a sufficient degree of conformity to the requirements of a super-power?

Herod's ambition was to keep the Jews intact and prosperous, in their own country, without losing the cooperation and protection of the Roman empire. He devoted his life to the task, and since he was a man of extraordinary gifts his achievement was greater than could have been reasonably expected of any man. However, to judge by the two frightful and catastrophic Jewish rebellions which occurred within a hundred and fifty years after his death – the rebellions that Jews call the First and Second Roman Wars – the task to which Herod addressed himself proved, in fact, an impossible one. This was mainly because of the mistakes made on both sides after he was dead. Roman emperors, as often as not, supported the Jews of the Dispersion, outside Palestine, against the violently anti-Semitic Greeks and easterners of Egypt, Syria and Asia Minor. But in Palestine Roman relations with the Jews, owing to total mutual incomprehension, soon lapsed into a failure Rome experienced nowhere else, a failure resembling in some respects the long history of unsuccessful relations between England and Ireland.

In order to achieve and maintain the equilibrium with which to prevent such disasters, Herod had to walk, for forty years, the most precarious of political tight-ropes. He had to be enough of a Jew to retain control of his Jewish subjects, and yet pro-Roman enough to preserve the confidence of Rome. Moreover, since his kingdom was in the eastern, Hellenised part of the Roman world, he had in effect to be (and longed to be) a Graecophile, in order to impress his numerous non-Jewish subjects and neighbours.

And even if it proved beyond his powers – was it perhaps beyond anyone's powers? – to solve his ultimate, long-term national problem, it is hard to blame anyone with assurance for events that take place a number of generations after he is dead. While he lived, he did very great things for Romans, Greeks and Jews alike. To the Romans he was the most loyal of dependent allies. For the Greeks and others he was a benefactor and builder of public works on a scale scarcely precedented in the area. The Jews in other parts of the Roman empire gratefully remembered him long after his death, and for all Jewry he built a Temple at Jerusalem which out-did Solomon's. He spent gigantic sums of money. And yet such was his efficiency that, without an extortionate system of taxation, he left the country rich.

Nevertheless, the Jews in the country never really regarded him as a Jew. They never let him forget that his forebears, only a short time back (herein resembling the people of Galilee), had not been Jews at all. And one may suspect that the Greeks, too, could never quite feel, in spite of the insistence of a loyal historian (Nicolaus) who gave him private lessons, that his Greek culture rang alto-gether true.

As for his Roman senior partners and overlords, they were successively Mark Antony and Augustus. Antony, in spite of his association with Cleopatra, was convinced that the policy of the western great power required a Jewish-Palestinian as well as an Egyptian state; and so he never allowed the queen of Egypt, in spite of an embarrassing amount of insistence on her part, to obliterate Herod's country – although he did feel obliged to truncate it for her benefit. One of the most remarkable meetings in history must have been Cleopatra's visit to Herod at Jerusalem in 34 BC. He told the rather unlikely story afterwards that she had tried to make love to him. And he went on to say that he had thought of having her murdered, but then decided he had better not. So she survived – though not for nearly as long as he did.

For when she and Antony succumbed to Octavian, the future Augustus, Herod achieved one of the many diplomatic successes of his career by transferring his allegiance, to the complete satis-faction of the victor. Thereafter, for many years, he was one of the chief bulwarks of Augustus' empire in the east. His frontiers – which were in a sense the frontiers of Rome, for the defence of these was one of the functions of a 'client' monarch – extended to Gaza and the Golan Heights and beyond, and included a strip of land across the Jordan nearly as far as the modern Amman. But to the south his kingdom stopped well short of Elat and Akaba and the Red Sea. And indeed, in spite of his own Arab blood, he never ceased to have strained relations with the Arab state controlling that area, a state which, like his own, was a dependant of Rome, but which Herod always hoped to reduce to dependence upon himself.

Herod the Great's kingdom of Judaea: one of its more barren regions.

Herod was a man of contrasts; the conflict between Jewishness and pro-Roman Hellenism was only one of them. Another was the strong contradiction in his temperament and career between enlightened, civilised rationalism and passionate, murderous savagery. It was because of this latter quality that the story of the Massacre of the Innocents came into existence; though that is only one of many legends, some diabolical, others half affectionate, which gathered round his subtle, violent personality. It was the brutality of his private life which finally surprised and sickened even the granitic Augustus. Perhaps Herod had lived too hard. Certainly he had indulged in too many wives and children; his matrimonial history is a strong argument against polygamy. And in the last ten years he failed to maintain balanced control over their intrigues, and consequently lost his command of events.

The troubled waters of the reign, which, until then, Herod had succeeded in pacifying to a remarkable extent, contain many cross-currents of absorbing importance. His policy of 'divide and rule', for example, owed a great deal of its success to the highly divisive nature of contemporary Jewry, about which new, though cryptic, information is constantly reaching us from the scrolls found at

Qumran beside the Dead Sea. The death of Herod and the birth of Jesus took place almost at the same time (some say in the very same year) and already for a long time strong Messianic hopes had been gaining widespread belief; though Herod's own view was that, if any Messiah existed, it was himself. Contrary to what is generally asserted, he formed and cherished a considerable number of influential Jewish supporters, and also had the passive backing of a good many other non-objectors. But towards the end of his reign the opposition increased, and was voiced not only by leading Pharisees, of the more radical type, but also by militant student demonstrators egged on by their professors.

The reason why Herod was called 'the Great' will be examined at the end of the book. The title came to him by accident. But now that he has it, does he deserve it? It was difficult, in the world of the first century BC, for anyone who was not either a leading Roman or Parthian – a leading figure, that is to say, of the western great power, or its eastern rival – to achieve any substantial status in affairs. With the possible exception of Cleopatra, Herod came much nearer to doing so than any other non-Roman, non-Parthian, of the age. At any rate he was a figure rising far above nearly all his contemporaries by the force and versatility of his talents. Within the Roman cosmopolis, he made Judaea a large, peaceful and extremely prosperous kingdom. And if, in spite of everything, he proved unable to save Judaea and Judaism from the holocausts which were to come, they still lay quite a long way in the future when he died, and he had brought the full force of his brilliant personality to bear on the task of doing all that could be done to avert them.

I am very grateful to Miss Susan Phillpott of Messrs Weidenfeld and Nicolson Ltd for editing this book. I also want to thank Mrs Sally Curtis for a number of suggestions, Mr Claus Henning for drawing the maps, Mrs Colleen Chesterman for collecting the illustrations, and Mr Stewart Perowne for finding and giving me a copy of his book *The Life and Times of Herod the Great*.

MICHAEL GRANT
Gattaiola, 1971

16

I

THE RISE
OF HEROD

Herod's background: Jews and Arabs

I When Herod first attracted notice, he was a young man of twenty-five.[1] It was 47 BC, and for two years the vast Roman empire, after decades of internal disturbances, had been plunged into the horrors of widespread civil war. In 48 Pompey, defeated by Caesar, had been murdered by Egyptian leaders. When Caesar subsequently got entangled in an unpleasant little Egyptian campaign, Herod's father Antipater, the chief minister of the Jewish principality of Judaea, had been able to provide him with useful help. As a result, when Caesar again proved victorious, the position of Herod's family was strengthened, and he himself emerged with an important post. For he was made military commander and governor of Galilee, the northernmost territory of the small Jewish state just as Galil is today.

The mid-first century BC, for all its troubles, was one of the most fertile epochs in the history of human civilisation. At Rome, in spite of political and military convulsions, it was a Golden Age of writers: Caesar himself, Cicero, Lucretius, Catullus and Virgil, who was a few years younger than Herod. Moreover, Herod's con-temporaries included Jews of great eminence, notably two of the greatest of all Jewish thinkers, Hillel and Shammai, of whom we shall hear more before long. As for Judaea's northern province of Galilee, it was a tiny but attractive and prosperous piece of territory, full of individualistic people. More will be said of them in Chapter 2. At this stage all that need be mentioned is that the country had been in alien hands until two generations previously; and that its past history was somewhat dim. At all events, it was dim in comparison with its future, for this was to be the land of Christ's childhood, and then the chief centre of his ministry.

When Herod arrived, however, these events lay more than half a century ahead. Galilee, to him, was a small region in a highly disorderly condition: a not unusual situation since these hillmen were notoriously unresponsive to authority, and especially to any authority set up by Jerusalem, which was separated from them by only a trifling geographical distance but by a considerable gulf of mutual suspicion. And Herod himself did not even come from a place so relatively close as Jerusalem: the place of his origin was a good deal more distant and alien than that. For he came from Idumaea, which formed the southern extremity of the Judaean state. Idumaea and Galilee had nothing in common except that each had only quite recently become Jewish, and the Jews despised them both; and there is no reason to suppose that the Galileans – as regionally minded and parochial as everyone else in the country – welcomed his arrival. Certainly, some of them very soon actively regretted it, for he immediately began wiping up dissident elements with a blend of efficiency, speed and brutality which gave promise of what was to come.

We do not know what Herod looked like because, as we shall

Sunrise over the hillsides of Judaea.

have occasion to see elsewhere, a strict interpretation of the Second Commandment, forbidding graven images, made it impossible for his statue to be sculpted on Jewish territory, or for Jewish coins to display his head. Statues were erected to him in non-Jewish areas, but unfortunately none of them has survived. All we know about his appearance, on the authority of one of his sons, is that in later years he dyed his hair. But we have a description of him from Josephus, our principal authority for the reign, which suggests that he was a formidable figure of a man. A pinch of salt may be added, because, as we shall see, Josephus probably derived the account from a royal minister and friend, Nicolaus of Damascus, but all the same there must have been a lot of truth in his assertion that Herod possessed every possible bodily and mental advantage.[2]

He was clever, he was tough, and, as Josephus goes on to say, he possessed that quality of good luck which the ancients so firmly associated with leadership. Nevertheless it was still a remarkable thing that in this particularist, traditionalist little country of Judaea a man from the imperfectly Judaised southern fringes should, at the early age of twenty-five, have found himself in sole charge of the northern frontier province. For an explanation of how this came about, one must look at the tangled developments of the previous years which had brought Herod's grandfather and father, and then himself, into positions of influence and power.

Idumaea, the homeland of Herod, was the district south of Jerusalem and Bethlehem. It was based on the town of Hebron, near the south-eastern edge of the central Palestinian mountain range, from which it descends by broad undulations into the semi-desert regions. Nowadays, Hebron is in the southern bulge of Yehuda, in that large segment of territory on the west bank of the Jordan which was occupied by the Israelis in the 1967 war.

The Idumaeans were the descendants of the Old Testament Edomites. But Edom had not stretched nearly so far north as Hebron, extending, instead, much further to the south, into the towering inhospitable heights of Negev and Sinai. In the sixth century BC, however, the people of Edom were displaced from these southern lands by the Arabs. But at the same time they profited by the downfall of the kingdom of Judah at the hands of Babylon (and the consequent exile and dispersion of many Jews), for these events enabled the Edomites to extend their occupation as far north as Hebron, less than twenty miles south of Jerusalem. And there, even after the subsequent cession of a few towns to returning Jews, they stayed, and the territory in which they had settled became known as Idumaea.

The Edomites, it was said, had egged on the Babylonian destroyers of Jerusalem with malicious glee; in any case the Jews always hated them.[3] Indeed, the hatred had been a good deal more ancient even than that, for the men of Edom were reported to have refused Moses himself a passage through their land.[4] The writer of *Deuteronomy* (? seventh century BC) appealed to the Jewish people not to hold the Edomites in abomination, for they were brothers – pagans, it is true, yet fellow-descendants from Abraham, speaking a Semitic language that was related to Hebrew just as it was related to Arabic. But the fact that the plea had to be made, and stressed, shows how badly it was needed: the lack of sympathy between the two peoples was very marked, and became, if anything, even stronger after they had expanded in a northerly direction. Excavations at the Idumaean fortress at Marissa (Maresha) show that foreign influences, coming from the Phoenician trading ports – in what is now Lebanese territory – were potent during the third century BC.[5] At that time Judaea was still an appendage of an alien empire, the Syrian-based Seleucid state, ruled by the descendants of Alexander the Great's general Seleucus. But soon it became an independent state once again, under Judas Maccabaeus the Hasmonaean (166–60 BC)[6] and his patriotic brothers, whose overthrow of the hated Seleucid yoke was one of the most stirring events in Jewish history. And then Judas' war-like nephew John Hyrcanus I (134–104 BC) forcibly converted the Idumaeans to Judaism, and ordered them to be circumcised.

Theoretically, this admitted them within authentic Jewry. Its exclusiveness was continually insisted upon. 'The Lord', declared the Psalmist, 'has chosen Jacob to be his own, and Israel as his special treasure'.[7] This was the special vocation of chosen, holy apartness which led the Jews to a flat denial that the gods of their neighbours had any existence at all; and the denial was supported by a correspondingly firm resolve to defend this separateness with the utmost jealousy. And so in about 100 BC it was still being declared that 'the lawgiver fenced us about with impregnable palisades and walls of iron, so that we should in no way have dealings with any of the other nations'.[8] Yet once the Idumaeans had been converted, whether forcibly or otherwise, their admission within the barrier according to the religious tradition should have been beyond question. There was great stress on the full acceptance of converts who had 'come to shelter under the wing of the Divine presence'. The Old Testament could provide an example in Ruth the Moabite, just as, later on, the New Testament was able to cite an Ethiopian eunuch who had received conversion;[9] and even a later, more cautious tradition allowed the third generation descendant of a proselyte family to be a full Jew. Nevertheless, in spite of these august rulings, the prejudice against the Idumaeans evidently died hard. They were so close in terms of geographical proximity – only a few miles away – but they seemed so foreign all the same.

One of the hereditary Idumaean chieftains was Herod's grandfather Antipas.[10] Indeed it seems that he governed the whole of Idumaea, having been granted this charge by the ferocious Hasmonaean Alexander Jannaeus (Jehonathan, Jonathan) (103–76 BC) and his wife Alexandra Salome who subsequently reigned by herself (76–67). Antipas held an important post, since Idumaea was a vital border-zone on the Arab frontier. But, looked at with hindsight, the appointment spelt the eventual ruin of the royal Hasmonaean family at the hands of Antipas' grandson, Herod. In Idumaea, as Arnold Toynbee remarks, the Jews caught a Tartar, like Napoleon who came to the French from Corsica, and Stalin who descended upon the Russians from Georgia.

There were alternative traditions, however, about the origins of Antipas. According to one report he did not come from inland Idumaea at all, but from the Mediterranean coastal strip which lay to its west and provided it with its ports, the former land of the Philistines. Within this territory, it was said, his birthplace was the ancient city of Ascalon,[11] now Ashkelon just north of the Gaza strip. In ancient times Ascalon was successively Philistine, Phoenician (at least in part), and then a Greek city-state – or at least it displayed the current form of Hellenised orientalism that passed for Greek in these parts. The place was exceptional in that it had escaped forcible incorporation into the domains of the militant Alexander Jannaeus. The true fact of the origin of Antipas, according to one version, was that he had been a slave in Ascalon's Temple of Apollo.[12] The writer who reports this was a Christian, probably copying from a Jewish source. But the information is suspect, because it looks like a malicious attempt to stress the sordidness of Herod's beginnings. It is more likely that the family were noblemen of Idumaea. Nevertheless, it is also very reasonable to suppose that they were closely linked with Ascalon, which was the neighbour and port of the Idumaeans. Moreover, the probability is increased by the special favours which Antipas and his grandson Herod both accorded to that city.

One of the sons of Antipas was Herod's father Antipater. The

Remains of the ancient coastal city of Ascalon (Ashkelon), where traditions hostile to Herod recorded that his father had been a temple slave.

hostile Jewish source which declared that the family were temple slaves recorded that Antipater was snatched away from Ascalon by Idumaean bandits, who then proceeded to keep him with them because his father could not pay the ransom. But that, too, is no doubt a fiction, again designed to cast a slight on Herod's pedigree. On the other hand the reports that he and his ancestors came from an authentically Jewish family, indeed a family which was both noble and priestly and had returned from exile in Babylonia, must also be discounted – but for the opposite reason. For these stories can be traced back to Herod's own associate Nicolaus of Damascus, and were clearly designed to show that Herod was a more authentic Jew than any Idumaean could be expected to be – and a priestly Jew as well.[13] The assertion was firmly and rightly discounted by his enemies.[14]

As for the wife of Antipater and mother of Herod, she was a woman of aristocratic origin called Cyprus, which is the flower of the henna (*lawsonia inermis* or *alba*) prized for its scent and now known as *chypre;* the *Song of Solomon* compares the beloved one to this blossom of the henna.[15] The poet declares En-Gedi on the Dead Sea to be its home, but the plant also came from Ascalon, with which therefore Antipater's wife Cyprus may, like her husband, have had some link. She also seems to have possessed Idumaean connections. Yet she was not, it would appear, an Idumaean, but a member of a people speaking another Semitic tongue, the Arabs;[16] nor, as some have supposed, should she be regarded as a member of a Jewish family that had settled in Arabia. When, therefore, a bitter enemy of Herod called him a *half-Jew*,[17] the taunt was true – or less than the truth. And indeed, in spite of efforts to demonstrate the contrary, his family were well enough aware of this disqualification. One day many years later his grandson King Agrippa I stood in the synagogue reading from *Deuteronomy,* and when he came to the passage 'You shall appoint over you a man of your own race: you must not appoint a foreigner, one who is not of your own race',[18] he wept, though everyone present hastily reassured him. And scriptural experts stressed the indispensability of a Jewish mother.[19]

But Herod's mother was an Arab, and she came from the Arab kingdom. There were, in fact, many such principalities, but the state which figures in this volume, and is described in it as the Arab state or Arabia, is the largest of them, the powerful Nabataean kingdom. It was the neighbour of Judaea all along the latter's eastern frontier in what is now south-western Syria and Jordan, and along the southern frontier too, where Judaea did not extend right down to the Gulf of Elat (Akaba), as it does now, but stopped short at the southern end of the Dead Sea.

The people who inhabited this Nabataean kingdom were Arab in race and speech, though their inscriptions show that they used another Semitic language, Aramaic (related to the Aramaic which was used in Palestine itself) as their official and literary language. At first they were nomadic, but then they established their capital at Petra, half-way between the Dead Sea and the Gulf of Elat.

> Match me such marvel save in Eastern clime,
> That rose-red city, half as old as time.[20]

The art of the Nabataean Arabs who were the neighbours of Judaea: a bronze handle in the shape of a human head from Oboda (Avdat).

Buildings carved in the rock at Petra, the capital of the Nabataean Arabs, now in south-western Jordan. The 'Temple of Isis' or 'Khazneh' (Treasury), second century A D.

On this silver coin Scaurus, an officer of Pompey, claims the submission of the Nabataean king Aretas III, seen kneeling beside his camel.

Petra is in an isolated, almost inaccessible position on Mount Edom, occupying a little oval space which lies within a circle of steep rocks and is only approachable through the narrow gorge of the river Musa.[21]

The territory of this Arab state extended far southwards over the grey limestone uplands of what had once been Edom, and the red heights of Sinai, as far as the waste-lands of central Arabia, and the Red Sea coast.[22] Although for a time they lost Elat to Egypt, these Arabs successfully escaped incorporation by the great Egyptian and Syrian kingdoms which took up the heritage of Alexander the Great. But their ambitions, and their worship of the pagan deities, brought them into sharp conflict with the expansionist Jewish regime of Alexander Jannaeus. Arab monarchs of the day, from Aretas (Harith) II (110–96) to Aretas III (87–62), had won battles against Jannaeus, but had lost others, and had been obliged to cede him Gaza and a strip east of the Jordan; though the last word rested with the Arabs, who after the death of the Jewish monarch momentarily outflanked his successors by conquering Damascus, which dominated the main longitudinal line of Transjordanian communications.

The Arabs could never be far from Jewish thoughts. Their army, operating a system of fire-signals by night,[23] was very experienced in desert warfare, and their subsidies were always available for brigands or guerilla groups ready to make trouble inside Judaea. But above all their strength depended upon their control of the spice and perfume caravan route from southern Arabia to Syria and the Mediterranean, and for this task of middle-man (combined with a readiness to seize any stranded or in-adequately defended goods) they possessed the necessary per-severance and cunning. They were also competent irrigators and fine potters, and now their peculiar brand of art, blending native characteristics with the successive influences of Egypt, Persia, Greece, Syria and Rome,[24] was preparing to reach new heights.

The Arab and Jewish kingdoms clashed at many points, but they had an enormous frontier in common, and they could not do without one another. Furthermore, Herod's father Antipater, as we have seen, was married to an important Arab; and even if this caused sneers from the Jews it proved very advantageous in other respects. Antipater possessed great influence over Jannaeus' wife and successor, Alexandra Salome (76–67), and graduated from the governorship of Idumaea to a high post at her court, perhaps the highest of all. When she fell ill and, before long, died, her two sons by the formidable Jannaeus came to blows. The older of the two, Hyrcanus II (likewise known as Jehonathan or Jonathan) was a weak character; the younger, Aristobulus II, was violent like his father. At the time of the queen's death Antipater had established himself as Hyrcanus' masterful adviser. Hyrcanus himself, how-ever, matched against his brother, soon gave up the struggle. Now,

An artistic triumph of the Arabs of Nabataea: a panther, made in the first century BC.

in this critical situation, was Antipater's opportunity to cultivate his Arab connections, as his father had done before him and as he himself had continued to do, for example by giving his elder son, Herod's elder brother, the Arab name Phasael.[25] And so Antipater induced the Arab King Aretas III to march on Jerusalem in the name of the rightful Jewish monarch Hyrcanus (65 BC). Success was virtually assured, when news came which utterly changed the situation. The Romans had arrived in Syria.

In the course of the previous century the Roman republic had won virtual control over the whole Mediterranean area, a feat which no other power had ever achieved or was ever to repeat. Great kingdoms fell to them, but two of the states which had parcelled up the empire of Alexander the Great (d. 323 BC) had been allowed, by the Romans, to pursue their existence, officially independent though attenuated and in fact largely dependent upon the will of

27

Pompey the Great, described as *Cnaeus Magnus Imperator*, portrayed on a silver *denarius* issued in Spain by his sons.

Rome. These were the kingdoms ruled by the descendants of Alexander's generals Ptolemy and Seleucus. Both the Ptolemies and the Seleucids had once ruled vast territories; but now the former were restricted to Egypt and the latter reduced to a small tract of Syria.

Finally, however, the repeated and unedifying quarrels of one Seleucid with another brought disaster upon their house and inflicted a radical change on the power-structure of the entire area. For several years past the greatest Roman military leader of the day, Pompey, had been stationed in the Near East, making an end of Rome's enemy Mithridates in northern Asia Minor. This done, he had decided to abolish the Seleucid monarchy and anarchy. And so it was learnt in Jerusalem that he was deposing the last king, and annexing Syria to the Roman empire as its latest possession. The new province (63 BC), a coastal strip seventy to a hundred miles deep with rows of mountains and then desert to its rear, was to perform the vital task of guarding the Roman frontier. For the Near East was overshadowed not only by the great western power, the Romans, but by the great eastern power as well – the only other major power the Romans had to encounter at any point of their borders. This was the empire of Parthia, which in spite of the ramshackle character of its loosely federated structure possessed a considerable potential of military strength.

So it was decided that the chaos in Syria had to end; and one of Pompey's generals, Scaurus, was already in Damascus, at the gates of both the Judaean and Arab kingdoms. Neither state of course was altogether without experience in dealing with the Romans. As regards the Jews, their national hero Judas Maccabaeus himself, battling for independence against the Seleucids, had formally enrolled himself as Rome's ally,[26] and his successors had repeated the gesture. They had also on occasion appealed to the Romans for help against their enemies, but they for the most part, having once encouraged the Jews to revolt against the Seleucids, had thereafter not taken much interest. But now that Syria was a Roman province, everything was instantly changed. This was clear enough, at all times, to Antipater – and he bequeathed this appreciation of the changed circumstances to his son Herod. Meanwhile, the new preponderance of the Romans could not fail to impress the current contestants for the Jewish throne, Hyrcanus II and his brother Aristobulus II, and they both appealed to Pompey. These appeals have been condemned as foolish, and indeed the fates of earlier countries that had appealed to Rome should have furnished food for thought. On the other hand, such action was not really shortsighted so much as realistic: once Syria was Roman, it was hardly possible for Rome to avert its eyes altogether from Judaea. For

Opposite: Pompey's troops entering the temple at Jerusalem: illustration from Josephus' *Jewish Antiquities* by Jean Fouquet (*c.* 1420–81).

Ous auons moustre
au uolume de diuant
iusquep a la mort de la
royne alexandre. Or
racomptons les choses qui sensuiuent
et ne tendons a nulle autre chose for

a neus trespasser des choses qui ont
este faictes en publicant a la memo
ye de ceulx qui les liront. Car a
ceulx qui escripuant hystoures on ra
comptent choses auaennes il conui
ent pour lanaenuete mettre ou faire

geographically, as countless migrations have testified, the Jewish homeland is an undetached portion of the Syrian land-corridor. And so Rome's eastern frontier against the Parthians needed the incorporation not only of Syria but of Judaea. Closer relations with Rome had become inevitable.

In the course of a prolonged series of intrigues and bribes, both Hyrcanus II (supported by Antipater) and Aristobulus II appeared in person before Pompey at Damascus. Pompey deferred a formal decision. To come down on either side must mean a continuation of civil war among the Jews, and first he intended to bring their Arab neighbours into line. This, however, he failed to do (they were not finally incorporated until the second century AD); and for his failure the Arabs have the Jews to thank. For Pompey was distracted from his Arab plan by the obviously uncooperative, hostile and nationalist intentions of Aristobulus. While Antipater, in fear of his children's lives, entrusted them to the care of the Arab king – his ten-year-old son Herod among them – Pompey besieged Aristobulus in the Temple, which had been the centre of resistance, and took it by storm. A general massacre followed. The priests were struck down as they officiated, and Pompey, though he safeguarded the treasures of the Temple, walked into the Holy of Holies. Probably he just wanted to see for himself what mysterious secrets it contained; but his visit was an intolerable affront to the Jews, since no one but the high priest was allowed to enter the place. When fifteen years later Pompey died miserably on the Egyptian sands, Jews welcomed the death of the Dragon, the Scourge of God.[27] The year 63 was a fateful year for the world. Cicero was consul; Augustus and Agrippa were born. And Pompey's few minutes in the Holy of Holies were an almost equally memorable event, to judge by the repercussions they aroused.

Aristobulus had capitulated, but he was far too keen on the tradition of the Maccabee conquerors to be left at large. And so he was taken off to grace the Roman triumph, his two sons, Alexander (II) and Antigonus, with him. Hyrcanus was duly reinstated, with Antipater still as his adviser. But the Judaea they were now permitted to control was lamentably truncated. During the second century BC a series of Hasmonaean kings, culminating in Alexander Jannaeus, had forged a Greater Judaea, the largest Jewish national state since Solomon. The numerous Gentiles it included, mostly the inhabitants of the Greek and Hellenised city-states which proliferated along the edges of the Jewish homeland (as elsewhere throughout the Near East), had been far from happy at the destruction of their own political organisations which incorporation in the Jewish state involved. But the Hasmonaean high priest Simon (142–34) had an answer which, even if it did not satisfy the Greeks, seemed sufficient to the Jews. 'We have not occupied other people's land or taken other people's property, but only the inheritance of our ancestors, unjustly seized for a time by our enemies.'[28]

Pompey, however, took exactly the opposite line, ruthlessly shearing off from the fringes of the Jewish state all the former Greek cities which the Hasmonaeans had incorporated. In this way, its entire coastline was removed, right down to and including the Gaza strip and Rhinocolura (El Arish) beyond. The cities thus detached included the very ancient Joppa (Jaffa, Yafo) which Simon the Hasmonaean had made into a Jewish harbour-colony, and Jamnia (Yavne) which had likewise been pretty thoroughly Judaised (Ascalon alone had remained free of Judaea, and still continued to be now). A large eastern belt, mainly on the other side of the Jordan, was also taken away and made into a league of ten cities, the Decapolis. In other words, all the Greek-style communities, both to the east and the west of Judaea, were revived and liberated from Jewish rule, regaining their autonomy under the general supervision of the governor of Rome's new province of Syria.

The same autonomy was conferred on a town little more than thirty miles north of Jerusalem, Samaria (Sebastya), which had been Hellenised since the fourth century BC but was obliged, like the others, to submit to the second-century Hasmonaeans. More remarkable still, it seems probable that the whole district in which Samaria lay, Samaritis (Shomron), was likewise detached from Judaea by Pompey. Samaritis was a fertile, well-wooded country which professed its own fundamental, apocalyptic brand of Judaism, still represented by a group of families today. The Samaritans accepted only the first six books of the Bible, revering not the Jerusalem Temple but a shrine on Mount Gerizim (which John Hyrcanus I destroyed in 128 BC). God, said the Jews, had sent lions among the Samaritans because they did not do proper homage to Him, and orthodox Jewry continued to shun them not only for their religious aberrations but on the grounds that they were descended from alien settlers who had been planted in the area by the Assyrian kings.[29] When some of the descendants of the exiled Jews had returned home from Mesopotamia in the fifth century BC, their leader Nehemiah had forbidden intermarriage with the Samaritans owing to their racial impurity, and even now, several hundred years later, travellers between Judaea and Galilee still often preferred to make a long and tiresome detour rather than pass through Samaritis. Such were the reasons why Jesus could receive the amazed enquiry: 'What! You, a Jew, ask a drink of me, a Samaritan woman?'[30]

This separateness was enough for Pompey to take Samaritis, too, from the diminutive new Judaea. And the Jezreel (Esdraelon) plain and valley to its north, that fertile break in the central range running south-east from near Mount Carmel, was lost with it. Galilee, further to the north, remained part of Judaea, but it was now quite isolated from the rest of the country by the extensive corridor comprising Samaritis and Jezreel; the kingdom was divided, like modern Pakistan.

Not content, then, with restoring the boundary between the rustic Jewish homeland and its Hellenised fringes on either side, Pompey had stripped the country right down to its orthodox Jewish core. This was a carefully thought out act. For, as A. H. M.

Samaria, restored by Herod the Great as Sebaste; it is near the modern town of Nablus (Shechem).

Jones observed: 'He was now convinced, if he had not made up his mind on the point from the first, that the Jewish kingdom as it existed was a menace to the peace and prosperity of Syria; the Jews were a troublesome and unruly people; they were furthermore backward and superstitious, and their conquests had had a disastrous effect on the civilization of southern Syria.'[31]

Moreover Hyrcanus II, when entrusted with this meagre dominion, was deprived of the title of king.[32] His uncle Judas (Jehuda) Aristobulus (I) (104–3) may have been the first to assume this royal title;[33] certainly it had been employed by Alexander Jannaeus (103–76). And now Hyrcanus II was deprived of it. Though retaining the position of high priest (of which more will be said later), he forfeited kingly status, being granted the title of *ethnarch* instead. This meant 'prince': a superior sort of prince, but less than a king.

This demotion of the ruler meant demotion for his minister Antipater as well. But he took it philosophically, true to his guiding principle: since everything depended on the Romans, it was above all necessary to keep in with them. And it still seemed better to work under the cloak of Hyrcanus, that is to say with a measure of national autonomy, than under the direct rule of the Romans which would follow if their favour disappeared. In the very next year Antipater was able to perform a useful service, simultaneously, both to Rome and to his Arab friends and connections. For after Pompey had been diverted from his proposed invasion of the Arab state, the governor whom he left behind in Syria, Scaurus, had returned to the attack. This presented Antipater with a problem. Complete success on the part of Scaurus would be unwelcome, since it would mean the total encirclement of Judaea by Rome, not to speak of the possible loss of Antipater's financial interests in the Arab kingdoms. But a Roman set-back was also undesirable, since it would invite the arrival in the area of massive retaliating Roman armies. Antipater handled the problem with a skill which may not have passed unnoticed even by his eleven-year-old son Herod. Scaurus got into difficulties in the desert and his supply services broke down. Antipater provided him with grain – and offered his mediation between Romans and Arabs; which both parties were by now happy enough to accept. On payment of a substantial sum (which Antipater guaranteed), the Arab king Aretas III was declared an ally of the Roman people – a dependent ally no doubt, but by no means the suppliant whom Scaurus shortly afterwards portrayed on a coin. For the kingdom retained a special status among 'client' states. Obodas (Aboud) II (62–47 BC), who now succeeded Aretas, was allowed to issue silver coins, a privilege scarcely ever extended to other dependents of Rome.

Antipater and his official superior Hyrcanus II were faced with a far more serious problem when the latter's more vigorous brother Aristobulus II, as well as his sons Alexander (II) and Antigonus, managed to get away from Rome, and raised the standard of rebellion in Judaea (57–6). The whole lot of them, as Antipater complained, had a positive passion for sedition, though they no doubt called it patriotism; and the Romans themselves were partly to blame for having created the habit of rebellion by encouraging these same Hasmonaeans, a century earlier, to revolt against the Seleucids. Already, at an early stage (57 BC), when the younger son was the only one of the family group to have arrived in the Levant, the current Roman governor of Syria, Gabinius, had decided that the political unit set up six years earlier was useless: large enough to provide fuel for revolutions, and too small to put them down. Hyrcanus was therefore deprived of his ethnarchy, retaining only his other title of high priest, and the small territory to which Judaea had been reduced was divided into five districts, each under a council of local notables.

These arrangements of Gabinius were probably popular among the Jewish aristocracy who for once found themselves in control of the regions. Antipater, even if he was allowed to retain Idumaea as a personal fief,[34] cannot have liked the new order nearly so much. Nevertheless, he did not allow his pro-Roman attitude to flag. On the contrary, he assisted and accompanied Gabinius on an expedition to Egypt to restore an unpopular ruler – Cleopatra's father – helpfully influencing the Jewish mercenaries who were garrisoning Pelusium (on the way to Port Said); and no doubt he subsequently shared the profits which came to the Roman general from the restored monarch. While Gabinius and Antipater were away, the Hasmonaean prince Alexander (11) revolted again – and now complete independence of Rome was probably his aim. This proved useful to Antipater who, after the defeat of the rebellion, was entrusted by the Romans with some sort of official oversight over Jerusalem. This was, in effect, a peace-keeping duty, combined with the lucrative task of collecting the Roman tribute in the place of the tax-gatherers, the publicans of the New Testament, who in Roman fashion had been 'farming' the taxes since 63 BC.

The years that followed were uncomfortable. First, Crassus, the associate of Pompey and Caesar in the triumvirate that was dictatorially ruling the Roman empire, ransacked the treasures of the Jerusalem Temple while on his way to fight Parthia. And then, while his army was thus engaged, yet another Judaean rebellion had to be crushed by Roman intervention, this time in Galilee, the northernmost of the five administrative districts, where a Jewish nobleman led the rising. Next came the sensational news that Crassus had been defeated and killed at Carrhae (Haran) by the Parthians (53). After his death, the two remaining members of the Roman triumvirate, Pompey and Caesar, gradually drifted into the enormous convulsions of the Civil War. These hostilities, as soon as they began in 49, rapidly exercised an effect on Judaea. For since Pompey controlled the eastern half of the empire, Hyrcanus 11 and Antipater, like all other princes and ministers in the area, had to support him – though the hatred felt for Pompey among the Jews must have made this embarrassing. On the other hand, Hyrcanus' more vigorous and nationalistic brother Aristobulus 11, who had special reason to bear a grudge against Pompey, was at this time again a prisoner at Rome; and Caesar, after gaining control of the Roman capital, took advantage of the existence of this potential ally by launching him into the Near East with two legions. However, the enterprise proved a disaster, since the Pompeians in Asia Minor poisoned Aristobulus, and then his son Alexander (II) was executed at Antioch (Antakya), the capital of the Syrian province.

These developments were highly satisfactory to Hyrcanus and Antipater, who had taken up a pro-Pompeian position. But by the same token Caesar's total victory over Pompey at Pharsalus in Thessaly (48) placed them in a perilous position. However, they were soon given an excellent opportunity to extricate and redeem themselves. For after Pompey had fled to Egypt and met his death upon its shore, Caesar, who had pursued him there, found his liaison with Cleopatra interrupted by very dangerous armed opposition in Alexandria. He sent to Asia Minor for help, but his relief column was held up at Ascalon. And it was at this point that

Julius Caesar: head of a statue commemorating him after his death.

Hyrcanus and his adviser Antipater arrived in very timely fashion with fifteen hundred soldiers to clear the way for the army that was held up. Then they proceeded to raise the Jews in Egypt in Caesar's favour – and these Jewish allies, excited to have a high priest visiting them for the first time, contributed largely to Caesar's final victory over his Egyptian foes. The Jews hated Caesar's Roman enemies, Pompey and the Pompeians, so much that the expedition was popular in Judaea, Caesar being hailed as the avenger of the Jerusalem that Pompey had profaned.

The Jewish intervention also did a lot to improve the positions of Hyrcanus and Antipater. For Caesar showed marked gratitude. Hyrcanus was promoted to the status of ethnarch again (47) – the five regional councils being abolished or deprived of political importance – and Antipater obtained a more explicitly recognised role as regent or chief minister of all Judaea. He himself was given the complimentary status of Roman citizen and exempted from the payment of taxes. He had to collect a land tax for Rome; this enabled him to collect more for himself on the side, but the official tax which he had to pay in was probably assessed at a quarter of the corn harvest of every other year, that is to say twelve and a half per cent per annum.

For a further consideration (20,675 bushels of grain every year except in the sabbatical one year out of seven[35]) the town of Joppa, taken away by Pompey, was restored to the ethnarchy. It was not very much of a port, since along the whole of this stretch of coast ships had to ride at anchor menaced by a south-west wind which threatened to dash them against the cliffs. But at least it had long been a port of a kind – and Judaea had gained its access to the sea once again. And at the same time the ethnarchy was given control over the fertile plain and valley of Jezreel (Esdraelon), part of what for the previous sixteen years had been a corridor of Roman territory running between the main part of Judaea and its Galilean province. Judaea was also exempted from winter billeting by Roman troops, and later it was decreed that the walls of Jerusalem could be rebuilt.

Such were the new privileges conferred upon Judaea; and in practice, it would appear, their recipient was Antipater rather than his ineffective master Hyrcanus II. Some allowance, it is true, has to be made for a tendency in our tradition (subsequently evolved at the court of Antipater's son Herod) to enhance Antipater at the expense of Hyrcanus. Nevertheless, there are certain clear signs that his power had now become very extensive. Above all, he was able to give key posts to his two eldest sons; the first, Phasael, being made governor of Jerusalem, and the second, Herod, obtaining the governorship of the detached province of Galilee.

Such were the tangled circumstances which in 47 BC brought Herod, at the early age of twenty-five, to this elevated and influential post.

Herod the King

Herod had still to become king of Judaea; but meanwhile he was already prince of Galilee.

This was a small territory measuring about twenty-five miles by thirty-five, the size of Hertfordshire or Rhode Island. But it was an area of key importance because, detached from the parent country, it formed a frontier zone along all its circumference. It also constituted a vital, integral part of Jewish territory. And yet, like Idumaea at the other end of Judaea, it had not been really Jewish for very long. Though there may have been partial Judaisation at an earlier period, full conquest and conversion, whether forcible or voluntary, only dated from the time of John Hyrcanus I (134–104 BC), or, less probably, of his successor Judas Aristobulus I (104–3). This absorption by Judaea and Judaism was fateful, for it meant that a century later, probably not long before Herod died, Jesus of Galilean Nazareth was born into Jewry.

The land of Galilee was so fertile that it played a large part in the Palestinian economy; and its people were lively and obstinate. Indeed they had a reputation for insubordinate behaviour, or so it was said in central Judaea where these peripheral areas were seen

View of the Sea of Galilee (Lake of Gennesaret, Tiberias), bordering upon the country which was the scene of Herod's first governorship.

through intolerant eyes. 'Nazareth!' said Nathanael to Jesus' disciple Philip, 'Can anything good come from Nazareth?'[1]

Josephus gives a somewhat suspect account of Herod's Galilean governorship. 'His youth', says the historian, 'in no way hindered him, and being a young man of high spirit, he quickly found an opportunity of showing his prowess. For on learning that Ezekias, a bandit leader, was overrunning the borders of Syria with a large troop, he caught and killed him and many of the bandits with him. This achievement of his was greatly admired by the Syrians, for he had cleared their country of a gang of bandits of whom they longed to be rid.'[2] But were they really 'bandits', or, if they were, might they not have had an ulterior aim as well? It is true that brigands have always found it easy to dodge to and fro between Galilee and the mountains of Lebanon. It is also true that in the whole of Judaea the slightest climatic fluctuation brings drought and consequent brigandage. But it is very possible, too, that Ezekias (Hezekiah) was a nationalistic, underground, political agitator, and in some circles a national hero in the tradition of Judas Maccabaeus himself. That is what Ezekias' own son (Judas the Galilean) became half a century later. Besides, the people of Galilee were full of admiration for the Hasmonaean regime which had freed them from foreign rule, and would be correspondingly ready to resent the pro-Roman Idumaean upstart Antipater whose son Herod had now come so forcibly amongst them.

That is probably why Herod's repressive measures involved him in one of the worst crises of his life, a crisis, indeed, which very nearly put a stop to his career almost before it had started. For great anger raged against him in the central Jewish council at Jerusalem. This body is described as the 'Community of the Jews' on Hasmonaean coins, including one issue on which a certain monarch, apparently Hyrcanus II himself, pronounces himself to be the head of the 'Community'. This may have been about the time when the council also began to be known as the *Synedrion*, from which the Hebrew term *Sanhedrin* later came to be derived.[3] Its seventy-one members, meeting in Gazith near the Court of Israel in the Jerusalem Temple, comprised at one and the same time a council of state and a supreme court of justice, the only body that could both theoretically and practically administer, throughout Judaean territory, the ancestral Laws of the Faith.

Now the members of this council, who all came either from priestly houses or from lay families of wealth and impeccable racial credentials, felt hostile to the influence of the Idumaean Antipater, and were therefore readily disposed to find fault with his two sons to whom he had granted high appointments. The government of Jerusalem by Herod's brother Phasael, though they cannot have welcomed his popularity, gave them no occasion for criticism. But Herod's behaviour, understandably bewailed by the mothers of the resistance fighters he had killed, inspired great anger

'Tomb of the Sanhedrin' at Jerusalem, popularly believed to be the burial place of the members of the Jewish Council slain by Herod in reprisals.

in the council because his executions of the rebels were quite illegal. By taking the law into his own hands in this way, he had usurped the most important power that the council possessed.

Its members therefore demanded that Herod should be brought before them; and Hyrcanus, caught between two fires, summoned him to attend and answer the charge. Antipater, too, felt obliged to advise his son to obey the summons. However, he also counselled him to bring a bodyguard – one small enough to avoid giving the appearance of intimidation but large enough to preserve him from harm and, in the event of condemnation by the council, capable of helping him to get away. When Herod arrived at Jerusalem, even the most careful examination of Josephus' conflicting accounts does not leave it entirely clear whether he was tried and acquitted or allowed to leave without the trial actually taking place. The role of Hyrcanus is also somewhat obscure. We are variously told that he 'loved' Herod but was 'vexed': probably he helped the young man to escape from Jerusalem without exerting himself unduly to let him keep his Galilean job. In any case, Herod fled to Damascus. What happened next, according to the story, was that he proposed to march on Jerusalem, and was only prevented from doing so by the pathetic pleas of his father and brother. But their appeals, in the form in which they are reported, seem to contain echoes of pleas to a legendary Roman hero, Coriolanus, on similar patriotic grounds, and so they may not represent what really happened. It is likely enough that Antipater and Phasael were afraid of ritual defilements if Herod's soldiers entered Jerusalem. But for the real directing agent behind these events we must look to the most important man in the Near East, the Roman governor of Syria.

At this time he was Sextus Caesar, Gaius Julius Caesar's young cousin. His distinguished relative was now on the point of wiping out his last Pompeian enemies and establishing uncontested dictatorship. Sextus Caesar was well aware of Gaius' friendship for the Idumaean house, and he shared the admiration of his province for Herod's energetic handling of Galilean sedition. Sextus had done his best to bring pressure on Hyrcanus to calm down the Jewish council's anger against the young man, but he did not want a retaliatory *coup d'état* by Herod, which would destroy the balance between the Hasmonaeans (Hyrcanus) and Idumaeans (Antipater), which Roman policy sought to maintain in order to avoid Jewish disturbances. So it was probably Sextus Caesar who dissuaded Herod, or instructed Antipater to dissuade him, from marching on Jerusalem. However, Herod was too valuable to lose or dispense with; since, therefore, he had been forced to leave Judaea, Sextus appointed him to a command on Syria's Judaean border, probably including Gaulanitis (the Golan Heights) and adjoining territory. And so Herod became a Roman civil servant. Moreover, it appears that at the same time Sextus entrusted him, in a personal capacity, with the governorship of Samaritis, which, it will be remembered, was part of the Roman territory of Syria, forming a corridor between Judaea and its outlying northern territories in Galilee and Jezreel. Samaritis still remained Roman, but Herod's personal command there was manifestly designed by the Romans to place him in a favourable position to exercise pressure on Jerusalem whenever a suitable occasion should arise.

Silver coin issued for Cassius by Lentulus Spinther in Asia Minor, 43–42 BC. Designs: tripod, sacrificial jug, augur's wand.

The Jews, who had experienced Gaius Caesar's gratitude, were shocked by his murder in 44 BC. This meant a big political change in their part of the world, since after a period of confusion it was one of Caesar's assassins, Cassius, who became the governor of Syria. Antipater and his family, however, succeeded in adjusting themselves once again to the changed circumstances, and became Cassius' loyal followers. Cassius, like his associate Brutus in the Aegean region, was busy raising funds for the reckoning that was bound to come with the dead dictator's supporters, and Herod was ordered to return to Galilee, which he had been forced to leave three years earlier, to collect the money that Cassius hoped for from there. Herod performed the task with such success that his former appointment in Roman Syria (including Samaritis) was confirmed, and he was also entrusted with fund-collecting duties in the province, in addition to the task of supervising fortresses and stores of arms in Judaea itself.

These were signal proofs of Cassius' confidence, but they disturbed the balance between the Hasmonaean and Idumaean interests which his predecessors had endeavoured to maintain.

Soon therefore another party in Judaea, headed by a certain Malichus, started showing recalcitrance about collecting these special taxes; his name (Malik) suggests that he was an Arab, but at all events he was clearly anti-Idumaean and anti-Roman into the bargain. He was saved from Roman vengeance, however, by the intercession of Hyrcanus II, whose attitude during this crisis seems so ambiguous that one must suspect him of wanting to play off Malichus against Antipater. The latter, too, remained curiously inactive in face of Malichus' hostile actions, allowing a formal reconciliation to be staged, and even dissuading a deputy of Cassius from having Malichus executed; it has been suggested that Antipater's wife Cyprus, herself an Arab, may have taken the initiative in these conciliatory moves. But, if so, they were mistaken. For Malichus, enlisting the services of Hyrcanus' butler, now proceeded to have Antipater poisoned.

It was the end of an epoch, and the end of an exceedingly clear-sighted man. Herod's father had correctly grasped the lesson that the great western power had come to stay: this was a situation that no amount of resistance movements could alter. But in order to avoid looking like an open collaborator with Rome he had preferred to act under cover of Hyrcanus, and it was fortunate for him that, at least until the very last stage, Hyrcanus was a malleable enough patron to make this possible. Many people hated Antipater – he was sacrificed to the hatred of the Jewish aristocracy. But he was an expert financier and manager, a capable commander, and a man of unlimited patience. This last quality enabled him to be unusually merciful; our records, although the traditions they represent are by no means all favourable to his family, cannot find any of the usual atrocities to attribute to him.

After Antipater was dead, his murderer Malichus occupied Jerusalem, claiming to act in Hyrcanus' name. Herod wanted to march against him, but his brother Phasael dissuaded him on the grounds that, since neither of them possessed the official powers to make such a move, it could be interpreted by the Romans as rebellion. So another ostensible reconciliation followed, and Malichus and Herod both accompanied Hyrcanus on a visit to Cassius at Laodicea (Lattakia) in Syria. On the way back, outside the ancient Phoenician city of Tyre, a Roman military escort turned on Malichus and stabbed him to death. Presumably Herod had persuaded Cassius that this must be done. Hyrcanus, who witnessed the deed, was disconcerted, but on being told that Cassius was responsible he managed to acquiesce, duly denouncing the dead man as a plotter.

Phasael returned to his governorship at Jerusalem, and Herod went back to his duties in the Syrian province. There he fell ill. When he had recovered, however, he returned promptly to Judaea to help his brother suppress revolts led by Malichus' brother supported by the military commander in Jerusalem. More serious still was the return to the country, with backing from over the border, of Hyrcanus' surviving nephew Antigonus, standard-bearer of traditional Hasmonaean nationalism. Early in the year 42 BC Herod repelled Antigonus' dash into Judaea, and returned in triumph to Jerusalem, where Hyrcanus gave him a good welcome. And this time, at least, his welcome was no doubt sincere since

The tower Herod named after his brother Phasael in his palace at Jerusalem, now dominating the citadel. The lower courses date from his construction.

Antigonus, if he had won, would have had many reasons to treat him vindictively.

And so now Hyrcanus – perhaps he had formed the plan a little earlier when the threat from Antigonus still existed – sealed his special relationship with Herod by betrothing him to his grand-daughter Mariamme. She represented both traits of the family, the aggressive side as well as Hyrcanus' passive side, for she was the daughter not only of Hyrcanus' daughter Alexandra but of Antigonus' late brother Alexander (ii). There might have seemed to be an obstacle to her betrothal to Herod, since he was already married. His first wife was Doris, of disputed ancestry: it seems most probable that, like Herod himself, she came from a noble Idumaean family.[4] Doris had borne him a son. Certain sections of contemporary Jewish thought were hostile to divorce, but according to *Deuteronomy* a man was allowed to divorce his wife.[5] So Doris was sent away from Jerusalem with her son. Henceforward, not

Julius Caesar as Imperator, with laureate crown: the patron of the Jewish régime led by Herod's father.

unnaturally, they were embittered in the extreme; and they were only authorised to reappear in the city on days of public festival.

Engagement to a Hasmonaean girl was of enormous political benefit to Herod during the years that lay immediately ahead. It mitigated, the qualms of an important section of the Jewish aristocracy and it showed that Hyrcanus II, who had no son himself, was regarding Herod as his heir. Now Mariamme was not only royal but beautiful too, and Herod, who was very susceptible to female beauty, fell deeply in love with her. However, egged on by her mother Alexandra, she showed no signs of recoiling from the perilous task of telling Herod home truths whenever she regarded this necessary. But the profound consequences of this situation did not become apparent until after their marriage, which did not take place for another five years.

The crisis of the moment was due to another convulsion in the greater Roman world. In October 42 BC, Cassius and Brutus succumbed at Philippi in Macedonia to the supporters of the late Julius Caesar, the young Octavian (the future Augustus) and Mark Antony. In the Second Triumvirate, which they shared with Lepidus, the rule of the east was allotted to Antony, and Phasael and Herod had to try to change sides again. Needless to say their Jewish enemies sent Antony delegation after delegation to discredit them. But Antony shared his former master Caesar's favour towards the family of Antipater, whose timely aid and hospitality he had enjoyed a decade previously while serving in the area under Gabinius. No doubt, on the same occasion, he had also got to know Antipater's sons. In any case, Hyrcanus now spoke up for them; and Phasael and Herod duly received confirmation of their appointments in Jerusalem and Galilee respectively, with the added title of *tetrarch* (originally, but no longer, meaning 'ruler of a quarter') which gave them a formal princely status under the ethnarch Hyrcanus.

Some have seen in this decision a plan to withhold supreme power from Herod, since he had been so loyal to Antony's enemy Cassius. Whether this recollection played a part in Antony's mind we cannot tell, but at all events he felt that a balance between the brothers was the better plan. His decision, however, did not prevent the other Jewish faction from sending yet another delegation to see him. It contained no less than a thousand men, and waited for him at Tyre, a politically inflammable city since Antony had just been obliged to dispose of its ruler, a nominee of Cassius who had fallen into disgrace after invading Galilee. Antony refused to see this vast deputation, and their dispersal resulted in casualties and death sentences.

However, the entire situation was now changed once again by the arrival on the scene of the major eastern power, Parthia – against which Rome's entire defensive system along the Syrian frontier was directed. Thirteen years previously, the prestige of the Parthians in the area had been greatly enhanced when they destroyed the large Roman army of Crassus, and he himself met his death. Now, in the spring of 40, Pacorus, son of the Parthian king, invaded Syria, with a Roman traitor as his political adviser. The local princelings hastened to submit, and Pacorus occupied almost

Opposite: Head of a Parthian monarch of the first century BC.

the entire province. In doing so he was helped not only by the glamour of the Parthian victory over Crassus but also by his own considerable reputation for moderation and fairness.

And now the invading army turned towards Judaea. Parthia had longstanding relations with the Jews, chiefly because of their ancient settlements east of the Euphrates; the historian Josephus, by placing these eastern communities near the head of his list of those to whom his *Jewish War* was addressed, shows how important they were. The Jewish state of the Hasmonaeans, too, under Alexander Jannaeus, had honoured a Parthian delegation.[6] And later Jewish sources show how passionately it was felt in some circles that by conquering Rome the Parthians would prove a providential instrument to make the way clear for the awaited Messiah.[7]

And so, as they moved into Judaea, the Parthians naturally supported the anti-Roman Antigonus. They did not, it is true, say this at once. However, Antigonus duly reappeared in Galilee, joined by Jewish bands from the oak woods that in those days covered large tracts of the maritime plain. Then he marched rapidly on Jerusalem. There the hasty arrival of Phasael and Herod compelled him to withdraw inside the Temple precinct; but very soon a Parthian force arrived to support him. Its commander proposed that Hyrcanus, Phasael and Herod should all proceed to the local Parthian commander-in-chief to plead their cause in person. Hyrcanus and Phasael duly complied and left. But Herod, full of suspicion, stayed behind. Nor did further invitations to proceed to Parthian headquarters entice him to make a move. For a wealthy Syrian, Saramalla, had already sent him advance warning of hostile Parthian intentions, and now Herod learnt that this intelligence had been accurate; for Hyrcanus and Phasael had been conducted to Ecdippa (Haziv, Ez-Zib) on the Phoenician (Lebanese) coast and placed under arrest. So now there was no doubt that the Parthian nominee for the Judaean throne was to be Antigonus, and it was revealed that the price he had promised included not only a large sum of money but five hundred women, the wives of his political enemies.

So Herod decided to escape from Jerusalem and take his women with him. He had already sent money south to his native Idumaea. Now, with his fiancée, her mother, his own mother, his younger brother and ten thousand men, he got out of the city. How he gave the slip to the ten Parthian officers and two hundred cavalrymen who had been left to guard him is a mystery. However, this luck did not hold for very long. Seven miles south of Jerusalem, he beat off a large force of his Jewish enemies; later he was to build a great fortress, Herodium, to mark the critical spot. On they pressed, often menaced by Parthian horse. The women were mounted, but his mother was transferred to a carriage, for we are told that it overturned and that Herod, in despair at her injury and the delay, thought of committing suicide – but the story may be a court legend to stress his family feeling. At all events the party managed to keep a rendezvous with Herod's younger brother Joseph (II) at Oresa (Kefar Harissah or Horshah) in Idumaean territory, five miles south of Hebron. There it was decided to disband most of the troops the two brothers had brought with them, but to lodge

Coin of Malchus I of the Nabataean Arabs (47–30 BC). It was unusual for a client-kingdom to be allowed to issue silver by the Romans.

their families in the towering desert fortress of Masada beside the Dead Sea, with eight hundred men to guard them under Joseph's command.

Herod felt that the time had indeed come to utilise his close family connections with the Arabs. He was at least half Arab himself, his family possessed large estates in their country, and his father had been intimate with its kings and had lent them money. Now Herod wanted some of the money back, in the hope of ransoming his brother and persuading the Parthians to abandon the cause of Antigonus; and so he left for the Arab capital Petra, taking with him his brother Phasael's seven-year-old son as a possible security. The Arab monarch of the day was Malchus (47–30 BC); his name, Malik, is the same as that of Herod's former internal opponent, Malichus, but he is best called Malchus in order to differentiate them. He refused to allow Herod to proceed as far as Petra, claiming that he had received Parthian orders to keep him out – though it was suspected that he saw a good opportunity to repudiate his debts to Herod and other leading Jews, and perhaps take over their investments in his country.

At all events Herod had to turn back westwards across the Negev. After collecting an escort at an Idumaean holy place, he got through to the Mediterranean coast at Rhinocolura (El-Arish), a former possession of Judaea which had been detached from it by Pompey and was now a frontier post of the ruling queen of Egypt, Cleopatra VII.

Herod was only just in time, for meanwhile the Parthians, too, had descended upon Idumaea, capturing and destroying the ancient fortress of Marissa (Maresha), a key-point on Judaea's southern frontier. No doubt they had selected it for destruction because it possessed ancestral connections with Herod's family.

Moreover, when he reached the coast, the refugee heard even more disastrous news. His brother Phasael was dead. A heroic version of the story declared he had died in battle, but apparently what had really happened was that he committed suicide in the cell in which the Parthians were detaining him. Hyrcanus had suffered in a more bizarre fashion. His ears had been cut off, or mutilated, by his Parthian captors. This meant that he could no longer be high priest, since the law ruled that no one with a physical defect could hold that office.[8] We may discount the anti-Hasmonaean version indicating that Antigonus himself actually bit Hyrcanus' ears off, just as it is not necessary to believe that the same villain killed Phasael by pretending to doctor a wound he had received, and poisoning it instead.

Anyway, Hyrcanus was now obliged to abdicate the high priest-hood, and the Parthians deported him to Babylonia. And Phasael was dead. Since one of Herod's strongest feelings was love for his Idumaean family, the sorrow that he displayed on learning of his brother's death was surely genuine. Nevertheless, it was also true that a potentially embarrassing rival, who possessed a considerable gift for acquiring popularity, was conveniently out of the way. Another blessing in disguise was the heavy-handed way in which the Parthians were behaving; for this belied Pacorus' reputation for just behaviour, made him unpopular with a good many Jews, and left no doubt in the minds of the Romans that the man they must back was Herod.

It was essential that he should now bring this point home in person. In other words, he must go to Rome, where both Antony and Octavian, their differences temporarily patched up by a treaty, happened to be at the moment. By far the quickest way to get there, if not the only way, was by sea from Egypt. So Herod moved west-wards through the border-zones of that country – just missing an Arab deputation sent by King Malchus to convey his second thoughts about the rebuff he had given the young man. When Herod reached Pelusium, at the north-eastern end of the Delta, Cleopatra's fleet commander there (after some hesitation) con-veyed him to the Egyptian capital Alexandria, where he was received by the queen.

When the Seleucid kingdom had been abolished by Pompey and made into Rome's Syrian province twenty-three years earlier, Ptolemaic Egypt was the only one of the successor-states of Alexander the Great that still survived. Though not so rich as it had been, the country was still very rich. But it had lost its extensive imperial territories in Palestine, Syria and Asia Minor, and its very survival as an 'independent kingdom' depended to a humiliating extent on the favour of Rome. Queen Cleopatra VII, like Herod in Judaea, had every intention of restoring her realm to its former glories; and, like him again, she clearly saw that the only way to do so was by cooperating with the principal Roman leaders. Being a woman, however, her methods were different, or at least more varied. In addition to collaborating with Caesar, she had become his mistress, and recently she had acquired Antony as a lover as well. Her intention was to persuade him to enlarge Egypt to its former dimensions.

This meant that Herod was taking a great risk in appealing to Cleopatra, since her plan to restore the ancient Ptolemaic kingdom must necessarily involve the curtailment, if not the abolition, of his own little state. However, Cleopatra welcomed him. Presumably she reasoned that they were both political friends of Antony; and that this able young man, at present obviously offering no threat, might come in useful – especially if she could keep him under her own control. Indeed it was said that she even offered him an Egyptian command, presumably over a contingent she was mobilising to help Antony against the Parthians. This would not have been the first time that the Ptolemies employed a Jewish general. Nevertheless, the story may not be true: it is the sort of thing Herod might have put in his memoirs to show how cleverly he had evaded her famous wiles.

At all events, if he did receive such an offer, he declined it. What he told the queen was that he wanted to go on his way to Rome, though the season was already autumn, when sailors normally avoided the Mediterranean. Cleopatra fell in with his wishes, and gave him a ship to start him on his journey. After a stormy passage he got as far as Rhodes, where he built himself another larger vessel. He could no doubt have hired one, but he wanted an excuse to delay and sound his friends at Rome. Meanwhile he felt it desirable to lavish benefactions on Rhodes – which was friendly to Antony and had been damaged by his enemies – while at the same time raising the large sums he would need when he got to the capital. These funds, presumably, he was able to collect from the extensive Jewish communities along the coast of Asia Minor.

And so Herod, although it was now deep winter, sailed on to Brundusium (Brindisi) and came to Rome. There he immediately told Antony, the friend of his family, about everything that had been happening in the Near East. Antony introduced him to his fellow triumvir Octavian, who, although a cold-blooded young man, could not fail to be influenced by the grateful friendship that his adoptive father Julius Caesar had extended towards Herod's house. Besides, Herod was pro-Roman, whereas his enemy Antigonus was anti-Roman. Moreover, great men always found it difficult not to be affected by Herod's charm.

Arrangements were therefore very quickly made to present him to the Roman senate. His sponsors before that august gathering were the orator and art-patron Messalla and an administrator and admiral named Atratinus. To judge from their subsequent careers, both these men were partly motivated by their distrust of Cleopatra's Egypt, which convinced them of the utility of a Palestinian counterpoise. Moreover, this was not the first time Messalla had spoken for Herod, for two years earlier, before Antony, he had defended him and his brother against their Jewish enemies. Now, the two senators put his case before their own colleagues, and denounced Antigonus as a collaborator with hostile Parthia. Then Antony rose to his feet, and argued that in the campaigns that he was planning, aimed at driving the Parthians out of Syria, Herod's assistance on his flank would be essential. And so Antony proposed that the kingship of Judaea, suspended since the demotion of Hyrcanus to ethnarch in 63, should be revived – and that the king should be Herod. The senate voted unanimously in favour of the proposal.

'The house adjourned,' reported Josephus, 'and Antony and Octavian went out with Herod between them, the consuls and other magistrates leading the way, in order to offer sacrifice and to deposit the decree in the Capitol. This first day of Herod's reign Antony celebrated with a banquet.'[9] It was the greatest day of Herod's life; and the banquet must have been a mighty celebration – though it was trifling dangerously with Jewish feeling to join the Roman leaders in a sacrifice to Capitoline Jupiter. Whether he felt worried about doing this, we do not know; but another aspect must certainly have caused him apprehension. The many Jews who saw something sacred in the Hasmonaean royal house, which had liberated the Jewish people from the foreign yoke, were clearly going to be shocked beyond measure to see a 'half Jewish' Idumaean explicitly granted the same royal title, and at the hands of a foreign patron at that. For this reason, and to rebut charges of improper ambition, Herod let it be understood that the Roman decision had come as a complete surprise to him. His own intention, he said, had been to have his betrothed Mariamme's ten-year-old brother Aristobulus (iii) appointed to the kingship – to which by birth he was entitled, being Hyrcanus' grandson and Antigonus' nephew. He himself, he declared, wanted nothing more than to be the boy's adviser. But this is unlikely to have been true. For within seven days of his arrival in Italy, Herod was already on his way back home again. Quite clearly the whole thing had been prepared in careful consultation with Roman notables during those months spent on the island of Rhodes on the outward journey.

Another very serious aspect of the Roman decision, from the point of view of Jewish opinion, was the fact that the kingship now had to be divorced from the high priesthood. For Herod most certainly could not be high priest, since he did not come either from the house of Aaron, which had previously held a monopoly of the office, or from the Hasmonaean family, which had subsequently taken it over. They had fabricated some slight justification for doing so, since they at least came of a minor priestly family. Herod the Idumaean could not expect to do likewise; even the reports that he, too, was of priestly origin, which he allowed to be spread by his entourage, were too half hearted to carry very much conviction.

Yet the Roman argument was clear. The reasons why Herod had to be placed in charge were these. First, the Hasmonaean Antigonus was anti-Roman (having backed the eastern against the western great power) and could not therefore play the part. Secondly, Antigonus' Hasmonaean nephew Aristobulus could not do so either, because he belonged to the same anti-Roman side of the family, and was in any case only ten years old. Thirdly, Herod was the only man with the necessary capacity and energy – and perhaps, in view of his Idumaean origin, with the necessary detachment – to keep down the incessantly turbulent Jews. But if Herod had to be in charge, he had to be king, for since he could not be high priest he had to be given a title that was its equal in prestige. Moreover, the coins of Antigonus, whose Hebrew name was Mattathias, show that he, for his part, did claim the kingly title; so nothing less would do for Herod whose task it was to supersede him. These were the circumstances which, in December 40 BC, caused the kingly title to be revived in favour of Herod, and his later coinage was inscribed with dates showing that he reckoned his reign from this time.

Herod's enemy calls himself King Antigonus in Greek and the High Priest Mattathias in Hebrew (40–37 BC). The design shows a wreath and double cornucopiae.

But the Roman decision was an unusual or exceptional one, for when there was a vacancy in a dependent, client kingdom it had normally been the custom to choose the new prince from the old line. The decision also involved a separation of the Jewish kingship from the high priesthood. This represented a reversal of the tradition that the later Hasmonaeans had established (a tradition only broken, inevitably, when a woman, Alexandra Salome, was on the throne, and Hyrcanus II became her high priest). Rome might have preferred, and found it tidier, to retain the union of kingship and high priesthood. But this could not be done, for there was no possible candidate for the combined job. So Herod had to be king and somebody else had to be high priest. But this was a problem that could, and must, be postponed for the time being, since first he had to gain possession of his kingdom, which was still in the hands of his rival, the man who in the eyes of most Jews was the legitimate king: the Hasmonaean Antigonus.

As an encouragement, the Romans promised Herod substantial enlargements of his territory. North of Jerusalem, Samaritis, which, before the Parthian invasion, he had been holding as a personal barony within the province of Syria, was to return to the Judaean kingdom, thus erasing the unfortunate Roman corridor between the nucleus of the state and Galilee. There was also some extension of his territory in the extreme south-west, to the west of his native Idumaea. It comprised a coastal strip, to supplement Joppa. This acquisition almost certainly included the important, ancient, recently reconstructed harbour town and Hellenised city-state of Gaza, terminus of the spice route from Arabia.

Herod takes over his kingdom

And so Herod had been given his kingdom by the Romans; but he still had to seize it from Antigonus.

Losing no time, he undertook a second winter voyage, and reached the Levantine shore in about February 39. But he could not land in Judaean territory at all, and in fact disembarked outside the northern extremity of his putative kingdom, at the Phoenician harbour-city of Ptolemais Ace (Acre, Akko) in Roman Syria (now just inside the state of Israel, which it serves as the natural port of approach to Galilee). In the previous year, Ptolemais had surrendered to the Parthian invaders without a struggle. But now its inhabitants had evidently been induced to change their minds, and Herod was able to disembark.

View of Acre (Akko), the ancient Ptolemais Ace, where Herod landed in 39 BC to conquer Judaea.

Soon after his arrival one of Rome's best generals, Ventidius, a self-made henchman of Antony, landed in Asia Minor and caused the main Parthian army in the area to evacuate Syria and hasten north to meet him. Ventidius defeated them and turned towards Judaea to dethrone Antigonus. However, a timely bribe from Antigonus persuaded him to withdraw, for his financial morals were inferior to his military talents. So Herod had to be content with the assistance of Ventidius' deputy Silo, who was less competent as a soldier and equally corruptible. With a force of mercenaries and volunteers, Herod made his appearance outside Jerusalem, where he and Antigonus issued counter-proclamations: Antigonus offered to abdicate if his pro-Parthian record made it necessary, but only in favour of one of his own Hasmonaean relatives – never if it meant handing over to the upstart Idumaean.

However, Herod found it impossible to undertake a siege without more serious Roman aid – Silo, well bribed by the other side, insisted on scattering his troops in remote billets – and directed his brothers to conduct other operations elsewhere. One of them, Joseph (II), installed at Masada before Herod's visit to Rome, had on one occasion nearly been forced to surrender owing to a shortage of water, and was planning a desperate dash to the Arab capital of Petra with a few men to seek help; but then the rain had fallen, and, with Herod's help, he had broken the seige. Now he was no doubt expected to recapture Idumaea. Meanwhile their younger brother Pheroras was sent to rebuild the great fortress of Alexandrium (Sartaba), towering over a conical mountain-top two thousand feet above the Jordan valley, three miles west of its confluence with the river Jabbok. Named after its reputed founder Alexander Jannaeus, but destroyed some nineteen years previously by the Romans, the summit of Alexandrium commanded an enormous view, as far as Mount Hermon eighty miles away. In particular, it was the best place to supervise the supply route from Samaria to Jericho (near the north end of the Dead Sea), and it soon gained a sinister reputation as a place for the supervision and incarceration of internal enemies.

Meanwhile Herod himself, in about January 38, moved up to Galilee and took the capital of the province, Sepphoris (Zippori), in a snowstorm. Next he set himself what had been regarded as the impossible task of suppressing the bands of the anti-Roman, pro-Hasmonaean resistance movement – 'brigands', as Josephus calls them. They were occupying unapproachable caves in the cliffs above Arbela (Arbel) north-west of the Sea of Galilee; but Herod attacked the caves by letting down capacious lifts suspended from iron chains. The lifts were filled with soldiers armed with grappling hooks and firebrands, and by these methods the guerrillas were exterminated.[1] The Parthians now invaded Syria for the second time, causing a serious scare; but in June 38 BC, Ventidius crushingly defeated them on the north-western borders of Syria, and the king's son Pacorus was killed. Ventidius then moved east to suppress a disloyal princeling at Samosata (Samsat in south-east Turkey). The operation hung fire owing to bribery, but meanwhile Ventidius sent a force to help Herod. It consisted of two legions under the command of a man who was perhaps called Machares, a name found in the Pontic royal family of northern Asia Minor. Since, however, he proved no more satisfactory than the other commanders who had been sent to help Herod before, Herod decided to hasten north, in difficult and dangerous conditions, to join Antony himself, who had now taken personal charge at Samosata. Antony duly took the recalcitrant town, and at last

The tomb at Nimrud Dağ of Antiochus I of Commagene, who was deposed by Mark Antony when he took Samosata (Samsat) in 38 BC.

adequate support was forthcoming for Herod. For now Antony ordered one of his leading supporters and generals, Sosius, to conduct a large army to take part in the Judaean campaign, and a legion, and then another, was sent ahead to begin the task.

They were only just in time to deal with a wave of disasters. Herod's brother Joseph (II), attacking Jericho against orders, had lost his life and those of many Jewish and Roman soldiers; and there were also further revolts in Galilee, which caused a serious dispersion of forces. Finally, by great efforts on Herod's part, the army of Antigonus under the command of his general Pappus was

The ruler of Samosata diplomatically greets the Graeco-Roman god Heracles – in addition to the Persian Ahuramazda, shown in the last picture.

beaten back in the direction of Jerusalem; and early in the winter a decisive battle was fought. It took place at Isana (Burg el Isaneh), twenty-one miles north of the capital, at the narrowest point of the narrow precipitous Valley of the Thieves on what is now the Jerusalem-Nablus road. The result was complete victory for Herod. In the bloodiest engagement of the war the enemy commander was killed, and only a blizzard prevented a decisive follow-up.

After the battle was over, Josephus reports that Herod had a narrow escape from assassination.

In the evening Herod dismissed his weary comrades to refresh themselves while he himself, still hot from the fight, went to take a bath like any other soldier, attended by a single slave. He was on the point of entering the bath-house when one of the enemy dashed out in front of him sword in hand, then a second and a third, with others in their train. These men had fled from the battlefield into the bath-house fully armed. There they had cowered unnoticed for a time, but when they saw the king they lost their nerve entirely and ran past him – unarmed as he was – shaking with fear, and dashed for the exits. As it happened no one else was there to seize the men and Herod was content to have come to no harm, so they all got away ...[2]

A coin of Herod, perhaps at Samaria, with his name and royal title in Greek. The symbols left of the altar (?) mean 'year 3' (38–37 BC).

How true is that story? Probably it is not true at all. The escape from assassination after the great battle is a theme of saga (the same story was told of Frederick the Great after the battle of Leuthen, in the castle of Deutsch-Lissa). In 37, again, in an earthquake, it was said that Herod had a narrow escape from a falling house. Perhaps he did, and perhaps there was an earthquake, but the historical importance of the stories lies rather in the fact that Herod was already becoming the sort of legendary figure around whom such tales gather.

He now felt his military position was strong enough for his troops to be dismissed into winter quarters. In spring 37 BC, just over two years after his landing at Ptolemais, he moved his army up to the gates of Jerusalem, and made ready to besiege the city. But Sosius had not yet arrived, so meanwhile he withdrew to Samaria and took time off to wed Mariamme, to whom he had been engaged for five years. He was in love with her, but the wedding, at this juncture, also had a strong political purpose. She belonged to the Hasmonaean royal family. There were Jews who hated the Hasmonaeans, but there were more who revered them as liberators of their faith and country. These Herod hoped to divide: for although some of them would still back Antigonus, he hoped that others would reconcile themselves more readily to Herod's victory once he was married to Antigonus' niece, the grand-daughter of the last Hasmonaean high priest Hyrcanus II.

After the wedding Sosius, with his large Roman army, effected a junction with Herod before the walls of Jerusalem. The siege

The fortifications of Herod's epoch: the sloping base (glacis) of his Tower of Phasael, known by Crusaders and Moslems as the Tower of David.

could now begin in earnest. The Roman army was very large, comprising eleven legions, six thousand horse, and many Syrian auxiliaries; and Herod's own force may have totalled thirty thousand men. But the city was a honeycomb of walls containing numerous strong points, and it took six weeks to reduce the outer wall. Another fortnight was needed to take the second wall; and then all that was left to Antigonus was the Temple and the upper city. Herod agreed to a petition that animals should be sent in for Temple sacrifices, but resistance continued. Finally, after a siege of nearly five months, the Temple and upper city were stormed, and the massacre began.

Herod tried to stop it, and succeeded in getting his own troops into the Temple, since he would never hear the end of it if he allowed Romans to plunder the sacred place. But Sosius thought it unreasonable that his soldiers should be asked to call off the looting. However, the distribution of a bonus by Herod, including a large sum for himself, finally convinced him, and the Roman army evacuated the city and marched away.[3] As for Sosius, later on he became an admiral of Antony's fleet and had to issue coins, on which he depicted a trophy and Jewish captives.

Jerusalem fell in August or September 37 BC. Later Jewish traditions declared that the day of capture was 3 October, but this was an attempt to charge Herod with sacrilege, since it was the Day of Atonement. Another Jewish tradition said that resistance had only collapsed owing to pious observance of the sabbatical year, on which 'you shall not sow your field nor prune your vineyard'.[4] But the sabbatical year did not begin until October; it cannot have hindered the resistance, though the inability to lay in extra stores in anticipation must have added to the general anxiety. In fact, resistance was desperately fierce, for many of the besieged, buoyed up with every sort of national and religious propaganda, were not only aghast at the prospect of a half-Jewish, pro-Roman king but knew the fate they must expect at his hands.

Antigonus himself could hardly hope to be spared. Sosius took him in chains to Antony, who was in Syria. There, in the capital Antioch, he was beheaded, or had his throat cut. Hostile tradition attributes his death to a request from Herod, but the question whether this was true or not is immaterial; neither Antony nor Herod could possibly allow him to survive. He stood for everything that they had to suppress – the popular reaction against Rome and its servants.

The historian Josephus, who had the blood of the Hasmonaeans in his veins but took care what he said because Antigonus had been so anti-Roman, utilises the moment of his execution to present an obituary testimonial to his house: which was splendid and renowned, but had lost its power through internal strife.[5]

For Antony, there could now be no going back on Herod. Nor had he the slightest desire to do so. Ruler of Rome's teeming, vulnerable eastern provinces, he was following the traditional procedure of setting up dependent 'client' native princes along their fringes – men who were often better qualified to govern than an official sent out from Rome. For often there were peculiar local conditions, and that was only too true of Judaea. Client principalities were also cheaper than provinces, since their rulers and their staffs did not have to be paid. On the other hand they resembled the provincial governors in one respect: they were obliged to collect funds for Rome, in the form of tribute. Herod's tribute was now assessed at a fixed sum instead of the previous annual percentage. He also felt it advisable – although nearly bankrupt at this moment – to add a large present for Antony. He contrived it by melting down the royal plate.

It was the task of these princes to maintain order within their

Bronze coin of Gaius Sosius (issued at Zacynthus, now Zante) with a trophy commemorating his capture of Jerusalem with Herod in 37 BC.

own dominions, but above all else they must help to ensure that the frontier regions themselves were kept safe. In the extreme southern sector of the eastern frontier there was already a loyal dependent queen of Egypt, bound to Antony by special bonds. Across the Red Sea there was another (though less reliable) dependent state, that of the Arabs. It seemed clear to Antony that a strong Jewish state on the Arab border was equally indispensable to Roman Syria and the empire. The job of making it strong and keeping it loyal had been allocated to Herod, and he had won the right to be given every support.

This group of client states was part of a much larger picture. For the Levant possessed such a varied organisation that it seemed like a continent rather than a country; and the same was true, to an even bigger extent, of Asia Minor. In that peninsula Antony was at this moment setting up three new kings of large and important dependent monarchies beyond the Roman frontier: Pontus in the north, Galatia in the centre, and Cappadocia in the south-east, where it shared the frontier burden with Syria. Later, after Antony had broken with Octavian (Augustus), all sorts of offensive things were said about Antony's arrangements. But these client monarchies, except in the special case of Egypt, proved durable. This may have caused some surprise because no less than three of the monarchs concerned suffered the handicap of not being of the local royal blood. The introduction of outsiders in this way was an innovation that the Romans had launched with Herod. Now he had confirmed Antony's confidence in his powers by surmounting an enormous crisis, and establishing control. But he still had extremely severe internal problems to face.

Herod and the Jews

4

After Herod had won his victory, it was inevitable that there should be a savage reckoning among the Jews who were now his subjects. But some of them, actively or passively, were on his side. And so these Palestinian Jews must now be discussed, since the situations of their various divisions, groups and sects throw important light both on potential opposition movements and also on his own power base. It was hardly to be expected that the council of state would get off lightly. After the military operations in Galilee with which Herod had inaugurated his career ten years earlier, they had objected so strongly to his unauthorised executions that they had tried to ruin him, and perhaps kill him. And now most of them had proved strong supporters of Antigonus, forming the life and soul of his resistance to Herod's besieging army. So once Herod had gained the upper hand, forty-five of the council's members, including most of the leading noblemen of the country, were arrested and executed, and their property was confiscated by the victor. The vacant seats were filled, but there is no record that Herod consulted this Jewish council ever again, or that he allowed it to exercise its judicial prerogatives. From now onwards it was reduced to a scholarly college, its competence strictly limited to jurisdiction on matters of doctrinal law, with future appointments to its presidency vested in Herod himself.

By all these actions, including the liquidation of Herod's enemies, the section of the Jewish population most heavily hit was the Sadducees. These were a relatively small and select group of influential and wealthy men, mostly landed magnates, and they also included the hereditary priests who controlled the Temple. There is some doubt about the origin of the name Sadducee. One theory among many links it with Zadok, a high priest of David's and Solomon's time;[1] and this is plausible enough, since the focus of their power was the Temple. While regarding themselves as the sole legitimate interpreters of the scriptures – the written scriptures, for oral traditions had no interest for them – they believed that the ceremonies of the Temple were more important than any academic hair-splitting about the Law. Denying predestination, they maintained man's freedom of choice and ability to change history. They were comparatively uninterested in morality; nor did they respond to the current wave of belief in an after-life, for they could find in the holy books no justification for the resurrection of the body, the survival of the soul, or the Last Judgment. Modern adaptations of Judaism, in harmony with the times, did not appeal to them, for they feared that their own privileges would suffer. In consequence, their teaching lacked the emotional basis needed for survival. Their influence was due solely to the inherited authority of the priestly aristocracy; and now Herod's victory had dealt it a mortal blow.

For the Sadducees had been attached to the Hasmonaeans, and were the core of their party. They had therefore objected to the emergence of Antipater as the guiding spirit of Hyrcanus. It was not because he was pro-Roman that they hated Antipater: a certain measure of Hellenisation and collaboration did not come amiss to them. They hated him because he was an Idumaean encroaching on the Hasmonaean royal house, and they hated Herod for the same reason. They felt the general prejudice against Idumaeans more strongly than anyone else, and it was they who, in 47 BC, had inspired the council to plan Herod's ruin. It was they, again, who formed the backbone of his enemies in Jerusalem ten years later: it was inconceivable to them that a 'foreigner' should be king of the Jewish nation.[2] Now they paid the penalty – though we shall see, later on, that Herod managed to create a new and docile Sadducee aristocracy (see Chapter 8).

As for those members of the council who managed to survive Herod's massacre, the most important of them represented another section of Jewish opinion, the Pharisees. During the siege two leading Pharisees led a move to open the gates to Herod. Their names are corrupted or misrepresented in Josephus, but it has been convincingly argued, and it appears highly probable, that they were the greatest Pharisee leaders of all time, Hillel the Elder and Shammai the Elder.[3] Ten years earlier, Shammai had stiffened the attitude of the Council against Herod's improprieties in Galilee. But now he and his colleague urged submission.

The Pharisees and Sadducees were not so much separate sects as legal schools representing different attitudes inside a common framework. They had crystallised as identifiable groups in the latter half of the second century BC, when the Pharisees, following the tradition of earlier groups of strict pietists, arose as a party opposed to the Hasmonaean merger of the kingship with the high priesthood. The name Pharisee has been the subject of as much speculation as Sadducee; the most frequently accepted interpretation derives it from a word meaning separated,[4] that is to say cut off from what is sinful or unclean. They themselves preferred the more modest title *Haberim*, meaning equals or associates or fellow-members.

In a later generation Josephus became a Pharisee, and he is speaking with their voice when he declares that the primary characteristic of Judaism is the Law. This Torah or Revelation – understood in terms of the legislation accompanying the sacred gift – consisted of the five Books of Moses, which came to be regarded as canonical towards the end of the fourth century BC. By 200, the canon of the Prophets was fixed, and later followed the canon of the 'Writings', the remaining portions of what Christians describe as the Old Testament. Many Jewish writers of all periods enlarge on their passionate love of the Law, notably the Psalmist[5] and the author of *Ecclesiasticus* (Ben Sira, *c*. 180 BC);[6] and to a Greek who slandered the heritage of Moses Josephus replied: 'We have laws perfectly designed to encourage true religion, social justice and international goodwill.'

The Pharisees took upon themselves the lofty task of expounding and interpreting this Law, insisting that it covered the whole of both national and personal life. In sharp contrast, however, to the Sadducees they believed that God had imparted to Moses on Mount Sinai not only the written Law of the Torah but an unwritten Law as well, known (from about Herod's time) as the 'ancient tradition' or 'tradition of the elders',[7] which had been handed down orally by divine authority, and must be preserved and transmitted to future generations. Later theologians even declared that the Holy One made the Covenant with Israel solely because of the oral tradition.[8]

Figure supporting on his head the sacred candlestick, or Menorah; from the catacombs of Beth Shearim, of late Roman date.

63

The strength of the Pharisees lay not in the Temple, which was the sphere of the Sadducees and priests, but in the synagogues, which were primarily places for the study of the Law. Though they are unlikely to have been initiated by the Pharisees,[9] the synagogues were increasingly employed by them to guide the minds of the Jews. For the most part the Hebrew of the Old Testament was only understood by well-educated people, but the Pharisees were able to offer Aramaic versions, which gave them an opportunity to add their own elaborations and interpretations. They were progressive in matters of religion, seeking, it is true, to resist Hellenising relaxations, but feeling that this could best be done by the adaptation of their faith to practical modern needs; for they declared that men have the right to amend any and every law. They were essentially a lay movement, mainly middle class – keen on schooling[10] and eager for conversions.[11]

Their assistants in these tasks were lay scribes (*Sopherim*). And indeed many Pharisees were scribes themselves. The scribes decided what was required to give practical effect to the Law in all details of conduct, and made it their business to seek out deeper meanings in the Torah by supplementations and inferences.[12] The typical scribe, often a poor man, is singled out for praise in *Ecclesiasticus*.[13]

At their best, the Pharisees were by no means dry formalists, but wanted to make religion a source of joy. They appealed to the popular sentiment of the day by stressing personal religion, and the sense of sin, and morality, and the resurrection of the body, and rewards and retributions in the after-life.[14] They envisaged the whole of history as pervaded by the divine purpose, and their faith, so much warmer than that of the Sadducees, is the Judaism that has survived today. But the Sadducees found their 'enthusiasm' distasteful, and accused them of playing up to the lower classes. They were also criticised in other quarters too, though their partisan Josephus does not dwell on the fact. Their interpretations were called 'smooth', and they were called painted ones, artificial and insincere teachers of hypocrisy.[15] Later, their observance of the letter of the Law, as interpreted by their more pedantic members, infuriated Jesus – hence the unfavourable definition of Pharisee in our dictionaries today. And they denounced him in turn because, Pharisee though he was, he had ignored their convention that interpretations of the Mosaic Law, as of Islamic Law, should be established not by command but by the creation of a consensus of opinion.

This, then, was the tradition maintained by Hillel and Shammai, who intervened during the siege of Jerusalem urging surrender to Herod. They were presidents of academies for the exposition of the Torah. It was later believed that they had taken on these posts from a series of similar pairs of men *(Zuggoth)* dating from 165 BC. But Jewish writings have very little to say of any teachers of earlier generations: which suggests that the tradition was still, in the time of Hillel and Shammai, at an early stage of formation, and that they played a great part in its foundation. That is to say, the Herodian age is of great significance in the history of the Jewish faith;[16] and the fact that such men pursued their creative tasks unimpeded by the king, and assisted by the peace he brought to Judaea, is an important facet of his achievement.

Hillel, who was born in Babylonia, was mild and humble and disliked hair-splitting. He enunciated the Golden Rule: 'Do not do to others that which you would not have them do to you'[17] – an injunction later revised by Jesus from negative to positive, though Christians and Jews have differed about the merits of the change. Shammai on the other hand had the reputation of being stern and inflexible, a tower of strength in his zeal for the Torah; and he usually followed the closer literal meaning of the text.

After getting into trouble with earlier Hasmonaean monarchs, the Pharisees had received deferential treatment from Queen Alexandra Salome (76–67 BC), whose reign moderate Pharisaic opinion consequently looked back upon as a time of almost millennial bliss; it was she, too, who introduced scribes into her state council. Nevertheless, when her family was brought down by Herod, these agreeable memories did not prevent the sections of opinion represented by Hillel and Shammai from counselling acquiescence to the non-Hasmonaean victor. The need for government was acknowledged: 'If it were not for the fear of government,' said Rabbi Hanina (when law and order were breaking down in Judaea in the century after Herod's death), 'men would swallow one another up alive'. The holders of this view were not likely to oppose Rome. 'And so,' advised another, 'love work and shun authority and have nothing to do with the ruling power.'[18] To those inclined for such pronouncements, Hillel and Shammai declared that Herod was an infliction from heaven, God's scourge and instrument of judgment – and that this had to be endured. Such a scourge was

Inkwells from the community house of a Jewish sect at Khirbet Qumran near the Dead Sea.

widely expected,[19] and its identification with Herod is forcibly declared by a Jewish work *The Assumption of Moses,* written shortly after the king's death and reflecting a section of opinion during his lifetime.[20]

This was perhaps not the most complimentary and tactful way to speak of Herod, but he did not mind, for if people held such a view it meant in effect that they would collaborate, so long as he did not interfere with religion and the Law. Their quietism suited him; it virtually made them into a pro-Herodian party, though a passive one. When his followers spread the report that he was of priestly, Davidian origin, this may have represented an attempt to ingratiate him with Hillel, who was himself said to be descended from the house of David in the female line. In any case, while these Pharisees and Herod appeased one another with a mutual policy of live and let live, the Pharisaic work throughout the country prospered as never before.

But there was also a radical branch of Pharisaism: the fact that 'Pharisee' is likely to mean 'separated' suggests how this aspect of their thought might take a political turn, and come to signify dissidence or secession. However, this tendency did not cause Herod any dismay, for extreme Pharisees of this kind had particularly hated the Hasmonaeans, so that for a time at least they were inclined to join those who found Herod positively welcome. But these people needed very careful handling, not least because they tended to hold pronounced Messianic views. Many moderate Pharisees deplored such opinions, including Hillel himself, who declared: 'He who has acquired for himself words of the Torah has acquired life in the coming world';[21] that is to say, immortality can be secured without having to wait for a Messiah to provide it. And Josephus tries to write as if such Messianic expectations did not even exist.[22]

Nevertheless, the extreme, Messianically-minded Pharisees formed a rallying-point for those whose national hopes and aspirations led them to believe in a coming Golden Age under the kingship of the house of David. Messianism was strong all over the Mediterranean world; Virgil's *Fourth Eclogue* (40 BC) is redolent of it. The Jewish word *mashiah,* in Greek *christos,* means 'anointed': someone who is holy, a king or priest with access to God. In Judaism, although a more spiritual and transcendental version was growing, the general belief was that a king of David's line would come and suppress the nation's enemies by force.

Such beliefs always flared up when things were going badly. 'Unless,' said David Ben Gurion, 'we had inherited from the Prophets the Messianic vision of redemption, the sufferings of the Jewish people in the Dispersion would have led to their extinction.' Moreover, since the time of the captivity by the Babylonians in the sixth century BC, many new ultra-Messianic passages had been

The caves near the monastic house at Qumran, seven miles from Jericho, where the 'Dead Sea Scrolls' were discovered.

interpolated into the older prophetic books. Then came the Hasmonaeans, and those who favoured them found it politic to allow that the Messiah might be not of David's house after all, but of Aaron's Levite line, as the new royal house claimed to be; or indeed it was possible to interpret a passage in Numbers to mean that a Priest-Messiah and Lay-Messiah would *both* make their appearance.[23] In any case, the successful Hasmonaean struggle seemed an assurance of divine aid and an encouragement to martyrdom; the war of liberation was surely a prelude to the final glorious cataclysm. And so, from that time onwards – the *Book of Daniel* is an early example – there was a great proliferation of Messianic, apocalyptic writings, enlarging in various ways on the promises of the scriptures. And there arose in consequence a whole host of self-declared Messiahs, who attracted followings of widely varying sizes.

The word Messiah first appears, as far as we know, in a collection known as the *Psalms of Solomon*, which seems to date from about

A thanksgiving hymn: one of the 'Dead Sea Scrolls' (so far ten complete and six hundred fragmentary) from the library at Khirbet Qumran.

50 BC and looks upwards from the tawdry Hasmonaean decline to the future return of David which is surely to be expected: 'God bring it to pass'.[24] And the same message is enlarged upon in many other pious works. 'The Son of Man', 'the hope of those who are troubled at heart', will found an empire under God's rule, from

The Qumran scrolls were placed in these jars before their ascetic custodians hid them away, perhaps after an earthquake.

which alien races will be expelled.[25] Hatred of the nation's enemies must be fostered,[26] and at the appointed time, when an apocalyptic war shall be waged against the whole lot of them, God will make his terrible visitation.[27] Meanwhile it is necessary to discern clearly who is the true follower of the Covenant, and who the false, which the legitimate beneficiary and which the usurper.[28]

The assertions quoted in the foregoing paragraph, together with others collected in an entire Messianic anthology,[29] are all drawn from the scrolls found in the library of a monastic community at Khirbet Qumran not far from the northern end of the Dead Sea, seven miles from Jericho. This frightening wasteland, between the salty waters and the limestone cliffs, was often the setting for passionate Jewish religious experience; it is the sort of territory in which John the Baptist formulated his message. We learn the austere rules of the Qumran community from its own *Manual of Discipline*. The precise dates of the works in its library are disputed,

Commentaries on Isaiah from Qumran. They expand the famous Messianic prophecy, and apply to the community the prophetic vision of the New Jerusalem.

but many or most of them belong to middle or later Hasmonaean times. Structural damage suffered by the tower, and a large diagonal crack which appeared in the steps, may perhaps be attributable to an earthquake of 31 BC, described by Josephus. This assumption is given added probability by the appearance in Qumran finds of Hasmonaean coinage, but the almost complete absence of coins of Herod (under his successor, finds are resumed). What happened must remain conjectural, but a clue seems to be provided by the uncompromising criticism of the Hasmonaean authorities that appears in many of the monastery's books,[30] as in those of at least one other related sect.[31] It could be that Herod, whatever his own origins might have been, welcomed this attitude and saw such communities as potential allies, or at least not as enemies. If so, when Qumran was devastated by the earthquake, it is conceivable that he gave the survivors refuge in Jerusalem, or built them another centre elsewhere.[32]

The most famous of these withdrawn monastic sects was that of the Essenes, who may have split off from the Pharisees in the early second century BC. Towards the Essenes, too, we know that Herod was favourable; it was stated that he was prepared to credit them with superhuman powers. Josephus was another who believed in their prophetic gifts. He says that one of their leaders, Menaemus (Menahem), when Herod was a boy, gave him a friendly smack on the bottom (a liberty few would have hazarded later on) and told him that he would be a great king but a bad man.[33] Though this story clearly did not emanate from Herod himself, it is likely he was impressed by the supposed prophetic talents of the Essenes, not only because of the deep-rooted prophetic tradition of the Jews, which was still vigorously active at this period,[34] but because occultism, too, was equally rife among them at this very time.[35] Indeed a symbol that appears on Herod's coins, a cross like the ones found on clay lamps and stone coffins excavated near Jerusalem,[36] seems to be of magical significance, denoting protection against evil spirits; it was customary to draw the cross-like letter X (*Chi*) on the crowns of kings.[37]

Bronze coin of Herod showing a cross placed within a wreath. The cross may be a royal charm against evil spirits.

However, the main reason why Herod favoured the Essenes was that they made it their invariable practice to refrain from disobedience to the political authority, actually going so far as to maintain that no ruler attains his office except by the will of God.[38] For this reason, we are told by the Jewish writer Philo, they had never clashed with any ruler of Palestine, however tyrannical, up to his own lifetime in the first century AD.[39] This was a passive attitude which could not fail to commend itself to Herod, and it is reported that he even went so far as to exempt the Essenes, like the Pharisees, from the oath of loyalty to himself, since such a worldly oath would have been contrary to their principles. The Qumran settlement is often identified with the Essenes. But if, as has been suggested above, he approved of the Qumran community too, that was for a different reason – because they were sternly militant, and because their militancy was directed against his Hasmonaean enemies. In view of this marked difference of attitude the complete identity of the Essenes and Qumran recluses seems unlikely. Probably there was quite a considerable number of such monastic sects, with differing views, many more than we are aware of; and the fact that we know about two of them and not the rest is

Scroll of the War of the Sons of Light and the Sons of Darkness foretelling God's onslaught upon the enemies of the Jews.

due to two accidents – the discovery of the Qumran library, and the fact that Josephus was interested in the Essenes because he had been one himself in his youth, living for a time with the Essene ascetic Bannus.[40] He says that there were four thousand of them, forming virtually a monastic order dedicated to the exact conduct of ritual and the interpretation of the Torah.

Such, then, were the religious elements from which Herod hoped to win support or at least obedience. And with this assurance of a certain amount of Jewish support, active and passive, behind him, he felt able to make a gesture which looked generous and might be useful. The former king, ethnarch and high priest, Hyrcanus, taken off to Babylonia in 40 by the Parthians, had been set at liberty there, and was treated with much honour by the large local Jewish community. But now he wanted to return home. The Parthians were willing – perhaps they found he inconveniently divided the loyalties of their Jews – and Herod agreed. So not long after his capture of Jerusalem he welcomed Hyrcanus back, addressing him as his father and ushering him into the place of honour. Probably he had not much liked the head of the Hasmonaean house maintaining what was virtually his own Jewish court under Parthian auspices; one can see that he might have been glad to get him back under his own control.

But Hyrcanus could not return to the high priesthood, owing to the mutilation of his ears. Nor could Herod become high priest himself, because his family, whatever inspired rumours to the contrary might say, was not regarded as possessing the requisite qualifications. But the office was of enormous importance. Jews regarded it as the very embodiment of their peculiar past and future destiny. The faithful had always been called upon to protect the legitimacy of this high priesthood. Indeed, it is no accident that the term 'theocracy' comes to us from a Jew, Josephus; for the prophet Ezekiel had declared that the worldly power must be subordinate to the spiritual.[41] As events were turning out under Herod, however, exactly the opposite had occurred. It is true that he received repeated suggestions that the high priesthood should be given back its secular powers,[42] but he was not likely to entertain such proposals for a moment. On the contrary, he was henceforward going to keep the office under his own close control. And from now on it was going to be neither lifelong nor heritable any longer.

To stress the point, the sacred robes themselves were to be kept under Herod's personal supervision. They were descendants of the robes with which God himself had clothed Aaron,[43] and they were too greatly and passionately revered for the king to feel safe if they were allowed in other hands.

From now on, these vestments were to be kept by Herod himself, and only released to be worn by the high priest on four ceremonial occasions each year: the feasts of the Passover, Pentecost and Tabernacles, and the Day of Atonement.

The robes were lodged in a new fortress-palace Herod built for himself, to replace the old Hasmonaean palace (Akra) which was in the upper city.[44] The new building, named the Antonia after Herod's patron Antony, stood beside the Temple, beyond its north-western extremity. It superseded a former castle, the Bira (Baris), which had been ruined during the siege of 37 and was the site of Antigonus' capitulation. But the Antonia was built sixty yards to the north of the Bira, so that Herod could escape the imputation of living inside the precincts of the Temple, where non-priestly, earthly rulers were not permitted to dwell.

The platform which was artificially levelled for the Antonia can still be seen. Upon it stood a great square structure, with four

The lower courses of the wall on the left form part of the foundations of one of the towers of Herod's Antonia fortress.

corner towers rising precipitously into the sky, three to a height of seventy-five feet and the other to a hundred feet or more. This building, with its frontage three hundred and seventy-five feet long, was compared by Josephus to a whole town, so numerous were its courts and porticoes and baths – the prototype of fortress-palaces such as Split and the Tower of London. Dominating the Temple as the Temple dominated the city, the Antonia was linked to the sacred precinct by underground passages as well as two stairways.[45] It was well placed to put down Temple riots, and indeed seemed the very symbol of the temporal power exercising domination over the centre of the faith.

This new state of affairs, arising from the unavoidable separation of the kingship from the high priesthood, cast a grave strain on Jewish emotions. Many thought that Herod would try to alleviate the tension by allowing the high priesthood to remain within the Hasmonaean house. After all, its leading figures had, until recently, combined the offices of king and high priest, and now that they no longer held the kingship there was a strong case for supposing that, as long as there was a male Hasmonaean available, he ought to

Model of the Antonia fortress, erected by Herod at the north-west corner of the Temple compound and named after Mark Antony.

occupy the high priesthood. And there was such a Hasmonaean: the young Aristobulus (III), the teenage grandson of the last high priest Hyrcanus II (whose Hebrew name Jonathan he adopted) and brother of Herod's own wife Mariamme.

But Herod, although he had married a beautiful Hasmonaean, wanted to hear no more of the political pretensions of her family, and the high priesthood was red-hot politics. So he now made the decision – which must have been regarded as sensational – to give the office to a member of another family altogether. A certain Ananel was selected and appointed. He was a little-known Jew from Babylonia,[46] and since he possessed no local connexions, he would be subservient enough. But the appointment was ingenious because Ananel actually belonged to the line of Zadok, reputed to be descendants of Moses' brother Aaron – the family in which, *before* the Hasmonaeans, the high priesthood had always been vested, men who held a place apart: 'the sons of Zadok, who alone of the Levites may come near the Lord.[47]

It may even be that Herod's own claim of priestly origin was intended to link him with Ananel. But what is clearer is that the appointment seemed a shrewd riposte to the pretensions of the Hasmonaeans. In comparison, their own high priesthoods, so vigorously extolled by their supporters, did not look so impeccable after all. They had only received them in the first place through the gift of Seleucid, Syrian monarchs or usurpers, and the priestly family to which they belonged was an obscure and undistinguished one, by no means Aaronic.[48] Besides, the Hasmonaean candidate, Mariamme's brother Aristobulus (III), was only sixteen, and it could be argued that this was too young. Theoretically, it is true, a high priest could be very juvenile indeed, and some held that at any time after puberty a man could hold a priesthood. But most later rabbinical authorities were inclined to hold that no priest should officiate until he was twenty; and this doctrine was no doubt already current among the authorities of Herod's time.

But Herod discovered he had miscalculated, for fury broke about his ears. His decision must have angered a great many admirers of the Hasmonaeans, but the centre of the storm was in his own family. In particular, his mother-in-law Alexandra (II), the mother of his wife Mariamme, was enraged beyond measure. She was an exceedingly formidable and persistent woman, bearing little resemblance to her ineffectual father Hyrcanus, but clearly taking after the many aggressive members of her house.

Herod, Antony and Cleopatra

And so Herod, by his appointment of Ananel to the high priest-hood, had antagonised his dangerous mother-in-law Alexandra. If she had stood by herself, he could have dealt with her. But she possessed a most powerful ally – Cleopatra: and now, in her dis-tress, it was to Cleopatra that she wrote, appealing for the reversal of Herod's decision about the high priesthood. Cleopatra was in Syria, and so was Antony (October 37), and Cleopatra spoke to him and urged him to get the new high priest deposed in favour of Alexandra's son.

Now Herod may have been prepared to put up with strife within his own family – and strife there surely was, since his mother-in-law exercised much influence over his wife. But one thing he knew, and that was that he simply could not afford to antagonise Antony's mistress Cleopatra. She was an extremely grave threat to Herod, and the threat was just reaching its acutest phase. The fact of the matter was that, like other Egyptian rulers of subsequent epochs, she wanted the Jewish kingdom right out of the way altogether. Passionately devoted to the idea of reconstituting the Egyptian empire as it had been in the days of her ancestors, she never forgot that Judaea had formed part of that imperial territory (before the Seleucids had succeeded in annexing it for themselves) and that it was her mission to suppress its independence and make it a Ptolemaic province once again. It is true that, when Herod had come to her in 40, a young fugitive wanting to get to Antony, she had done nothing to harm him; indeed she had given him en-couragement and help. But it had not seemed, in those days, that he was ever really likely to come back to Palestine, much less to rule it. Yet now he had returned and taken over, and this had happened just at the time when, encouraged by close association with Antony, her own ambitions were taking shape. Foremost among them was the destruction of Herod, and the annexation of his country.

Antony's reaction to this aim shows that, so far at any rate, he was not the besotted lover his enemies made him out to be. Herod's kingdom formed a very precious part of his system of imperial defence, and Herod himself inspired him with affection, as far as we can tell, and certainly with confidence. Cleopatra's blandish-ments, therefore, were quite unable to make him eliminate Herod altogether. Other Levantine dynasts, on whose territories Cleopatra had similar designs, were less fortunate. One of them was executed and she got his land. She also obtained a whole series of Hellenised coastal city-states in Phoenicia, the modern Lebanon – in fact she acquired nearly the whole Phoenician maritime strip, except Tyre and Sidon. She was even given a considerable tract in the interior which had been directly under the control of the Roman province – an alienation of imperial territory which was made much of, for propaganda purposes, by her numerous enemies at Rome. And the Arab kingdom had to cede important areas of Transjordan, which passed under her control and became enclaves in her kingdom. The most lucrative of these territorial transfers carried with it the sole right to exploit the bitumen or asphalt which rises to the surface of the Dead Sea – a material much prized as mortar, and as a medicine, and for protection against worms and grubs in vineyards, and for the embalming of corpses.

Coin of Cleopatra
VII of Egypt,
issued at independ-
dent Ascalon
(Ashkelon) in 38 BC.

Cleopatra's operation of this Dead Sea monopoly would bring her officials unpleasantly close to Herod's territory. Indeed it became quite clear that, even if Antony was not going to allow Herod's total suppression, the latter, like the other princes of the Levant, was going to have to make certain substantial concessions to her special relationship with the Roman leader. It also became painfully clear, while Cleopatra was with Antony in Syria during 36, what these unavoidable concessions were going to be. For it was now decided that Herod should cede to her a very considerable coastal strip, including Joppa and the greater part of his shore-line, though he was, for the present, able to retain Gaza, which was left as the terminal of a Jewish corridor to the sea.[1]

These were grave losses, and Herod was struck a further financial blow as well. For he was also forced to let Cleopatra have his extremely profitable groves of date-palms and balsam at Jericho, north of the Dead Sea. The palms of Jericho (*palma caryota*), known as 'hang-over palms' because of the strength of the date wine they produce, were the finest grown on a commercial scale anywhere in the ancient world. The two balsam groves covering twenty square miles produced the famous 'balm of Gilead' which cured headaches and cataracts and was prized for its fragrant scent. The pain caused to Herod by these serious encroachments can only, perhaps, have been somewhat relieved by the consideration that everyone else was in the same boat – and that Cleopatra would one day go too far.

Meantime, while it was very regrettable to have functionaries of Cleopatra in the coastal towns, it would be even more unpalatable to have them in the interior, managing these groves she had annexed only fifteen miles from Jerusalem. Herod dealt with this awkward problem by proposing that he should rent the groves back from Cleopatra for a very substantial annual sum. For good measure, he also offered to be responsible for the sum the Arabs on the eastern side of the Dead Sea were committed to pay her for their bitumen. The arrangement was satisfactory enough to Cleopatra

View eastwards from the Jerusalem temple: the Mount of Olives, venerated as the place from which Jesus ascended to heaven.

because she would get all the money without having to do anything to earn it; and with any luck she would succeed in embroiling the Jews and Arabs with one another.

But Herod, too, was making the best of a bad job. The arrangement he had made with Cleopatra was expensive, but at least it kept Egyptian officials right away from the area, and it gave Herod a chance to intervene in Arab affairs. All in all he had not fared too badly, especially considering that there was treachery within his own palace. For this was just about the time when, as we have seen, his mother-in-law Alexandra was writing to her friend Cleopatra urging Antony to get Herod's newly-appointed high priest deposed in favour of her own son Aristobulus (111). Antony took no direct action; though it may have been now that he sent a devious diplomat in his service, Quintus Dellius, to discuss matters with Herod. And Antony thought it advisable, in order to keep the peace and conciliate Cleopatra and Alexandra, to invite the young Aristobulus to come and pay him a visit.[2] Herod, however, declined the invitation on the youth's behalf, with the very reasonable explanation that such a trip would be a security hazard since it would stimulate seditious hopes and intrigues.

Nevertheless, as regards the high-priesthood, Herod knew he was defeated. He simply could not run the risk of having his position further undermined with Antony. And so he gave in. By the end of 37, or in the first weeks of the following year, the high priest Ananel was deposed. Having been criticised for making the appointment, Herod now incurred criticism for deposing him. It was a breach of the Law, and religious historians could only find two precedents, neither of which they regarded as satisfactory.

So Aristobulus, shortly after his seventeenth birthday, became high priest. But Herod did not like doing things under compulsion; what had happened did not inspire him with love for Alexandra, and he still did not like having a Hasmonaean as high priest. The outcome is vividly described by Josephus.

For the time being Herod seemed to have healed his domestic troubles. But still he did not long remain free of suspicion, as is natural after a reconciliation, for he had reason to fear from Alexandra's past attempts that she would try to overthrow his government if she found an opportunity. He therefore ordered her to remain in her palace and not to do anything on her own authority; and as a careful watch was kept, nothing escaped him, not even what she did in her daily life. All this gradually made her wild with rage and caused hatred to grow in addition, for she had a full share of womanly pride and resented the supervision that came from his suspicion, and she thought anything was better than to be deprived of her freedom of action and to live the rest of her life in slavery and fear in spite of appearing to have honour. She therefore wrote to Cleopatra, making a long sustained lament about the state in which she found herself and urging her to give her as much help as she possibly could.

Thereupon Cleopatra told her to escape secretly with her son and come to her in Egypt. This seemed to Alexandra a good idea, and she contrived the following scheme. She had two coffins made as if for the transporting of dead bodies, and placed herself and her son in them, after giving orders to those of her servants who knew of the plan to take them away during the night. From there they had a road to the sea and a ship ready for them to sail into Egypt. But her servant Aesop incautiously reported this to

Sabbion, one of her friends, thinking that he knew of the plan. When Sabbion learned of it – he had, as it happened, formerly been an enemy of Herod because he was believed to be one of those who had plotted to poison his father Antipater – he saw a chance to change Herod's hatred into goodwill by informing him of what was going on, and so he told the king all about Alexandra's plot. The king permitted things to proceed as far as the carrying out of the plan, and then caught her in the very act of fleeing. But he overlooked her offence because he did not dare take any harsh measures against her, even though he would have liked to, for Cleopatra, out of hatred toward him, would not have allowed her to be accused: and so he made a show of magnanimity as if forgiving them out of kindness rather than for another reason. He was determined at all costs, however, to get Aristobulus out of the way. But it seemed to him that he would be more likely to have his motives escape detection if he did not act at once or immediately after what had happened.

When Tabernacles came round – this is a festival observed by us with special care – he waited for these days to pass, while he himself and the rest of the people gave themselves up to rejoicing. But it was the envy arising from this very occasion and clearly working within it that led him to carry out his purpose more quickly. For Aristobulus was a youth of seventeen when he went up to the altar to perform the sacrifices in accordance with the law, wearing the ornamental dress of the high priests and carrying out the rites of the cult; and he was extraordinarily handsome and taller than most youths of his age, and in his appearance, moreover, he displayed to the full the nobility of his descent. And so there arose among the people an impulsive feeling of affection toward him, and there came to them a vivid memory of the deeds performed by his grandfather Aristobulus. Being overcome, they gradually revealed their feelings, showing joyful and painful emotion at the same time, and they called out to him good wishes mingled with prayers, so that the affection of the crowd became evident, and their acknowledgment of their emotions seemed too impulsive in view of their having a king.

As a result of all these things Herod decided to carry out his designs against the youth. When the festival was over and they were being entertained at Jericho as the guest of Alexandra, he showed great friendliness to the youth and led him on to drink without fear, and he was ready to join in his play and to act like a young man in order to please him. But as the place was naturally very hot, they soon went out in a group for a stroll, and stood beside the swimming-pools, of which there were several large ones around the palace, and cooled themselves off from the excessive heat of noon. At first they watched some of the servants and friends (of Herod) as they swam, and then, at Herod's urging, the youth was induced to join them. But with darkness coming on while he swam, some of the friends, who had been given orders to do so, kept pressing him down and holding him under water as if in sport, and they did not let up until they had quite suffocated him. In this manner was Aristobulus done away with when he was at most eighteen years old and had held the high priesthood for a year.[3]

Aristobulus met his end towards the end of the warm weather of 36; and Ananel became high priest again.

So distasteful had Herod found it to see an attractive young Hasmonaean holding the office that he had decided to get rid of him, and face the consequences. For consequences there were bound to be. It is true that Aristobulus was given a splendid funeral – and his death was described as an accident, but Alexandra, for one, was not going to believe this version of her son's death for a moment. In a frenzy of rage and grief she wrote to Cleopatra again. Antony, who was just back in Syria from an inconclusive and costly campaign against the Parthians, was obliged to listen to Cleopatra's tale. And so Herod found himself summoned to Laodicea (Lattakia on the Syrian coast) to give his account of what had happened.

If this meeting took place in spring 35, as is quite likely, Cleopatra was there as well. Yet, even if she was, things did not turn out at all as she and Alexandra had hoped. Antony declared himself uninterested in the private scandals of Herod's court; the internal affairs of dependent kingdoms, he said, were of no concern to him. What was uppermost in his mind was his own strategic planning against the Parthians. They had inflicted an expensive setback on him in the previous year, and now, in the season that lay ahead, he intended to attack them again with a very large force. It was therefore essential that affairs along his frontiers should be in trustworthy hands. He knew he could rely on Herod. Whether the king intended to deny the murder of Aristobulus, or to justify it on the grounds of political necessity, we do not know, for, as it happened, Antony refused to listen to any formal case against him at all. On the contrary, he invited Herod to sit with him on the tribunal at law suits and entertained him lavishly (later Herod recalled the pleasant circumstances of his visit by presenting the town of Laodicea with a new water supply). In order, however, to take Cleopatra's mind off the snub, Antony did feel it advisable to instruct Herod to let her have another gift. So to round off the coastal territories that had been ceded to her before, she was now given the Gaza strip too. If Herod, after this, had any considerable access to the Mediterranean, we do not know what it was. He was still alive, and still king; but it seems that he was totally landlocked.

Gaza was the port of Idumaea, and Cleopatra wanted that large territory too. Indeed, she had taken steps to secure it, by inducing its governor, Costobarus, to enter into treasonable correspondence with her. He was a leading Idumaean who, after the siege of Jerusalem two years earlier, had been entrusted by Herod with the key job of hunting down and exterminating the supporters of the defeated Hasmonaeans. Thereafter he was made governor of the country, which was not only his own and Herod's native land but regularly supplied the king with a large proportion of his troops.

However, Costobarus had powerful ambitions of his own. He would have liked to reign over an independent Idumaea, and he toyed with the idea that Cleopatra might find it in her interests to help him fulfil such an aim. His ancestors had been priests of the pagan god Koza, the divine archer, whom the Idumaeans had worshipped before their forcible conversion to Judaism in the previous century; and Costobarus probably intended, on achieving independence, to revert to paganism. However, the scheme misfired because Herod got wind of it. But the king acted discreetly, passing the matter over and retaining Costobarus in his post. His mother Cyprus and sister Salome (II) were said to have intervened. But presumably Costobarus had a formidable array of supporters – perhaps men who were disappointed that Idumaeans had not got more of the pickings at court. And Herod could not afford just now to have another upheaval on his hands, instigated, once again, by Cleopatra.

Besides, his triumphant return from Laodicea had very rapidly been spoilt by the news of deplorable developments at home during his absence. Herod had entrusted the control of the country, while he was away, to a certain Joseph (I) who was not only his own uncle but also the husband of his sister Salome. The exact nature of the trouble in which this prince became involved is obscure because the historian Josephus tells a story which he subsequently repeats when Herod goes away again five years later and leaves a different regent in charge. On both occasions, says Josephus, Herod instructed his regent to kill his wife Mariamme if he himself failed to come back; and on both occasions the regent disclosed to Mariamme that he had received this damning instruction. Such a duplication of events seems so unlikely that the story is best applied to the later occasion, when, as will be seen, it had identifiable results.

During the king's absence in 35, however, his uncle evidently disgraced himself in some way or other. Whether Herod, as was reported, suspected him of excessively intimate relations with Mariamme is quite uncertain – but far from improbable, since the king was a very jealous and suspicious man. But even without this addition, another plan his wife and uncle formed together, while he was away, was quite serious enough. For when Herod returned, he was told that Joseph and Mariamme and her mother had at one moment, during his absence, intended to seek refuge with the resident Roman legion; such a unit was still stationed in Jerusalem. They had formed this plan, on the instigation of Alexandra, after a false report from Syria that Herod had been put to death by Antony, and they only abandoned the design on the arrival of the king's letter indicating the successful outcome of the Laodicea meeting.

If this account of their proposed behaviour was true, it had been an unpardonable slur on Herod's vanity. For whatever qualms he himself may have felt about the prospects of his reception at

Laodicea, it was inexcusably humiliating that his own family should be prepared to believe reports that his journey had ended in such total and final failure. Consequently his uncle Joseph was executed.

The informant against him had been his own wife, Herod's sister Salome. Whatever her faults, and they were numerous – including an extremely ready ear for gossip – she was never lacking in what she regarded, often wrongly, as her duty to her royal brother. As for Alexandra, Herod seems to have believed, and he may have been right, that she had intended to pass Mariamme over to Antony if he himself died. That, it seemed to him, was why she had proposed to entrust the girl to the Roman legion. So his relations with Mariamme had begun to take an unhappy turn. And Alexandra, already repeatedly guilty of disloyal communications with Cleopatra, remained under the deepest suspicion.

The royal Egyptian coinage of Cleopatra: a bronze issue minted at Alexandria.

It now became necessary for Herod to see Cleopatra himself, and to see rather a lot of her – at a time when his feelings towards her must have been savage in the extreme. In 34 Antony was ready to try conclusions with Parthia again, and Cleopatra escorted him northwards from Egypt as far as the Euphrates, proceeding through territory largely consisting of her own recent annexations. Then she returned south through Syria, and paid a visit to the land she so greatly coveted: Judaea. She was received by Herod. The king later wrote in his memoirs that he had intended to kill Cleopatra, and that his friends had only dissuaded him from doing so with great difficulty. He also reported that she had tried to have sexual relations with him. It is doubtful if either story is true. The main aim of both of them, Jewish king and Egyptian queen alike, was to keep in with Antony, and Herod would most certainly not achieve that by killing Cleopatra any more than she would achieve it by seducing Herod. Of course, the queen, if she had attempted such a manoeuvre and had succeeded, might have planned to claim that the initiative had been Herod's, so that she could discredit him with

A silver coin of Syria inscribed in Greek with the names of Antony, Roman triumvir, and Cleopatra, 'goddess manifest', 34-32 BC.

Antony. But on the whole it seems more likely that Herod's assertion was a deliberately unchivalrous misinterpretation of an
occasion on which he had merely been at the receiving end of her
famous social charm.

And a little charm cannot have come amiss, since the meeting
must have concerned matters that were most unpalatable to Herod.
What they chiefly had to talk about was Herod's cession of his last
port, Gaza, to Cleopatra, the money he had to pay her for renting
back his own palm and balsam groves, and the further sums he was
committed to raising on her behalf from the Arabs. These were
indeed painful subjects. Nevertheless, eager to maintain Antony's
present intention of remaining friends with himself as well as
Cleopatra, Herod carried off the whole occasion well, showering
rich gifts on the queen he hated so much and escorting her back
home all the way to Pelusium beside the delta of the Nile.

Herod was particularly glad to get the queen out of the way,
because internal troubles, due to the increasing alienation of the
Hasmonaean remnant, were by no means over.

Not content with his great new castle-palace Antonia in Jerusalem itself, he had spent the past few years in the construction of a
further fortress, Hyrcania (Khirbet Mird). It was strategically
located in a bare desolate waste eight miles south-east of Jerusalem,
eleven miles south of Jericho, and close to the Dead Sea. The name
given to the castle suggests that it had been built, or rebuilt, in the
reign of John Hyrcanus I (134–104 BC). The Romans had destroyed
it in the fifties BC, but now the stronghold was reconstructed with
impregnable fortifications by Herod, who intended it to play a
major part in his security system.

Hyrcania also acquired a particularly evil reputation as a place
where captives were incarcerated before disappearing for ever. One
of the prisoners held there was a royal Hasmonaean personage, the
sister of Antigonus who had been defeated and executed in 37; she
was thus the sister-in-law of Alexandra (11), and Mariamme's aunt.
In about the year 33, encouraged by all the difficulties Herod was
experiencing, this princess attempted a rising. The indefatigable
persistence with which the Hasmonaeans fomented rebellion over
and over again shows how much support existed for them in the
country, and also, perhaps, what large hopes they based on Cleopatra. But this revolt, like all the others, was put down and the
princess lost her life. The surviving members of the Hasmonaean
house were becoming fewer and fewer.

At this point, however, all eyes were turned towards Roman affairs.
For some years past the government of the Roman world had been
divided between Antony and Octavian, occupying the eastern and
western provinces respectively (the third member of the triumvirate, Lepidus, had been dropped). The arrangement was an unstable

one, and now it was coming to an end, since each of these two potentates wanted the whole of the empire for himself. Each therefore was massing vast armies and fleets against the other, Octavian in Italy and Antony opposite him along the coast of Greece. It was clear that a major clash was approaching.

Antony's forces were enormous, but their morale was weakened – and this included the morale of the senior commanders – by the presence of the foreign woman Cleopatra in his camp. Until now, as we have seen, Antony had not granted Cleopatra everything she wished, but now the situation was becoming rather different. Whether his feelings towards her had become deeper we cannot say. But in any case there was also a practical reason for the increased closeness of their association: he had entrusted her with the construction of many ships, built of the wood she disposed of in her new Syrian possessions. These ships formed a substantial part of Antony's fleet, and he also depended largely on Egypt for provisions.

Every dependent prince of the region, naturally enough, was expected to enrol in Antony's military effort on this decisive occasion. Thus Herod, too, hastened to play his part. Enrolling an important and well-equipped contingent, he was actually on his way to join his patron in person when word came from Antony that he was to halt, go back, and march against the Arabs instead. So, without forgetting to send money and provisions on to Antony, he turned about and did as he was told.

Trouble had arisen with the Arabs over the lands they had been compelled to cede to Cleopatra, including the rich Dead Sea bitumen concession. Herod, it will be remembered, had agreed to make himself responsible for collecting the revenue from these properties and passing it on to Cleopatra. But now the Arab king, Malchus, had begun defaulting on his payments: and that was why Antony had ordered Herod to turn back, so that he could march into Arab territory and use force of arms to collect what was due. It is easy to see the hand of Cleopatra in this plan, since she was delighted to have an opportunity to keep Herod out of Antony's camp. Moreover, although Herod's victory was required in order to get hold of the funds, she took the special precaution of ensuring that it should not be too decisive a victory. For she herself sent a force to the neighbourhood, with instructions to prevent Herod from doing too well.

Antony's action in sending Herod against Malchus sowed the seeds of trouble for the future because it struck at the very principle underlying the conception of the Roman client states, to which category both the Jewish and Arab kingdoms belonged. States of this kind were not intended by the Romans to have any foreign policy of their own, and there should have been no question of them fighting against one another. It was true that Herod was only taking this action at the request of a Roman leader. Nevertheless the action, requested and performed merely because the Arabs were being financially refractory, completely negated their 'client' status. Worse still, Antony's instruction to attack the Arabs had a very bad psychological effect on Herod because it instilled in his mind the idea that he was free to attack them again whenever he felt like it; and later on, as we shall see, he felt like it and did it.

At all events, while Antony and Octavian prepared for their decisive sea-battle of Actium off the north-west coast of Greece, Herod was moving east across the Jordan to invade Arab territory (32 BC). First he gained a satisfactory success at Dium, probably the modern Tell-el-Ashari in south-western Syria, beyond the

The upper reaches of the River Jordan, crossed by Herod to enter Arab territory in 32 BC.

Golan Heights. But then, pushing onwards, he suffered a defeat at Canatha (Qanawat) in Auranitis (Hauran). In this rocky basalt-lava country, where the Arab cavalry found it difficult to operate, the battle started well for Herod. Evidently, however, he pressed the pursuit too impetuously; though, when disaster followed, he himself variously blamed it on the insubordination of officers and on intervention by the hovering force of Egyptian troops. Herod's headquarters camp was overrun, and he himself had to fall back behind the Jordan and resort to guerrilla tactics. In order to gain time, he sent a deputation to the Arabs to discuss possible peace terms. Moreover, at this juncture (spring 31), a serious earthquake took place, killing many thousands of persons and countless cattle. The Jewish troops out in the open were unaffected, but the Arabs, believing they had suffered serious losses, put Herod's envoys to death. Jewish morale was now low, but Herod succeeded in restoring it. Then he led his troops across the Jordan and up the long defile to the Arab provincial capital of Philadelphia, now Amman the capital of the Jordanian kingdom. On the rolling plain south of the city, Herod won an important victory, and the Arab King Malchus had to agree to meet his financial undertakings after all. It is also recorded that he gave Herod, who was partly a fellow Arab himself, an honorific title.

But the respite was brief, for very soon afterwards, in the greater Roman world, there occurred an earth-shaking event which could not fail to have violent repercussions upon the Jewish kingdom as on every other dependent state or subject province: for at the battle of Actium, Octavian and his admiral Agrippa won a conclusive victory over Antony's fleet (September, 31 BC).

Cleopatra's ships, which had stood in reserve, turned away, and she and Antony fled back to Egypt.

II

HEROD'S GREATER JUDAEA

Success with Augustus: tragedies at home

6

Antony and Cleopatra had lost the eastern world, and the entire Roman empire now belonged to Octavian.

The Arabs rapidly showed they had read events correctly. For when attacking a part of Cleopatra's fleet which had been drawn over a neck of land by the Nile delta in case she decided to escape down the Red Sea, they destroyed the entire force. This gained them valuable credit with the new world-ruler Octavian. It was now up to Herod to gain it too—a formidable task since he had been such a good friend of Antony. However, he hastily managed to perform a useful service to the victor by giving assistance to the Roman governor of Syria, who had gone over to the winning side. At Antony's request, a party of gladiators was on its way from Asia Minor to reinforce his meagre garrison in Egypt, and what Herod now did was to help the Syrian governor intercept and detain them. Then he planned to undertake the inevitable journey to see Octavian, who was on the island of Rhodes. But it was a perilous journey, and might even prove a fatal one; for Octavian might not easily forget his past services to Antony. So, before Herod left Judaea, he prepared for every eventuality.

The most important thing, he decided, was to make sure that Octavian could not be in a position to call upon any possible alternative candidate to the Jewish throne. It was only three years since the last Hasmonaean attempt at a rising, and the head of the Hasmonaean house was still alive and in Jerusalem. He was Hyrcanus ii, the former king, ethnarch and high priest, whom Herod had brought back from exile in Babylonia. Hyrcanus, now in his early seventies, was a mild and unambitious old man, but all the same it no longer seemed safe to have him about. Not only was he the obvious person to promote to the kingship again if anyone wished Herod ill, but he was liable to the continual nagging of his daughter Alexandra (ii). She was all too well aware of the increasingly bad relations between her daughter Mariamme and Herod. Nor was she likely to let Hyrcanus forget that his grandson Aristobulus (iii)–her son–had been murdered by the king. So Herod now felt that Hyrcanus, subject to these pressures, had become a security risk; and he therefore produced evidence that the old man had been in treasonable communication with the Arabian king Malchus. The Arab mon-

arch had sent Hyrcanus four horses as a present, together with a message of greeting. But according to Herod, there was a great deal more to it than that, for Malchus had also made arrangements that Hyrcanus should escape, in the company of numerous supporters, to Arab territory; and the entire plan, Herod claimed, had now been betrayed to himself by a go-between. This version of the story, set down in his memoirs, is generally assumed to be untrue. But its untruth cannot be regarded as certain. The scheme as Herod described it is one which might well have taken shape as an actual project in the hostile mind of Alexandra, and Hyrcanus could well have passively acquiesced in it, as he had acquiesced in so much else during his long and varied life.

However, his life was now at its end, for Herod, after showing the guilty letters, forged or otherwise, to his council of friends and relations – not the historic council of state – had him strangled: a form of capital punishment, incidentally, which was not authorised for such a crime by Jewish tradition.[1] And so died the man who, after his own not very whole-hearted fashion, had presided over the opening stages of Herod's career; the man, moreover, who formed a unique, historic link with the traditional, royal, high priesthood and the glories of the Hasmonaean liberation. And by getting rid of Hyrcanus Herod had ensured that he himself could go to Octavian with a less anxious heart, for now there was no one readily discoverable who could be called upon to replace him on the Judaean throne.

Nevertheless, he made his preliminary dispositions with some care. The last time he had gone away, when he went to meet Antony at Laodicea, his wife Mariamme, or more particularly his mother-in-law Alexandra, had made trouble on a serious enough scale to cost the life of his uncle and regent Joseph (I). This time, therefore, Herod took the extraordinary precaution of placing the two women in one fortress, Alexandrium, near the border of Judaea and Samaria, but separating them widely from Mariamme's children who were, in their turn, sent to another stronghold, Masada, near the southern end of the Dead Sea. There they were set under the care of his mother Cyprus and his sister Salome (II). The children were thus hostages to ensure that Alexandra and Mariamme should not raise a rebellion. The castle in which they were lodged, Alexandrium, was placed under the command of an officer named Sohaemus – he came from Ituraea, a country of which we shall hear more later on – while Masada was entrusted to Herod's own brother Pheroras. And if news should come that Herod was dead, Sohaemus was ordered to kill both Alexandra and Mariamme, so that Pheroras would be able to take over without Hasmonaean intervention, and the Idumaean house would thus remain in power. Ultimately, the heirs would still

Opposite: The hill-fortress of Masada. Right: Herod's three-terraced villa-palace, hanging over the abyss. The long, narrow chambers behind are store-rooms.

Mosaic floor from Herod's main (western) Palace at Masada. The lines were incised in the plaster to guide the mosaicist.

be his sons by Mariamme, half Idumaean and half Hasmonaean. But Herod believed that she and her mother, after his death, were capable of attempting an immediate anti-Idumaean *coup d'état* involving the destruction of his own brother and sister and other relations; and this was what his arrangements, and his instructions to Sohaemus, were intended to stop.

And so, in spring 30, he set off for Rhodes. The prospects were not, in fact, so alarming as he had thought, because, with the single and obvious exception of Cleopatra, Octavian had taken the sensible decision to confirm all Antony's major client rulers. Nevertheless,

Herod, when he arrived in the conqueror's presence, took the tactful precaution of leaving his royal diadem off. He then delivered a statement. He had been loyal to Antony, he said, and he would now be loyal to Octavian. He added that he had remained loyal to Antony until the very last moment (which was not entirely true because he had intercepted Antony's gladiatorial reinforcements very promptly, and was indeed written off as an ally by Antony's land commander immediately after Actium[2]). Herod also declared that he had consistently advised Antony to get rid of Cleopatra. He had certainly felt like giving him this advice, and it would be very interesting to know if he had really ventured to give voice to it. Anyway, it was a sentiment that Octavian must have regarded as very proper, especially since it harmonised with the official version of the civil war according to which the foreign woman Cleopatra, not the Roman Antony, was the real foe.

And so Herod's visit to Rhodes was a success. Octavian felt convinced, quite justifiably, that the Jewish monarch would be as useful to him as he had been to Antony. And so he announced his confirmation of Herod's kingship, later arranging that the Roman senate should formally sanction the decision. There was only one casualty, a certain Alexas (1) of Laodicea. After Antony returned with the remnants of his navy to Egypt, he had sent Alexas, who was his and Cleopatra's friend, to Herod to try to persuade him not to desert to Octavian.[3] Alexas, however, had not only failed in his mission, but had himself deserted to the winning side. And now, at Rhodes, Herod, encouraged by the way in which he himself had been received by Octavian, put in a plea for indulgence to Alexas. But the plea was not granted, since the Roman had already sworn to make an end of the man, on the grounds that Alexas had done everything in his power to block a reconciliation between Octavian and Antony at the time when such a possibility existed.

Nevertheless, this was only a minor disappointment; in more important matters Herod had succeeded wonderfully well. Furthermore, the time was approaching in which he could make himself useful again. Octavian was on the very point of launching an expedition against Egypt, to complete the elimination of Antony and Cleopatra, so that he would then be able to annex the country as a rich appendage to the Roman empire under his own personal control. When he landed at Ptolemais Ace in Phoenicia, Herod was already there, with a huge gift, and abundant provisions, and a hundred and fifty apartments ready to house Octavian and his friends. Then, as the Romans marched towards Egypt and came to the desert, Herod laid on supplies of water and even of wine.

It was not long before Antony and Cleopatra both committed suicide. Then Herod escorted Octavian back to Antioch, with the happy consciousness that he had outlived the queen whom he hated; he was to outlive her by twenty-six years.

Next, in the autumn of the same year (30 BC), all the territory he

The palm depicted agricultural prosperity - represented by the Jericho palm-groves - but is also the Tree of Wisdom, and the sacred Torah.

had lost to her became his once again. He resumed possession of his precious palm and balsam groves at Jericho, and he received back the coastline he had been obliged to relinquish to her. He even acquired certain towns on the coast which had ceased to belong to Judaea ever since Pompey had truncated its territory thirty-three years earlier. Two of these were not far from Jerusalem, the ancient Philistine communities of Jamnia (Yavne) and Azotus (Ashdod). Jamnia, Judaised by the Hasmonaeans, had been rebuilt under Roman rule; later it was destined to become a great centre of Jewish learning. Azotus, in the remote days of the past, had been the Philistine capital. It bordered upon the territory of Ascalon, which alone remained a free and independent enclave, privileged, no doubt, because of its associations with the family of Herod.

Octavian also amended Pompey's dispensation by giving Judaea back two towns that lay east of the Sea of Galilee. They belonged to a district known as the Decapolis, 'Ten Cities', corresponding, for the most part, to the Bashan and Gilead districts of the Old Testament, at the point where the modern frontiers of Israel, Jordan and Syria meet.[4] Pompey had detached the ten towns from Judaea and formed them into a self-governing league, and now Octavian still allowed eight of them to remain autonomous under the general supervision of the governor of Syria. But two passed into the possession of Herod. One of them was Hippos, which today is Susita – in Israel, but very near the Syrian border. It stands on the east side of the Sea of Galilee, its ancient walls rising upon the edge of a lofty precipice. The other town of the Decapolis which Herod gained was Gadara, a little further to the south, on an elevated plateau covered with buildings. Gadara (now in the extreme north-western corner of Jordan) had been adorned with new buildings by Pompey to please a favourite former slave who came from the place; but he was by no means the only influential Gadarene, for the city also produced the poet Meleager and the poet-philosopher Philodemus, and enjoyed the reputation of a southern Athens. Such towns retained their civic institutions and internal self-government, though they were not altogether free of interference from Herod's nearest provincial governor.

His kingdom had now been extended to dimensions not far short of those attained by the expansionist Hasmonaean monarchs of the previous century. This encouragement of the Jews was a natural Roman corollary to the elimination of Egypt, but Octavian also saw it as a sensible and indeed indispensable measure of imperial defence. For he realised there was a reckoning with Parthia still to come, and Herod seemed to him just the sort of political realist and effective man of action who was needed in this critical area. Moreover, Octavian's addition of Greek and Hellenised elements to the Judaean realm was deliberate. He wanted to water down the Hebrew nationalism of the central homeland by infusing non-Jewish elements, in the hope that a more or less Hellenised type of client state would emerge – rather like the kingdoms in Asia Minor, where the population was again non-Greek but could be governed by an administration of the normal Greek type.

As for Herod, Octavian gave him as a special *bonne bouche* four hundred Galatians who had been Cleopatra's guards. This was appropriately symbolic, for the eclipse of Cleopatra had left him the most important non-Roman in the entire Mediterranean world. As hitherto, Herod's policy was, quite simply, collaboration with the great western power, since he saw with perfect clarity that such collaboration was the only means of securing his own national interests. Honorific inscriptions[5] show that he adopted and welcomed the title *Philoromaios* – lover of the Romans – and to this he added the designation *Philokaisar* – lover of Caesar – for 'Caesar' was the name of Caesar's heir Octavian.

As a client monarch, Herod enjoyed the official appellation of 'friend and ally of the Roman People'. But Rome's relations with such allies, we learn, were personally conducted by the emperor himself. Later, the historian Tacitus wrote contemptuously about the servile role of client monarchs, observing with characteristic acidity that 'Rome made even kings the instruments of servitude'. And indeed it is true that they enjoyed no treaty to safeguard their relations with Rome; there was nothing bilateral about the 'alliance'. The kings held their office on a grace and favour tenure, and could be dethroned at the will of the Roman emperor.

They were also required to help Rome, when Rome needed their help, and to contribute to its finances. However, they did possess internal autonomy; and Herod believed, rightly, that under the completely unavoidable shadow of Roman greatness he might, by efficient cooperation with the suzerain power, create a Jewish state which could maintain a real existence.

Meanwhile, he had navigated one more very dangerous reef by making himself as thoroughly acceptable to Octavian as he had earlier been acceptable to Antony. And so his three successive reappearances in Judaea, after meeting Octavian at Rhodes, escorting him to Egypt, and escorting him back to Antioch, were in the nature of triumphal progresses. Herod was in the highest favour with Rome; and his territories had been enormously expanded. 'It seemed,' thought Josephus, 'as if he were one who by the kindness of God always achieved more brilliant success in the midst of danger.'[6]

However, the historian adds, his success also caused utter consternation among those who had hoped for the contrary. And it was within his own family circle that Herod found a particularly sour atmosphere had developed. Neither Mariamme nor her mother Alexandra can have loved the king any more dearly after he had done to death their closest relations, Aristobulus (III) and Hyrcanus (II). Nor did Alexandra, at least, by any means share Herod's satisfaction at the removal of Cleopatra. And now, during his absence at Rhodes, Sohaemus, the governor of Alexandrium, had disclosed to Alexandra and Mariamme that the king had instructed him to kill them if he failed to come back. Perhaps Sohaemus doubted whether Herod would return alive; that may have been why he was unwise enough to give the secret away. Besides, Mariamme was a woman of great beauty, and if she wanted to learn from Sohaemus what Herod had said to him it must have been difficult for him to resist. Anyway he told them, and their reactions can easily be imagined. Even the suggestion that Herod had only given this outrageous order because he could not bear the idea of his beloved Mariamme going to anyone else was hardly likely to placate her. And it was not entirely plausible either, for it failed to explain why her mother would have had to die as well.

A year of very difficult and disagreeable domestic life followed, and the situation was by no means improved by continual insinuations from the king's sister Salome (supported by his mother) that his Hasmonaean wife and mother-in-law were plotting against him. 'The king's wives resented Salome, for they knew she was very difficult by nature, and constantly changing and being by turns an enemy or a friend.'[7] And they, on the other hand, never once for a moment let her forget that her birth was inferior to theirs. Indeed Mariamme, asserts Josephus, could not forbear to reflect on Herod's humble origins when she was compelled to embrace him; and she would utter deep groans. Well might Ben Sira, the author of *Ecclesiasticus*, declare: 'Any spite but a woman's!' and 'Curses on the gossip and the tale-bearer!'[8] Gradually things came to a head, and Josephus gives a long and harrowing account of the growth of Herod's suspicions and the interrogation and torture of witnesses, culminating in Mariamme's arrest, her confinement in the Antonia fortress, and her execution, followed by his own excruciating remorse and desperate illness.[9]

The whole tragic story became the subject of many a rabbinic legend,[10] and in our own time it has stirred the Swedish novelist Pär Lagerqvist, as it had moved Voltaire before him. Byron, too, pictured the torments of Herod.

> She's gone, who shared my diadem;
> She sunk, with her my joys entombing;
> I swept that flower from Judah's stem,
> Whose leaves for me alone were blooming;
> And mine's the guilt, and mine the hell,
> This bosom's desolation dooming;
> And I have earn'd those tortures well,
> Which unconsumed are still consuming![11]

Of the king's misery, and the iron that entered into his soul, there can be no doubt. But our only source of information is Josephus, who was partly of Hasmonaean stock himself and presented the story very much from the Hasmonaean point of view; and it is by no means certain that Mariamme, who for good reasons had come to hate Herod, was guiltless of high treason.

At all events, the position of her mother Alexandra was now impossible, and she could scarcely expect to survive. In fact, she may have lasted for about another year. In 28 BC, while Herod still lay ill in Samaria – suffering from boils on the neck or a nervous breakdown, or both – he accused her of tampering with the loyalty of the commanders of the two Jerusalem fortresses, Herod's new Antonia and the older Hasmonaean palace-castle of Akra in the upper city. If the charges were justified, her move had been a desperate one, because both commanders were old friends of Herod, one of them being his own cousin, Achiabus. Yet it is, on the whole, likely that the story was true. The Hasmonaeans invariably attempted to revolt against the Idumaeans whenever occasion could be found, and Herod's illness was an obvious opportunity. Moreover Alexandra, violently deprived by Herod of her son, father and daughter in turn, must by now have been desperate. Nor was she by any means incapable of seeking the monarchic role for herself: although regnant Jewish queens had always been a rarity,[12] she was unlikely to forget that one of them, very popular in many quarters, had been her own grandmother Alexandra Salome. The first step, then, was to explain to the fortress commanders that, since Herod was now incapacitated, the natural regent was now herself. But they reported her approach to the king, who rapidly brought his convalescence to an end and gave orders for her execution.

The formidable power of Herod's builders. This 'Wailing Wall' revered by the Jews was the western wall of the Temple enclosure.

This did not, however, bring the purge to a close, for he was under the impression that the rot had spread. And his suspicion was probably justified, since when autocrats are ill plots proliferate. And so further casualties followed.

One of those who now succumbed, again because of the supposed Hasmonaean danger, was Herod's fellow-Idumaean Costobarus. He had been governor of their native Idumaea since a short time after Herod's victory in 37 BC. Costobarus had already been fortunate to emerge unscathed on an earlier occasion, for Herod had heard that he was plotting with Cleopatra to declare Idumaea independent and restore it to paganism, from which it had been forcibly converted not so long before. One of those who interceded for him then had been Herod's sister Salome, and subsequently, after the execution of her own husband Joseph (I) for malpractices during the king's absence, she had been given to Costobarus in marriage. Now, however, in 28 or 27 – not long after the downfall of Alexandra – a strange fact came to light. After the siege of Jerusalem a decade earlier, Costobarus had been the man designated by Herod to hunt down the Hasmonaeans and their supporters in the city. But now the king discovered that he had not completed the job. Instead he had secretly preserved and harboured two young men – the sons of a certain Babas – who were actually members of the Hasmonaean family.[13] Even if he saved their lives merely on some personal grounds of family friendship – and this of course we cannot determine – his action, once discovered, could not fail to be interpreted as treasonable.

Moreover, Costobarus had made the mistake of quarrelling with his wife – a perilous mistake, since she was Salome. So she had divorced him, although it was contrary to Jewish law for the wife to take such a step.[14] And now she told Herod of the survival of the Hasmonaean youths, adding that Costobarus, together with a group of other leading notables, was planning to revolt. The king had for some time had reason to suspect that the sons of Babas were still alive, and when Salome revealed where they were hiding, he instantly had them hunted down and then killed. Costobarus was also executed, and so were the more important among his associates.

His disloyalty had been an extremely grave matter, not only because of the ever-recurrent Hasmonaean element – this was the last of it, because now there were no males of the family left – but because of the very special importance of his fief Idumaea. It was Herod's own country, where he owned extensive lands and relied on mobilising many soldiers; and it extended along the very delicate southern frontier bordering on the unreliable Arabs.

The capital of Idumaea, Hebron, standing almost at the end of the mountain range which runs through the centre of the kingdom, commanded the point of transition between the higher plateau and the desert. It was an extremely holy place; its holiness dated back long before the time when the Edomites, from whom the Idumaeans were descended, had moved up here from the south. And now that the trouble that had threatened in this quarter was over, Herod decided to stress the importance of the sanctuary, and at the same time emphasise his own links with the sacred centre, by a major project of construction and propaganda. For it was to Hebron, according to ancient tradition, that Abraham himself had come before his journey into Egypt; and it was in the Macpelah caves at Hebron that Abraham, Sarah, Isaac, Rebecca, Jacob and Leah were all said to have been buried. And it was here, too, that David had established his capital before he captured Jerusalem. This then was the site where Herod constructed a most imposing monument. The tombs of the ancients – to the north-west of the present town – were surrounded by a towering wall, much of which still survives in the outer enclosure of the Islamic Haram. The enormous blocks, perfectly fitted with an alternation of pilaster and recess and with other architectural refinements,[15] give a unique illustration of the portentous blend of massiveness and sophistication which characterised Herod's numerous buildings throughout his kingdom.

When Abraham came back from Egypt he had settled his tent for

Part of Herod's massive monument to the patriarchs at Hebron: now the outer wall of the Moslem Haram.

a time about two miles from Hebron among the turpentine (terebinth) trees at Mamre, where he built an altar to the Lord. Here, too, there was an ancient memorial to Abraham, and this, likewise,

Herod reconstructed on an impressive scale, again creating a massive enclosure for the shrine.[16] Of all the heroes of Jewish history Abraham must have held a special place in Herod's heart, for the patriarch had been the father of many nations,[17] the ancestor of Jews, Arabs and Idumaeans alike; in fact, of all the peoples who played a part in Herod's origins, and whose differences one with another so often tore him apart and obstructed the triumphant unity he was endeavouring to bring about.

Yet it remained clear that it was only through the Romans that success in this respect, or, for that matter, in any other respect, could be won by Herod and his Judaea. At Rome the battle of Actium, although he had favoured the wrong side, had in fact saved the reputation of easterners like himself, for it removed the impetus and *raison d'être* from the virulent anti-eastern publicity which the previous years of tension had generated in the imperial capital. In more specific terms, the battle, contrary to first expectations, enhanced Herod's personal position. He was therefore quick to join in the universal celebrations. He sent a princely contribution to the town of Nicopolis, which was being constructed beside Actium itself to commemorate the victory. But this had to be celebrated in Jerusalem also, and for the purpose, in 28 or 27, Herod introduced the Actian Games, which were to be held every four years.

The Games were to include horse-races, and theatrical, musical and athletic competitions, and contests between wild beasts. Three separate buildings for these various displays were rapidly erected. Herod's hippodrome was within the city, on a site south of the Temple,[18] and the other two buildings stood outside the walls. His theatre was on the ridge of Er Ras, about half a mile south of Jerusalem, where it has left its imprint on the slope of the hill. The amphitheatre was laid out somewhere in the Raphaim plain, west of the present railway line.

The introduction of these activities represented a large step towards the Hellenisation of the country; and in the view of many Jews it was a very perilous step indeed.

Attendance at the theatre, it is true, was not necessarily forbidden to members of their religion: the Jewish writer Philo said he saw no objection to watching a performance. As for the gladiatorial displays, which were now seen at Jerusalem for the first time, they were a ghastly Italian custom which was gradually percolating, at this time, into the Hellenised east.[19] What the Jews thought when they saw such spectacles is not recorded; although we do hear that sections of the population protested against the beast-fights.

But it was the gymnastics and wrestling that caused most of the trouble. This sort of activity had already been a major political issue at the time of the Maccabee (Hasmonaean) war of national liberation. For it was regarded as the very symbol of the pagan Hellenism which it was the purpose of the rebellion to eradicate,[20] and it seemed deplorable that Hellenisers of Seleucid times had established a sports-ground at the very foot of the Jerusalem citadel itself.

The Jews entirely lacked the Greek taste for athletics, and deplored the fact that their youths became partly Hellenised by coming into contact with Greeks in the gymnasium.[21] Young Jews were seen walking about in athletes' hats,[22] and probably in nothing else – a further serious ground for disapproval, since Judaism was far from sharing the Hellenic penchant for nudity. Worst of all, athletes developed a distaste for circumcision, that practice (of unknown origin) which, as God had declared to Abraham, was an essential requirement of the Covenant,[23] a mark of the national consecration to the divine purpose. After the Exile, the Jewish devotion to circumcision had increased, and the practice had gained still further in national significance. Unfortunately, however, circumcised visitors to the gymnasium were likely to find themselves embarrassed. As we know from their literature, the Greeks and Romans sniggered at the practice, which they found unattractive. As a result, young Jews on occasion actually underwent an operation to make themselves uncircumcised, thus 'repudiating the holy covenant'.[24] These were problems which Herod's Games inevitably threw into the foreground once again. Having once decided that Greek-style athletics must be included, all he could do, to avoid trouble, was to locate his theatre and amphitheatre outside the city-walls, in the hope of saving Jewish susceptibilities at least to some extent.

Another grave problem, however, arose over the actual construction of the buildings. Herod wanted them to be as fine as any others in the Mediterranean world. But this, according to every Graeco-Roman norm, involved the lavish use of sculpture and relief – which would normally require the representation of human beings and animals. Yet the Second Commandment was interpreted as completely forbidding any such thing. 'You shall not,' it ordained, 'make a carved image for yourself nor the likeness of anything in the heaven above, or on the earth below, or in the waters under the earth.'[25] However, the words that follow are: 'You shall not bow down to them or worship them; for I, the Lord thy God, am a jealous God'. According to a liberal interpretation, the first instruction introduces the second, and is qualified and explained by it; what the Commandment intended, according to this view, was to forbid the setting up of images for worship, and not to prohibit representational art in general. This had evidently been the view of Solomon, who adorned his Temple with bulls and lions. But a stricter opinion ruled that no such representation, either of animals or human beings, was permissible. The destruction of graven images had been an important incentive to the aggressive wars of the Hasmonaeans, and the total absence of men or beasts from their coinage shows that they took the strict view. Herod's coinage was equally careful (with a single isolated example, of which something will be said later on.) Clearly, therefore, he could not decorate his buildings with the sort of sculptures that were universal elsewhere. What, then, could he do instead?

He hit on the ingenious idea of adorning those structures with trophies instead of statues. Religious leaders, catching a view of them in the new theatre, complained bitterly that they were human images; perhaps the learned objectors were short-sighted. But Herod had one of the trophies taken down and dismantled, showing that it was not a statue at all, but a simple piece of wood with armour and weapons attached; and there was a great deal of laughter at the holy men's expense. Nevertheless, they were still far from satisfied, because they felt that the veneration of weapons was just as improper as the construction of statues. It would have been no use for Herod to explain that these particular weapons were not intended for worship, because, as one of the Qumran scrolls informs us, the Jews believed that weapons and trophies *were* objects of worship to the pagan Romans.[26] The same passage also refers to the Roman veneration of military standards, and later there was serious trouble when Pontius Pilate introduced legionary standards into Jerusalem.[27]

Such were the anxieties and discontents aroused by Herod's new buildings and Games. Indeed, feelings ran so high that an attempt was made to assassinate him on the very premises of the impious theatre he had now built. But the king's intelligence service detected the plot just as he was about to enter the theatre, and the conspirators were arrested. They died defiantly, declaring that their action had been for the sake of their religion. But the man who had informed against them was caught by the crowd and lynched and torn to pieces. This disturbed Herod, who had great difficulty in finding out who had been responsible for this outrage; but he found out in the end, and had the culprits executed. Thereafter Jewish resistance, for the most part, went underground for over twenty years – until the very last stages of Herod's reign.

Jews and non-Jews

7

The dangerous conspiracy that Herod had uncovered proved that the people of Jerusalem were unreliable. Herod could not dispense with the city as his national and religious capital. But he could seek to offset its deficiencies elsewhere, and that is what he did. For this purpose he fastened upon the region just north of Judaea proper, namely Samaritis (Shomron). It will be recalled that, in 63 BC, Pompey had detached this territory from the Judaean principality and incorporated it in the Roman province of Syria. Later, however, the young Herod had been put in charge of Samaritis by the Romans, and it had subsequently been reunited with his kingdom.

The capital of the region was the ancient city of Samaria, a conspicuous fortress-town beautifully situated in the mountains of central Palestine, where it stands upon a hill within a saucer of other hills, and serves as an observation point looking over the plains of Sharon and Jezreel. By nature, Samaria would seem more truly destined to be the capital than Jerusalem, being more central and more accessible. And indeed, nearly a millennium earlier, when Solomon's kingdom split into the two states of Israel and Judah, Samaria, after two changes, had become the capital of the northern Israelite kingdom, retaining this supremacy for two hundred years, during which Kings Omri and Ahab constructed their ivory-plated palaces. Then in 721 BC the city fell to the Assyrian Sargon, who destroyed the Israelite state. Four hundred years later, after the death of Alexander the Great, a military colony of Macedonians was planted in Samaria, but it was completely obliterated by John Hyrcanus I (c. 108 BC). Then, during the fifties, the Roman governor Gabinius had rebuilt the place, giving it his own name and surrounding the town with a wall.

Now, in 27 BC, Herod began its reconstruction on a large scale, endowing the new city not with his own name but with that of his Roman patron. At this time Octavian had just begun to call himself Augustus, a designation with reverential connections which symbolised the New Order known to us as the Roman empire or principate. The Greek for Augustus was Sebastos, and in consequence Samaria was henceforward to be known as Sebaste; the place, now in Jordanian territory occupied by Israelis, is still called Sebastiya. It was a corridor between the Greek cities which lay to the west and east of the Judaean homeland. But the principal gateway faced west, where most of the traffic came from.

The gateway was flanked by two towers, which are still extant,

and further round towers studded the two-and-a-half-mile circumference of Herod's walls, which were visible as far away as the coast.
Inside the walls were colonnaded streets and a forum and basilica,
and the outline of a stadium can be seen on the eastern slope among
the olive trees. But since the foundation was in honour of Augustus,

Herod's basilica (lawcourt, meeting-place and commercial centre) at Samaria,
which was reconstructed under the name of Sebaste from 27 BC.

The principal gateway of Herod's Sebaste, the new Samaria, facing westwards towards the sea.

the place of honour was taken by a temple in his name, coupled with that of Rome. Standing at the western end of the summit, on top of the debris of Omri's and Ahab's palace and a Hellenistic acropolis, the temple was approached, like other Levantine shrines, by a fore-court resting on an artificial platform. Upon this platform, at the foot of the temple steps, stood an altar to the imperial divinities, whose statues were to be seen nearby.

Such a shrine would have been inconceivable in Jewish lands; but Sebaste was a Hellenised foundation. It is true that a considerable proportion of the inhabitants, perhaps half, consisted of Samaritans – the heterodox Jews who were native to the area – but the ruling class, like the constitution, was Greek (and, as later events showed, by no means pro-Semitic). In this Greek enclave, then, Herod saw no objection to raising a temple to non-Jewish deities, Rome and Augustus, who were revered in conjunction throughout the Graeco-Roman world. The stricter Jews were shocked; yet Herod persisted in erecting temples to Rome and Augustus in a number of non-Jewish centres in different parts of his kingdom, as well as in various Roman provincial territories. But the most splendid manifestation of this imperial cult was the temple at Sebaste.

It was a fertile district, famous for its excellent fruit. Herod arranged for a copious water-supply from across the valley, and nearby he founded a model settlement called the Five Villages (Pente Komai, now Fondaqumia). He also distributed good lots of land among 6000 settlers. They could be called up for military service, and were allocated to a special corps, of which half the establishment, 1250 infantry and 250 cavalry, came from this settlement. No wonder the Jews called it a 'fortress to dominate Judaea'.

A colonnaded street in the lower town of Samaria, probably the work of Herod.

For Herod felt that he could trust Samaria-Sebaste. It had lent him a base against the Hasmonaeans; it had provided him with munitions; it had sheltered his family. And before long he forged a special link with the place by marrying a Samaritan woman. He had divorced his first wife Doris and executed his second wife Mariamme, and it may have been now that he married another, Malthace the Samaritan. Viewed with hindsight, this became the most significant of all his marriages, because hers were the sons who managed to survive and succeed him. At the time, it was just another offence against orthodox Jewish feelings, because the Samaritans were not orthodox Jews – as their few survivors still are not today. But, looked at from a different angle, Herod's marriage was yet another

The theatre of Śebaste: a post-Herodian building which probably stood on the site of a theatre erected by Herod.

move in his campaign to set up Samaria-Sebaste as a counterpoise to the dubious loyalty of Jerusalem.

However, this was only one of Herod's numerous strongholds. For the many revolts he had experienced inspired him to spread them thickly round the country. There has already been occasion to speak of his fortresses at Jerusalem (Antonia), at Hyrcania, at Alexandrium near the borders between Judaea proper and Samaritis, and at Masada beside the western shore of the Dead Sea. There were at least four others as well. One of them dominated the winter capital Jericho, fifteen miles away from Jerusalem towards the north-east. The castle overlooking Jericho was named Cyprus after Herod's mother, to whom it was probably a posthumous memorial.

The 'Valley of the Shadow of Death', the lower part of the Wadi Qilt ('Cultivated Valley') leading down from Jerusalem towards Jericho.

Earlier, Jericho had been guarded by two of these strongholds, on either side of the valley of the Wadi Qilt, but Pompey had dismantled them.[1] Now one of the two was reconstituted on a formidable scale at the place now known as Tell-el-Akabe on the mountain edge. Its garrison watched over the Jericho-Jerusalem road, and looked far out over the Dead Sea and the barren, desolate mountains of Moab that lie on its other side.

Those mountains now formed part of Peraea, the province which formed Herod's eastern frontier with the Arabs. And just as Masada, Oresa and other castles defended his souther frontier with the same state – together with a whole system of fortifications which have now been revealed in the Negev[2] – so also two fortresses were constructed in Peraea to protect this eastern border. One, Machaerus (Mkaur), stood in a desert area to the east of the Dead Sea. It is situated just north of the impassable rift of the Arnon river, upon a wind-swept peak high above the humps that rise up out of the grim and rugged territory all around. Machaerus had been a fortress of Alexander Jannaeus, but Herod much enlarged it and made it the strongest of all his castles after Jerusalem. It was here, after his death, that John the Baptist was imprisoned, until Salome (III), delighting another Herod (Antipas) with her dancing, secured for her revengeful mother the captive's head. Beneath the ruins on the summit, known as the Hanging Palace (El Mashnaka), the rock face is hollowed out into a large vaulted chamber which was probably John's dungeon.

Further north in the same province, to the north-east of the Dead Sea, rose a hill containing a second Peraean fortress, across the

The circular hill-fortress of Herodium, the more westerly of the two castles of that name, south of Bethlehem.

Jordan from Jericho. Now El Hubbeisa, the place was then called Herodium. But this was confusing, for there was a larger and more famous Herodium on the other side of the Dead Sea, at Jebel Fureidis in the Tekoa area seven miles south of Jerusalem. The site marked the spot where Herod, escaping from the Parthians with his family in 40 BC, had fought the most critical battle of his life, repelling a ferocious attack from hostile Jews. But the site was also chosen for security reasons. Like Hyrcania a few miles away, and like the Antonia in the capital itself, this western Herodium could scarcely be designed to repel an attack from an external enemy: it was a regional headquarters intended to keep the population of Jerusalem quiet, and to provide a prison for anyone who was recalcitrant. Later it served as Herod's own burial place, for he preferred it to the family mausoleum he had constructed in the capital.

The interior of the keep at Herodium, reached by a flight of two hundred steps and containing a royal residence.

A traveller from Jerusalem to Bethlehem sees the immense, sinister cone of this Herodium dominating the view towards the south. Originally there were twin cones side by side, like breasts, but Herod truncated the eastern summit and heightened and strengthened its western counterpart in order to build Herodium. On the top was a round fortress, with four round towers, one higher than the other three – a spherical version of the Antonia. A circular corridor ran along the circumference of the fortifications, and inside there were royal apartments and baths. A great stone stairway which rose up through the defences on the north can still be viewed, and at the foot of the hill there are traces of a settlement and a pool with a kiosk in the middle; no doubt a park extended all around. An aqueduct, of which fragments have survived, brought the water from a spring near Bethlehem, irrigating the surrounding countryside and supplementing the rain-water that was collected in cisterns beneath the citadel. Such cisterns, lined with hydraulic cement, were characteristic features of the hill fortresses of Herod. Equally characteristic were the massive stone banks or *glacis* ('slippery places') sloping steeply down from the castle keep. And each of the castles outside the capital was located so that it could signal to at least one other, while sometimes there were also relay stations between one and the next.

Another means of maintaining security was the military colony. A settlement of cavalrymen was planted at Gaba in west Galilee, perhaps the modern El-Harithiyye, not far from Beth Shearim, in the rich valley of Jezreel. A further military colony was located on two hills beside the eastern frontier, at Esbon, which had formerly belonged to the Arabs and must have been taken from them by Herod. Subsequently the same formula was employed again farther north. Samaria-Sebaste contributed to a special corps; the other half of the unit came from Herod's new coastal city of Caesarea, of which more will be said later; in due course the whole corps was stationed there.

Herod's forces were not very large, because his country itself was small; but they were highly efficient. The soldiers included a good many Jews of Judaea, for Herod had inherited the right of conscription from the Hasmonaeans, and probably also took over a system by which lands were distributed to Jewish peasants in return for service in the army. Along the frontiers, especially, the local population were expected to give military aid, in exchange for land-grants and various degrees of local autonomy. Since, however, Herod had so many difficulties in winning the loyalty of Palestinian Jews, he derived as high a proportion of recruits as possible from Jews from other countries who had settled in Judaea; they suited his purpose owing to their lack of the local ties which might have made them seditious. Babylonian Jews were especially useful, and towards the end of the reign five hundred Jewish horse-archers from Babylon were given permanent residences in the north-east.

But Herod also relied to a very great extent on his own compatriots from Idumaea: a reliance which must have made him particularly anxious when the governor of that territory, Costobarus, was suspected of disloyalty. The Idumaeans had already been used as mercenaries by the Ptolemies of Egypt in the third century BC, and their later mass-conversion to Judaism provided the Hasmonaeans with a military strength which was all the more valuable because it was free from sectarian preoccupations. The insatiable passion for conquest displayed by Alexander Jannaeus (d. 76 BC) required the recruitment of mercenaries from as far afield as Asia Minor, but he, again, also found Idumaeans particularly useful for the purpose. Under Herod, they were all the more vital, because his was an Idumaean house, and he could usually be sure of support from his own people. Indeed, at the outset of his career and reign, it was they who furnished him with his principal support. Later, their fortified villages along the frontier remained in a permanent state of semi-mobilisation and formed the nucleus of Herod's main mercenary army. Alongside them fought Greeks and Thracians and Germans, and the Galatians who had been transferred to Herod from Cleopatra's bodyguard.

The Roman legion in Jerusalem, which his wife and mother at one point had thought of joining while the king was away, had been withdrawn from the country after he succeeded in stamping out his major internal enemies. But it seems likely that he retained a certain number of Roman officers for instructional purposes. Moreover, the names of his infantry and cavalry commanders during the last years of his reign suggest that they were possibly Romans. His commander-in-chief, too, seems to have borne a Roman name, Volumnius, and may very well have been a Roman seconded to his employment; perhaps he also had responsibilities in the province of Syria.[3] But whether Herod's army was primarily organised on Roman or Greek lines it is impossible to say.

The civilian organisation of his kingdom, however, is known to have been very largely Greek. The keynote was struck by his coins, which abandoned the bilingual inscriptions, Hebrew and Greek, of his Hasmonaean predecessors, and described him as *Herod the King* in Greek only. His name, as it so happens, is Greek too, meaning 'heroic'; and he did not, like the Hasmonaeans, have a Hebrew name as well, or if he did he made no use of it. His brothers and sisters had all been given Jewish names – though Phasael's was probably a compliment to the Arabs, among whom it is more common. But his children, except those called after their uncles and aunts, were all named like Greeks. As early as 44 BC three of Hyrcanus' ambassadors had Greek names, and only one Jewish; and by the time of Herod's last decade there is only one single identifiable figure in his whole entourage who displays a Hebrew name, his cousin Achiabus. Not that there was anything new about this, for as early as the third century BC even eminent Jewish theologians had borne Greek names. The first five books (the Pentateuch) of the Septuagint, the earliest Greek version of the Torah, originated with Egyptian Jews who lived during the same century.[4] Already by 200 BC there was a thorough blending of Jewish and Greek ideas.[5] Many Jews dressed and lived in the Greek fashion, and not only if they were rich; even in remote villages the humble tombstones are inscribed in Greek. Numerous Hebrew commercial terms were taken from that language, while Hebrew itself was becoming increasingly reserved for literary, legal and liturgical purposes. The language spoken by less educated people was Aramaic, the western or north-western Semitic dialect which had been the official tongue of the Persian empire and became the *lingua franca* of the whole Near Eastern world; it can still be heard in villages in the neighbourhood of Damascus. But in Aramaic, too, one word out of five was of Greek origin.

The typical Jewish Hellenisers had been the Tobiad family, native chiefs who had come from near Esbon in the Peraea and enjoyed power before and after 200 BC, under Ptolemaic and then Seleucid rule. The Tobiads and their supporters looked as though they might Hellenise traditional Jewry out of existence altogether. But they were still resisted by the overwhelming majority of the Jews, and opposition to what they stood for was the main war-cry of the Maccabaean, Hasmonaean revolution. The unfaithful wife is the Jewish people, and her lovers are the Gentiles who have led the nation astray.[6] But the Hasmonaeans were not against all Hellenism; their main aim was to secure the observance of the Law. It was therefore one of the ironies of history that their regime, too, having started as the champion of pure Judaism, began before long to take on the characteristics of an ordinary Greek or Hellenised monarchy.

But they did not go nearly all the way, and now there were many signs that Herod was going a good deal farther. Often, it is true, he paid attention to the susceptibilities of Judaism. But he did not do so all the time, and it was the exceptions that counted in men's minds. They seemed, in the words of Arnaldo Momigliano, 'a series of outrages against the law by a disloyal convert'.

In 1970, says Nahum Goldmann, 'the great danger constantly threatening contemporary Jewry is its rapid erosion'. Many Jews of Herod's time would have said just the same. The more contacts there were with Hellenism, the more strongly surged the contrary tendencies towards particularism, beneath the surface and sometimes erupting above it. Extremist attitudes to the Gentiles tended to increase. In the third century BC, the *Book of Jonah* had been written in a liberal mood which ignored the distinction between Jew and non-Jew. And indeed even now the great Pharisee Hillel, like later rabbis following his tradition, believed that it was not impossible for Gentiles to be righteous.[7] But many other writings, notably the scrolls found in the Qumran library beside the Dead Sea, are fiercely opposed to them, and reject the smallest contact with these 'vain heathens'. On the Day of Judgment they will be well out of the way.[8] Even Josephus, who collaborated thoroughly with the Graeco-Roman world, felt obliged to dictate to his Greek scribes some very sharp remarks about their compatriots.

Herod's kingdom was not, of course, by any means purely Jewish. It contained pure Jews, heterodox Jews such as the Samaritans, Jews of recently converted stock like the Galileans and Idumaeans, and many other people – Greeks, Syrians and Arabs – who were not Jewish in any sense of the word. And this, as has already been suggested, was precisely what Augustus wanted, in the hope of achieving something like a standard Hellenistic client state.

In the non-Jewish parts of his territories Herod felt entirely free to behave in a non-Jewish fashion, allowing his statue, for example, to stand before a thoroughly pagan temple of Zeus (Baalshamin) at Si'a in the north-east.[9] But the real charge against him was that he felt, and behaved, in a more friendly fashion towards the Greeks than towards the Jews. And another trouble was that the Jewish part of his territory must have been invaded by a swarm of foreign immigrants. Certainly Herod, unlike the Hellenisers of the previous century, made no attempt to force Hellenism on Jews in Jewish lands.[10] Nevertheless, as soon as his iron hand was removed by death, all these Greeks became the specific targets of the xenophobe agitations that followed.

Herod's court was Greek in all its titles and grades. As in any Hellenistic court, there were his 'relations' and a class of those who were brought up with his children (*Syntrophoi*), and four ranks of 'friends' who comprised his leading advisers. His chief minister also bore a Greek title, 'manager of the affairs of the kingdom', combining Egyptian and Seleucid terminology, and suggesting a special concern for finance. The holder of this office, throughout the greater part of Herod's reign, was a certain Ptolemy. It is one of the unfortunate features of ancient historians that, in their search for drama, they say so little about the men who did the solid work; and so Ptolemy, for all his extreme importance, remains a shadowy figure. It is known, however, that Herod gave him a plantation at Arous (Haris), twenty miles south of Sebaste in the mountains, for we hear that the place was ransacked by the Arabs after the king had died. It is also recorded that, at the same critical juncture, Ptolemy was one of those who loyally supported Herod's chosen heir.

We cannot tell from Ptolemy's name whether he was a Greek or a Jew. But it is clear enough that Herod's court was full of Greeks and Hellenised orientals. The rhetorician Irenaeus is mentioned, and Andromachus and Gemellus (the latter perhaps a Roman) who were in charge of the education of the king's sons. But much the most remarkable figure in his entourage was Nicolaus of Damascus, a Greek or Hellenised Syrian who was a literary figure of very high and widespread reputation. He was the second son of two wealthy leading citizens of his city; his father had held many civic offices, and conducted numerous diplomatic missions. And we know more, as it so happens, about his personal appearance than we know about Herod's, for Nicolaus is reported to have been tall and thin and abnormally red in the face. Only fragments of his Greek literary compositions have survived. He may not have been a literary genius, but he possessed a large and versatile talent which might well have ranked above those of many surviving authors if his works had not been lost. In addition to musical compositions, he wrote tragedies and comedies, philosophical and anthropological essays, an autobiography, a biography of Augustus, and a universal history. This history possesses a very special significance for students of Herod because it was the principal source of Josephus' studies of the period (see Chapter 19).

Nicolaus was Herod's secretary, in the most elevated sense of the term; his daily companion, honoured by him above all his other friends[11] (his brother formed part of the same circle[12]). It was no doubt in Nicolaus' honour that Herod presented his home-town Damascus with a new gymnasium and theatre.

Nicolaus came into Herod's service from an unexpected quarter, for he had been tutor to the children of Cleopatra and Antony. When his former employers died in 30 BC he was about thirty-four years of age; and he transferred his services to Herod, whom he had already, perhaps, known for the previous ten years. Nicolaus' major influence, however, does not seem to have developed until 20 BC or thereabouts, when Herod asked him for tuition in Greek philosophy and rhetoric.[13] The king had received little formal education. He had attended a primary school as a child, but he was sent off to the Arab court for protection when he was ten. Few horrors must have escaped his notice when he was a boy, but he managed to form cosmopolitan cultural tastes; in spite of his fragmentary education, he conceived a large, if vague, passion for Hellenism. There is special point in Nicolaus' dedication to him of a work on foreign customs, for surely he was the adviser who encouraged this ardent interest and gave it form.

In his middle and later life, he accompanied Herod on his travels, and was selected by him as the leader of delicate negotiations. His position gained enormously in strength because not only Herod but Augustus came to like him very much. The emperor had made his acquaintance after Actium, perhaps at Rhodes, and was impressed. He called Nicolaus his companion – a designation that was virtually a title – and ranked him high among his friends; a specially large and fine sort of date, which Nicolaus presented to Augustus in Rome, was called the Nicolaitan after him. Moreover Nicolaus also possessed influence with Augustus' deputy Marcus Agrippa, to whom, later on, he appealed on behalf of the little town of Ilium (Troy), when it was in trouble for nearly letting Agrippa's wife get drowned in its river. Nicolaus also successfully championed the

An eastward view over the desolate Mountains of Moab, beyond the Dead Sea.

Jews of Asia Minor with Agrippa (see Chapter 12), though he was not a Jew himself.

Nicolaus was in the grand tradition of internationally minded Greek polymaths and philosophers. Yet, in spite of his relations with the very great at Rome, he did not spend much time in the capital. Moreover, when he did have to go there, he aroused criticism for consorting with ordinary people, including slaves, instead of associating with the aristocracy. He accepted the charge gladly; he was said to be a very good-natured man,[14] and he and Herod, with their complementary qualities, must have made a curious pair. Nicolaus was also criticised because he did not hoard up the large fortunes the king presented him with but spent them, and it was also said that the glory he won from Herod was undeserved. But there would obviously be many envious people likely to say that. Nevertheless we, too, ought to harbour a grudge against him. He was excessively loyal, and our information about the reign has suffered accordingly. Part of the time Josephus is too unfavourable to Herod, and part of the time he is too favourable: when he is being too favourable his source is nearly always Nicolaus.

Like the chief minister Ptolemy, he formed part of a new royal council which Herod became accustomed to call upon for advice. The old Jewish council of state, of whom more than half the previous members had been executed in 37 BC, was never employed for such purposes, being retained purely and simply to consider matters of religious law. Instead Herod employed, formally or otherwise, this new council of friends and relations, herein following the practice of other Hellenistic monarchs and, indeed, of Augustus himself. When Herod wanted support for a judicial decision, such as the executions of Hyrcanus or Mariamme, this was the body whose views, or whose agreement, he sought. Apart from his leading advisers, who were always present, its membership was no doubt somewhat fluid. For example, when some major propaganda effort was to be announced or when a perilous attempt at sedition had been discovered, additional notables could be drafted in to make the meeting as representative as possible.

Generosity and splendour

The policies which, aided by these counsellors, Herod adopted were a blend of autocracy, stringent severity and liberal open-handedness.

Like many absolute rulers, he was a great believer in addressing 'the people' direct. On important occasions such as his triumphant returns from seeing Roman leaders, popular gatherings were often assembled to acclaim him. But they were not formal assemblies; they possessed no constitutional significance or powers, being merely convened, in a manner not without precedent in Greece, in order to hear and applaud the ruler's will.

By the same token, men believed guilty of rebellion, including members of Herod's own family, found themselves haled before hostile people's courts, which more than once threatened to lynch them before the king indulgently intervened. Sometimes these hordes of angry people were purely informal, like other popular assemblies, but at other times there were meetings of formal royal lawcourts. For Herod surely founded courts of his own, like the Hasmonaeans before him.[1] The Jewish idea that the king was not competent to act as judge was brushed aside, for jurisdiction, like legislation, was entirely in his hands.

When his family got into trouble and were brought before such bodies, Herod was inclined, for publicity reasons, to cite Jewish Law, but that was not the code the courts employed. They probably operated, ostensibly, on the basis of Greek laws inherited or borrowed from Hellenistic kingdoms, with perhaps certain modifications based on Roman legal practice.

The system Herod employed for governing his dominions was again Hellenistic. Broadly speaking, his administration perpetuated the arrangements which had been in force under the Hasmonaeans, and which they, in turn, had inherited from the Seleucids and the Ptolemies before them.[2] Under the governors of the principal provinces, Galilee, Idumaea, Samaritis and Peraea (Judaea itself did not have a governor), the ten or eleven regional units in the Jewish parts of the country were known by the Greek title of *toparchies,* and the non-Jewish territories were divided into areas described by another Hellenistic term, *merides.*[3] These non-Jewish regions differed from Judaea because they were based on city states of the Greek kind, which did not exist in Jewish territory.

Although Herod had to make certain concessions to the autonomy of these Greek cities, autonomy was not a conception that appealed to him. The Jewish towns were allowed even less self-government, and several coastal communities – Joppa, Jamnia and Azotus – lost whatever degree of independence they had possessed before, and were reduced to the status of mere capitals of toparchies. The organisation of the country tended to be centralised and bureau-cratic, in accordance with the practice of Ptolemaic Egypt; devo-lution was not favoured.

Government was also suspicious and severe, with the closest attention paid to security. Public meetings, other than those sum-moned by the authorities, were prohibited, and even an informal gathering of a very few persons was regarded with official mis-givings. 'No meeting of citizens was allowed,' records Josephus, 'nor were walking together or being together allowed, and all their movements were observed.' Inside the cities, and out on the open roads as well, there were hosts of men spying upon any and every social encounter. The huge fortresses everywhere, with their frightening reputations, provided a further reminder that caution was desirable. When Herod died, the dungeons were found to contain a number of long-term prisoners.

Such was the fate of the dissident minority; certainly this was not a time when opposition flourished. But the reverse side of the coin was the extraordinary generosity which Herod repeatedly displayed towards the general body of the population if they were in distress. It was not so much that he sometimes reduced their taxes in emer-gencies, because that was common practice among Hellenistic and Roman governments. But when a real crisis came, he handled it with unlimited munificence and effectiveness. An opportunity of this kind arose in 25 BC, when Judaea was suffering from a particularly severe visitation of the droughts that can all too easily cripple this country, with its irregular rains. On the occasion in question, the drought seems to have continued for a second year. Crops were almost non-existent, stores ran out, and outbreaks of pestilence soon followed.

Herod dealt with this situation by providing a special labour-force on his own pay-roll, and by distributing large quantities of grain. He imported the grain from Egypt – a difficult thing to ar-range, but the governor of that country was a friend of his. Good relations with the Romans had turned out to be useful!

And then he helped cities beyond his borders as well, sending seeds to the inhabitants of Syria. This, as Josephus points out, 'brought him not a little profit'.[4] The usual interest rate for seed loans was as high as fifty per cent! But Herod's own subjects were scarcely likely to object that foreigners, outside the realm, should be heavily charged for the preservation of their lives, when the profit was going to this remarkable welfare work in Judaea.

Josephus ends his account by pointing out that all these measures understandably made Herod a very good deal more popular and induced people to wonder what sort of a man he really was, since he could blend savage repression with this extraordinary generosity. Elsewhere he reverts to this psychological problem, concluding that Herod felt no real goodwill towards his subjects, but was generous merely because he liked to be honoured – and that in any case his generosity had unpleasant repercussions, because the funds to pay for it had to be raised by harsh measures.[5] The latter charge, as we shall see elsewhere, is not really justified. The psychological motivation of his welfare work is a more disputable question. But it is easy to dismiss any liberal measures in this way, by questioning the motives behind them; the solid fact that remains is the beneficence, and Herod was a thoroughly beneficent ruler.

The Jews, of course, had a great tradition of looking after the poor – a tradition, incidentally, which contributed largely to the successful social services that later gave the Christians their footholds at Rome and elsewhere. One of the writers of the *Book of Isaiah,* in the fifth century BC, had proclaimed the Lord's interest in the oppressed.[6] Three hundred years later, Ben Sira, the writer of *Ecclesiasticus*, urged humanitarian attention to the problem,[7] but felt obliged to conclude that the gulf between rich and poor had become quite unbridgeable.[8] And thereafter, as time went on, this pessimism seemed more than ever justified. This was partly because of a certain ambiguity in the attitude of the influential Pharisees themselves. In a sense they were democratic, for they were not wealthy men themselves, and they believed in education and in consensus of opinion; they were responsible for many decisions of social importance, relating, for example, to the protection of native craftsmanship and agriculture. Indeed, their enemies accused them of indulgence to the poor.[9] On the other hand, they held a very low opinion of everyone who had no knowledge of the Law – and that meant, in effect, not only wrong-minded people, but the ill-educated lower classes. 'As for this rabble,' a Pharisee is quoted as saying, 'which cares nothing for the Law, a curse is upon them.'[10] The term translated as 'rabble' or 'people of the land' (*Am ha'aretz*) was primarily a term of abuse directed against people who were 'ignorant of the Law', that is to say 'ignoramuses' who held different views from the Pharisees themselves or who behaved like the Gentiles (or, in later years, like the officials appointed by the Romans). But the same term was also very readily, and to some extent justifiably, interpreted as an indication of inhumanity.

Herod's welfare measures, which took no account of knowledge or ignorance of the Law, could claim an advantage over this attitude; and Josephus has testified to the popularity that it brought him.

At this point, he felt strong enough to introduce a new religious policy. It was preceded by a new marriage, this time to a woman who possessed the same name as his beloved wife whom he had executed in 29 – Mariamme. Since then (according to the chrono-

The designs on Jewish ossuaries, in spite of Greek influences, interpret the second Commandment strictly by avoiding human or animal forms.

logical interpretation which seems most probable), he had already been remarried at least once, to Malthace the Samaritan. There is no evidence that now, on marrying the second Mariamme, he divorced Malthace. There was no need to do so. It is true that certain theologians, Pharisees and monastics spoke against bigamy and polygamy. But there was, in fact, no religious objection to the practice.

No doubt the new bride Mariamme (ii), like her predecessors and successors, was of sensational appearance, for Herod liked beautiful women. But there was more to the marriage than that. For it was followed, before long, by the appointment of her father Simon (ii) as high priest. It will be remembered that when Herod first took over his kingdom, his non-priestly origins had prevented him from becoming high priest himself, and he had appointed to the office a Babylonian Jew of the old high-priestly family, Ananel. After the brief and unhappy period in which the king's young brother-in-law

Aristobulus (III) became high priest and was subsequently murdered by Herod, Ananel had resumed the office. Then he died – or perhaps he was asked to abdicate – and someone else had been appointed in his place.[11] Now this nominee in his turn had been deposed, and the father of Herod's new wife Mariamme (II) was given the post.

The high priest upon whom the king's choice had fallen was the son of a certain Boethus, who is believed to be identical with a famous theologian of the same name. The theologian was the founder of a sect of the Sadducees named after him, the Boethusians. Now Herod, from this time onward, continued his practice (deplored by the orthodox) of periodically dismissing and replacing high priests; and it so happens that nearly all of them, for a considerable time, came from the family of Boethus, or from houses joined to it by intermarriage. Their near-monopoly became a conspicuous feature of the system. 'Woe is me,' observed a Jew who was out of sympathy with them, 'because of the house of Boethus! Woe is me because of their truncheons!'[12]

As these successive high priests resigned, they retained the high prestige of their former office. Moreover, this glamour extended to their families and the families with whom they intermarried. Consequently the members of these houses, centred round whichever dignitary happened to be Herod's high priest of the day, formed a select but gradually increasing group possessing a good deal of influence. The essential feature of the group was its loyalty to the king, who in this way contrived to extend his power over a significant element of the Jewish aristocracy. An important section of the Pharisees already afforded him at least passive support, and the attitude of the monastic groups such as the Essenes was again one of obedience. But the old Jewish nobility, the Sadducees, had hitherto been hostile or evasive. This was not surprising, since they figured so very largely among the forty-five members of the council of state whom Herod had executed after his capture of Jerusalem, and those who survived had been shocked by the liquidation of so many Hasmonaeans. Now, however, by his exploitation of the high priesthood, Herod was building up a new Sadducee aristocracy, which was loyal to himself; an aristocracy partly of birth but above all of service.

While taking these steps to gain support in leading Jewish circles, Herod also found time for the agreeable task of creating a worthy dwelling for himself in the capital city of the kingdom.

Jerusalem, situated upon the ridge that forms the backbone of Judaea, 2,500 feet above the Mediterranean and 3,800 above the Dead Sea, controlled the main longitudinal hill-traffic that passed through the country. Yet its projecting triangular spur, with the valleys of Kidron to the east and Hinnom to the west and south, combines this accessibility with a certain element of judicious iso-

Herod's palace, which dominated Jerusalem's western ridge: reconstruction of the apartments of Augustus and Agrippa.

lation; it is a city more of refuge and withdrawal than of open communications. 'As the sightseer looks over Jerusalem,' observes Werner Keller, 'he almost feels that he is breathing in its obstinacy, rigidity and inflexibility.'

There were already two royal palaces in Jerusalem: the Hasmonaean palace (Akra) on the high ground to the west of the Temple enclosure, and Herod's own castle, the Antonia, to the north-west of the Temple precinct. The palace of the Hasmonaeans was scarcely fit for royal habitation, and in any case Herod did not want to live in a residence of theirs. As for the Antonia, he had built this palace-fortress and had made it his residence, but its close proximity to the

Temple invited disagreeable remarks, and he may have been sensitive enough to dislike its associations with his tragic marriage to the first Mariamme. There was also a more practical disadvantage. The Antonia was enclosed on the north and west by hills, and even to the south its view was restricted by the high ground beyond the Hinnom valley. This meant that it was impossible to signal from the Antonia direct to any of the country's other fortresses. It may have been partly for this reason that the king now decided to build a new palace in another part of Jerusalem altogether.

The position he decided upon was at the western extremity of Jerusalem, the Upper City, in the area of the present Jaffa Gate and citadel. The site dominated the western ridge of Jerusalem just as the Temple towered above the eastern ridge; and it was possible to send signals to every other fortress for miles. This citadel-palace, on which work started in 23 BC, was to be twice the size of the Antonia, a whole city in itself, filled with every sort of building. It was surrounded by a wall forty-five feet high. On the north-west and west sides this wall formed part of the city-wall, and it was punctuated at this point by three adjoining towers named Hippicus (after a friend of Herod's youth killed in battle), Phasael (after his late brother) and Mariamme (supposedly after his current wife – though it must have been embarrassingly easy to think of her predecessor instead). The tower Hippicus, commanding a postern with access to a new aqueduct which furnished the palace with water, stood close to the existing Jaffa Gate. Phasael rose where the great north-east tower of the citadel, the Tower of David, rises now; and it still incorporates the masonry of Herod's tower to a considerable height. The tower of Mariamme was at the north-eastern corner. Stewart Perowne writes:

These towers stood on a scarp 30 feet high, and were themselves 128, 125 and 72 feet high. They were square and the bases consisted of solid cubes, fashioned of great stones so perfectly joined together that they appeared to be one block. Hippicus was 45 feet square at the base, Phasael 60 and Mariamme only 35. The upper parts were of rather smaller dimensions. Immediately above the foundations of Hippicus was a reservoir 35 feet deep to store rain-water, and then a two-storey building, surmounted by turreted battlements. The design of Phasael was similar, the lower storey contained a cloister and the second a bath and other fine rooms. It was so splendid that it looked like the Pharos, the famous lighthouse of Alexandria, only larger, says Josephus. (That the Pharos was a square tower of several storeys we now know from the representations of it in the mosaics at Gerasa [Jerash].) Mariamme, being named after a woman, was smaller but more sumptuously furnished, and with greater variety.

To the south of the towers was the main palace, in which there were two great chambers called after Augustus and Marcus Agrippa. There were besides many other rooms, some of them big enough for 100 guests to sleep in at a time. The walls were encrusted with rare and costly marbles, the beams were of exceptional width, imported probably from Lebanon, and richly adorned. Exquisite paintings and sculptures delighted the eye, and the domestic appointments were of silver and gold. Outside, a series of porticoes, embellished with curiously carved pillars, surrounded green lawns and groves which were watered by deep canals and pools into which brazen spouts discharged their refreshing cascades.[13]

Above the water-courses, he continues, were pigeon-houses stocked with tame pigeons. In the middle of this great park, reminiscent of Hellenistic palaces, these pigeon-houses were located somewhere on the site of the present police barracks or Armenian garden. The pigeons were carriers, and formed part of Herod's communications system. The domestication of these birds goes back to early Egypt, but Herod had derived the practice from the Idumaean town of Marissa which, until its destruction by the Parthians in 90 BC, had bred many such birds in caves designed for the sacred doves of Atargatis-Tanit, a pagan goddess equated with Aphrodite. More prosaically, the pigeons' droppings were used as agricultural fertilisers. The rabbis of later periods, otherwise very reticent about Herod's buildings, were at least prepared to credit him with the introduction of a breed of pigeons.

Reconstruction of (from left to right) the Hippicus, Mariamme and Phasael towers of Herod's citadel-palace.

Herod's Tower of Phasael, now the 'Tower of David' with a Mohammedan superstructure and minaret, contained a cloister and a second-storey apartment.

Seventeen miles north-east of Jerusalem – twenty-three by the steeply descending road – lies Jericho, 'the deepest hole in the world'. This oasis of date-palms and balsam trees seemed to Josephus to contain 'the rarest and loveliest things in abundance'; and it was here that Herod made his winter capital and residence – at the point where the Wadi Qilt debouches from the cleft of the Valley of the Shadow of Death (so called because of its dark gloom) into the Jericho plain, two miles south of the Old Testament city of that name.

Watched over by the great fortress of Cyprus, Herod's palace, like the palace at Jerusalem, contained two apartments named after Augustus and Agrippa. Beside the site where these main buildings must have stood, excavations have disclosed a terrace, two hundred feet long, with a hemicyclical, niched and tiered water-garden at its central point[14] (was this the pool Herod had arranged for the young high priest Aristobulus (III) to be kept under the water until he drowned?). All round were other elegant constructions. Most of Herod's buildings elsewhere make great use of stone, but since there is no stone to be obtained from anywhere near Jericho, its Herodian walls are built of the diamond-shaped brick (*opus reticulatum*) characteristic of Augustan construction in Italy. And indeed, wrote J. C. Kelso: 'Everything about this civic centre instantly calls up Rome and Pompeii. One might say that here in New Testament Jericho is a section of Augustan Rome that has been miraculously transferred on a magic carpet from the banks of the Tiber to the banks of the Wadi Qilt.'

Not far away, the discovery has been made of a second complex of buildings, covering an area of seventy-nine by forty-three yards.[15] It seems to comprise an elaborate gymnasium and palaestra, with sophisticated bathing facilities. Here the diamond brick does not appear, but the possibility cannot be excluded that this group and the other both belong to Herod's reign, though perhaps to different phases of it. There was also a hippodrome at Jericho, and a theatre or amphitheatre, or both; Josephus says both, but he may have been mistaken.

The site of Herod's Jericho was no doubt largely determined by the fact that the Valley of the Shadow of Death is exceptionally well supplied by springs. Three of them, and two others not far away, were channelled into aqueducts, so as to bring abundant supplies of water into the new city and the parks, and the plantations of the oasis. Twelve miles to the north, Herod founded an agricultural village and model farm in memory of his brother Phasael; it was here that the dates named after Nicolaus of Damascus were grown. The place is still called Fasail – almost the only surviving oral relic of Herod and his family.[16]

On the site of Herod's palace at Jerusalem: the fourteenth-century citadel, overlooking the Jaffa gate.

The Roman road leading north-eastwards from Jerusalem towards Jericho.

But Herod was by no means content with palaces in Jerusalem and Jericho alone. There also remained the provinces of Galilee, Peraea and Idumaea; and in all of these he built residences. In Galilee he chose the capital town of Sepphoris (Zippori), which he had captured during a snowstorm when he was first taking over the country. In Peraea, across the Jordan, he built a dwelling at Betharamphtha (Beth-haram, Er Rame), six miles north of the Dead Sea.[17]

Overlooking that same sea at its other, Idumaean end, he built two palaces at one and the same place, the bleakest place possible, on the top of the hill of Masada. 'Surely,' says Palestine's geographer George Adam Smith about this Dead Sea desolation, 'there is no region of earth where Nature and History have so cruelly conspired, where so tragic a drama has obtained so awful a theatre.' To modern

Israelis, Masada is a place of sacred pilgrimage because of its resistance to the Romans in the First Jewish Rebellion or First Roman War (see Chapter 17).[18] But more than a century before then, this huge, boat-shaped rock had been the place where Herod lodged his family in 40 BC when the Parthians swept through the country and he was hastening to Rome for support, and it was here, later on, that he chose to build himself two residences. But these associations do

Masada. Right (above long cliff): Herod's main palace. Front left: the precipice which his second palace overhangs; baths and storehouse at its back.

not quite explain his choice of this site: there was also something in his own personality that recommended a site so melodramatically remote from human contacts, amid a landscape so stricken and so fantastic that it is scarcely possible for a photograph to do it justice.

Masada, like Herod's other chosen abodes, was to remain a fortress as well as a palace; and he rebuilt the great walls extending a mile round the precipitous hill-top, twenty feet high and twelve feet broad, punctuated by no less than thirty-eight towers, each rising to a height of seventy feet and more. The larger of his two Masada mansions covered thirty-six thousand square feet at the western extremity of the plateau. The numerous important finds made by its recent excavators have included the throne room, and an entrance hall decorated with a floor mosaic, perhaps the earliest

133

The mosaic artistry of Herod's Masada was inherited by the Byzantines who built this chapel in the fifth century AD.

coloured mosaic to have been found in the country. Its designs show a careful avoidance of the human and animal forms that could have been regarded as infringements upon the Second Commandment. Other mosaics of considerable elegance were uncovered in a bath-room and corridor. A kitchen, too, has come to light – with enor-mous cooking stoves, and store-rooms large enough to enable the occupants of the palace to live a self-contained existence. 'In Herod's time', writes Yigael Yadin, 'these store-rooms held more costly and sophisticated items than were stored in Masada's public store-houses. We found evidence of this in the shreds of hundreds of delicate vessels, such as flasks and juglets of cosmetic oil, which were scattered over the floors.'[19]

Much stranger, however, was Herod's second palace at Masada, which stood at the narrow northern extremity of the same hill-top, and indeed jutted beyond it on three terraces, hanging, one above the other, right over the abyss, with the support of massive eighty-foot-high supporting walls. The lowest terrace, containing rooms and baths and pilastered, painted colonnades,[20] was designed chiefly for enjoying the grim and startling scenery. This, too, was the purpose of the middle terrace, which included a decorative

The lowest of the three terraces of Herod's villa-palace on the northern tip of Masada: an open court surrounded by columns.

circular building. The upper terrace provided living accommodation for Herod and his most intimate entourage (the rest were accommodated elsewhere on the hill). Their four living rooms were adorned with paintings and mosaics; at the northern extremity, a large semi-circular portico commanded an amazing view on three sides of the compass.

Behind this northern palace was a large bath-house, another *tour de force* in this waterless region, fed by rows of huge cisterns conserving rain and the 'flash floods' provided, at rare seasons, by two rocky streams. The cisterns are not far from the northern palace, and their proximity was convenient. But the main reason why the king decided to inflict upon his engineers and architects such an astonishing challenge was climatic. 'The northern point of the Masada rock,' says Yadin, 'particularly the middle and bottom terraces, is the only site on Masada which is sheltered for most of the daylight hours: sheltered from the sun, so that it is cool and pleasant, and sheltered from the south wind – the rock walls of each terrace serve as wind-breaks – so that it is always still. Only Herod, the great and ambitious builder, could have conceived the project of erecting a three-tiered hanging palace-villa for himself on this spot.'[21]

The principal bath-house at Masada: the hot room. The small pillars supported the floor, beneath which an adjacent furnace introduced the hot air.

And so Herod built himself these unique dwellings and refuges in his native Idumaea, in addition to his palaces and mansions in Judaea, Galilee and Peraea. He also possessed palaces in regions that did not belong to his kingdom at all. One was at Ascalon, which was the natural port of Idumaea. Situated in a rich and well-watered coastal oasis between two chains of petrified sand-dunes, its ramparts crowning a semi-circle of cliffs, this little city-state remained a free enclave within his territory. He could have incorporated it in his own dominions if he had so desired, but he preferred not to; no doubt his family connections with the place gave it a privileged position. His palace at Ascalon has not yet been located, but we learn that he adorned it with baths, fountains and colonnades. Fragments of one such colonnade, his 'Hall of the Pillars' leading to the senate-house, can be seen today collected in an excavated portion of a Herodian building at a corner of the municipal park.

Herod was also at a later date given a palace at Antioch, the capital of Syria, by one of its governors – no doubt in gratitude for the gifts which he in his turn lavished upon the Syrian and Phoenician cities (see Chapter 14).

Expansion beyond the Jordan

The gifts which Herod exchanged with the communities of Syria
and Phoenicia illustrate the careful attention which he was always
obliged to pay to his northern frontier; and it was in this direction
that he turned his eyes in 23 BC. His immediate neighbours to the
north-east were the Ituraeans. Based upon the Lebanon and Anti-
Lebanon mountains and the Bekaa plain that lies between them,
these people also possessed territory which extended down to the
shores of the Sea of Galilee and far beyond into a large hinterland
towards the east, the other side of the upper waters of the Jordan.
The Ituraeans were Arabs of an unruly brand, skilful archers inclined to brigandage. But the Hellenised founder of their dynasty
had organised them, just under a century earlier, into a state of more
or less orthodox pattern, with its capital at Chalcis beneath Lebanon
(formerly Gerrha) and a great religious centre at Heliopolis, the
City of the Sun (Baalbek).

The son of the dynasty's founder[1] had been confirmed in his
principality by Pompey, but later he had created many difficulties
for Herod. He was the brother-in-law of Herod's enemy Antigonus,
and had harboured him in 42–41 BC, providing a spring-board for
Antigonus' return to Judaea as the Parthian, anti-Roman nominee.
The next 'tetrarch and high priest', as their coins call these rulers,
was again regarded as pro-Parthian, and became one of Cleopatra's
victims. But his son Zenodorus, like Herod, succeeded in keeping
at least part of his ancestral territory out of her hands, at the price
of paying her a rent. And subsequently – again like Herod – he had
been confirmed in his principality by Augustus.[2]

Now, however, Zenodorus was in trouble. The city that usually
suffered worst from the banditry of his Ituraeans was their rich
commercial neighbour Damascus, and Damascus was suffering
from this now: its rulers issued a series of anguished complaints to
successive governors of Syria. We can assume that Herod's adviser
Nicolaus, who himself came from Damascus, supported their
protests. Finally, in 23 BC, Augustus gave orders that Zenodorus'
dominions should be drastically reduced in size. Their entire southern and south-eastern portion was to be taken out of his hands –
and granted to Herod instead.

This extensive territory now belongs to Syria, comprising its
southern extremity, to the east of the Golan Heights. In classical
times, it was divided into three regions, the plain of Batanea and the
more distant mountains of Trachonitis and Auranitis. The geo-

graphical units represented by these names were thought of by the ancient writers as possessing widely different locations and sizes. Batanea, however, may be said to correspond with part of the biblical Bashan, a treeless plain (En-Nukra between Leja and Gilead) but rich in cattle.[3] Trachonitis is the modern Leja and Safa, south-east of Damascus, a crumpled and cracked maze of lava ridges and gullies. 'It forms,' observes A. H. M. Jones, 'an ideal home for those who wish to evade the pursuit of the law. An invading force must march blind – for there are no commanding heights from which a general view can be obtained.' The purpose of the cession of this territory to Herod, says Josephus, was to enable him to purge it of what seemed to the imperial government to be robber bands, though to those of other political views they may have looked more like guerrilla organisations. Their hide-outs were almost inaccessible caves[4].

The third region granted to Herod, Auranitis, should be identified with the pile of volcanic mountains south-east of Trachonitis, still described as the Jebel Hauran. As its alternative name (Jebel Druz) recalls, it is now the home of the traditionally lawless Druses; it has always served as a convenient place of refuge for people on the run. The capital of Auranitis, Canatha, had been recognised as a city by Pompey, and it was near here, at Si'a, that Herod built or rebuilt a temple of Baalshamin, and adorned its courtyard with his own statue.

However, Herod's annexation of Auranitis caused his relations with his Arabian (Nabataean) neighbours to become extremely strained once again. Only eight years had passed since the end of a

Reconstruction of Herod's temple of Zeus Baalshamin at Si'a in Auranitis (Hauran). One of the statues flanking the door represents himself.

hard-fought war between Herod and these Arabs, a war which the Jews had won with considerable difficulty. After Actium the Arabs had hastened, like Herod, to ingratiate themselves with Octavian. But their king, Malchus, had died very soon afterwards; according to one account his death was caused by Cleopatra, one of the last actions of her life. His successor Obodas (Aboud) III was an old, sluggish man, entirely ruled by his clever, young and handsome chief minister Syllaeus (Shullay), who now begins to play an important part in Herod's story.

We are not quite sure of the meaning of the title which the Arabs

From Moab, beyond Herod's frontiers, a bust of the goddess Atargatis from the N. Arab (Nabataean) hill-temple of Khirbet-et-Tannur.

Top: Base of an alabaster funerary stele from S. Arabia (Arabia Felix), which controlled the trade-route between Egypt and India.

Below: Alabaster head from S. Arabia, first century BC or AD. The Himyarites had established a rich kingdom there, with its capital at Eudaemon (Aden).

Stone plaque in the shape of a head from S. Arabia; of about the time of its
invasion by Roman forces with Jewish and Nabataean contingents in 25 BC.

had conferred upon Herod at the conclusion of their war with him.
If, however, he thought it meant he could interfere in their kingdom,
he must have been rapidly disillusioned by Syllaeus, who was just
as ambitious as Herod to make his own kingdom an important
entity. But Syllaeus, in his turn, had to reckon with a somewhat too
keen interest on the part of Augustus, who was eager to see the
Arabs playing a more satisfactory part as a client kingdom and was
apparently prepared, failing that, to incorporate them in the empire.
At any rate it was alarming to learn that the emperor was expressing
the hope that he could either enjoy them as rich friends or conquer
them as rich enemies.[5]

Moreover, Augustus also had designs on the southern part of
Arabia, where a wealthy kingdom of Arabia Felix, based on Eudaemon (Aden, now in South Yemen), exercised a highly profitable
monopoly of the Straits of Bab-el-Mandeb controlling the trade-
route between Egypt and India.[6] In 25 an expedition against this
remote region was launched under Aelius Gallus, who had been
Augustus' governor of Egypt. Both Herod and Syllaeus were instructed to contribute to the force, and they sent five hundred and a
thousand men respectively, while Syllaeus was also requested to

141

organise transport and provide advice about the route. This placed him in a severe dilemma. On the one hand he had to keep in with Rome; and yet a complete Roman take-over of southern Arabia would mean that Syllaeus' own position as a commercial middleman was undermined.

As matters turned out his reputation with the Romans was endangered, because the expeditionary force got lost for a long time in the desert wastes, where an immensely long journey involved terrifying hardships. But the faces of all concerned were saved, because in the end the South Arabian kingdom, impressed by such a costly effort, formally accepted the friendship of the Roman people. It could, technically, be said that it became a client kingdom – its coins now showed a head resembling Augustus. But it only belonged to the outermost penumbra of states that could be so described, and its obligations must have been minimal. At least, however, it is probable that it agreed to abandon its monopoly of the Straits.

Although, nearly twenty years later, Syllaeus was accused of treachery in the matter, at the time he managed to survive without disgrace. Admittedly he had not saved the army from the unreliable and perhaps corrupt guides who led it astray, but that was perhaps the Romans' fault and not his: they may have insisted, against available advice and intelligence, on going most of the way by land instead of sea. At all events Syllaeus was able, in the end, to point out to them that they had gained their main aim; at the same time he could claim privately to his own associates that Roman encirclement had been averted.[7]

What Herod's attitude was to these events – apart from the natural concern he must have felt for his troops taking part in the expedition – we cannot tell. But very soon it became clear that the strained relations between Jews and Arabs, which had caused war in 32–31 BC, were by no means over, and were indeed entering into an acute phase once again. This, however, was far from being the intention of Syllaeus. In about 25 he paid a diplomatic visit to Jerusalem, no doubt in connection with the numerous financial interests the two kingdoms had in common. While he was there, Herod's sister Salome fell in love with the brilliant young Arab regent.[8] Hitherto her matrimonial career had been disastrous, since her two previous husbands had been executed by her brother; the first, Joseph (II), because of suspect behaviour while acting as Herod's deputy, and the second, Costobarus, after she had divorced him and then told the king he was a traitor.

And now she turned her attention to Syllaeus. We do not know how well he was aware of her curious character. At all events, he seems to have reciprocated her love; or at least he saw the possibility of remarkable future advantages for himself in such a marriage. And so a few months later he came to Jerusalem again, and asked Herod for her hand. But now a difficulty arose. Herod reminded the suitor that he himself and his Idumaean house belonged to the Jewish faith, and that anyone who married into the family must likewise be circumcised and become a Jew. Syllaeus pointed out that this was impossible in his own case, because his people would stone him to death if he did. Thereupon Herod declared that the proposed marriage alliance was impracticable; and so it came to nothing. Salome, deeply upset, and further infuriated by rumours

Augustus' wife Livia, here depicted by Tiberius as 'Imperial Well-Being', *Salus Augusta*, was unresponsive to an appeal from Herod's sister Salome about her marriage plans.

that she had already become Syllaeus' mistress, appealed to the emperor's wife Livia, with whom she was on friendly terms, to try somehow to put matters right. But Livia proved unhelpful. Acting no doubt on the advice of Augustus, she indicated that Herod's decision must prevail. The king had tried to solve Salome's problem by suggesting that she should instead marry a certain Jew, Alexas (11). Salome found him unattractive; but all Livia had to suggest was that she should do as she was told.

There is something a little mysterious about the incident. It is perfectly true that the religious question provided a problem which it would clearly have been difficult, and perhaps impossible, to overcome. This being so, however, it is strange that Syllaeus, who was anything but a fool and must have seen the problem quite as quickly as anyone else, should have tried to persist with the match. It looks as though, initially, he must have received some encouragement from Herod. Half Arab himself, the king may at first have been prepared to let his sister go away and abandon her Judaism; but then later on, after realising how vigorous the Jewish opposition would be, he changed his mind. But that may not have been the only reason why he withdrew his support for the plan. It also appears that the brother of Herod and Salome, Pheroras, led the opposition to the marriage; and it is not too difficult to see why. For it seemed to Pheroras all too probable that Syllaeus, once married to Salome, would only wait for Herod's death to seize the whole of Judaea himself and annex it to his Arab state.

However that may be, Syllaeus departed from Jerusalem, and any prospect of friendship between the Arab and Jewish states was at an end. Soon afterwards friction became acute when, as we have seen, Augustus ordered Zenodorus, the Lebanese ruler, to cede to Herod his large territories in northern Transjordan. In order to evade this instruction, Zenodorus hastily arranged to sell the easternmost of these territories, Auranitis in the Jebel Druz, to the Arab kingdom instead. Syllaeus jumped at the idea, because the possession of this area would secure his caravan route to Damascus. But Augustus refused to recognise the transaction, and Herod, with the help of experienced guides, took forcible possession. It also appears likely that in order to deal with this problem the emperor gave him the privilege, a most unusual one for a client king, of extraditing fugitives from states outside his own jurisdiction.[9]

Herod's stock with the Romans evidently stood very high; and now he improved it still further. In 23 Augustus' right-hand man, Marcus Agrippa, was sent out from Rome to the eastern provinces with wide powers as viceroy of the entire region, amounting virtually to the position of deputy emperor. He set up his headquarters at his favourite island Mytilene (Lesbos), and Herod visited him there, apparently in the winter of 22–21.

If this date for the visit is correct, as it seems to be, one may wonder why he had waited so long before going to see the great man. After all, when Octavian had been in the east, Herod had called on him with much greater alacrity. It is possible, however, that the king delayed owing to rumours that relations between Augustus and Agrippa were somewhat strained. Agrippa was a man of enormous gifts who had performed immeasurable services for the emperor, and it was said that he had become piqued because Augustus seemed to be favouring his own youthful son-in-law, Marcellus, as his heir. Indeed, it was believed that was why Agrippa had been sent away from Rome. But soon after his departure for the east Marcellus died; and it was also becoming apparent that Augustus' other principal adviser, Maecenas, had now definitely taken second place to Agrippa. It was clearly not desirable to postpone visiting him any longer.

And so Herod proceeded to Mytilene, and, judging from subsequent events, there is every reason to believe that he enjoyed the same personal success with him as he had enjoyed with Augustus. Agrippa cannot have been an easy person to captivate. But Herod's capacity to exert charm and impose his personality did not fail to rise to the occasion.

However, Herod's visit had to be brief, for in 21 Agrippa was summoned back to Rome; now Augustus himself was coming out to the east and he wanted Agrippa back to take charge during his absence. Moreover, Agrippa's special position was further demonstrated by his marriage to the emperor's own daughter Julia, recently widowed by the death of Marcellus.

During Agrippa's discussions with Herod at least one important matter was settled. It was arranged that two of the king's sons should go to Rome to study.

His eldest boy, Antipater (II), was not one of them, for, since his mother Doris had been divorced by Herod twenty years ago, neither mother nor son had enjoyed the royal favour. Nor were the sons of the Samaritan Malthace (Archelaus [II] and Antipas [II]) selected to go to Italy; and the son of his latest wife Mariamme (II), daughter of the new high priest, was still much too young. The boys who were now to go and complete their education in Rome were Herod's sons by the Hasmonaean Mariamme (I), who had been executed by the king in 29 BC.

These two youths, Alexander (III) and Aristobulus (IV), were to be lodged when they came to the capital at the home of a Roman called Pollio. It has been supposed that this was Gaius Asinius Pollio, an elder statesman of great distinction as a writer and literary patron. But Asinius Pollio, under the new Augustan regime, had maintained a marked aloofness, pursuing an unfashionable taste for *libertas,* the aristocrat's freedom of speech and action. 'He was preserved,' as Sir Ronald Syme expresses it, 'as a kind of privileged nuisance.' This relatively anti-Augustan figure does not seem the sort of man to whom Herod would have been likely to entrust his children, and it appears much more likely that they were placed in the care of Publius Vedius Pollio, one of the leading supporters of the new imperial order.[10] A knight (*eques*) who perhaps came from a humble family of Beneventum, famous for his ostentatious luxury and not without a reputation for cruelty, he was a leading financial expert of the regime, highly esteemed by Augustus, who had entrusted him, soon after Actium, with the enormously important province of Asia (western Asia Minor). Vedius Pollio's, then, may well have been the Roman household in which Herod lodged his sons. Although they were not his oldest boys, their Hasmonaean blood made it seem likely that they would be his heirs, and, in spite of the disaster that had befallen their mother this seems, at the present stage, to have been the view of Herod himself. But his arrangements for their education met with profound disapproval among many Jews. For they were going to live in a Gentile household at Rome; and the tutors who were placed in charge of them there would also be Gentiles.

As usual, however, internal criticisms could be brushed aside if Herod was able to point to a success with the Romans. And a further striking opportunity to achieve such a success arose in 20 BC, when Augustus himself appeared in Syria. Herod proceeded to Antioch

King Phraates IV of Parthia, 'King of kings, Benefactor, Just, God-Manifest, Phil-Hellene', with whom Augustus reached agreement in 20 BC.

to meet him for the second time, accompanied, on this occasion, by his friend and minister Nicolaus of Damascus (who recorded that he saw envoys who had come to see the emperor from India[11]).

At this moment Augustus, like so many Roman leaders when they visited this part of the world, was primarily concerned with relations with the eastern power Parthia. The bone of contention, as always, was Armenia: above all, Roman dignity required that the disaster to Crassus thirty-three years earlier should be avenged and that the Roman standards the Parthians had captured on that occasion should be got back. More cleverly than most Roman rulers before and after him, Augustus decided that the Armenian question could best be settled by diplomatic rather than military means; and in May of the year 20 the Parthians duly handed back the captured standards to the emperor's stepson Tiberius. They were influenced by the arrival of a large Roman army under Tiberius' command. If it had come to a fight, the presence of a strong and secure Judaea on the Syrian flank would have been essential, and Herod would have had his part to play. But it did not come to a fight. Nevertheless Herod was able to make good use of the presence of Augustus; for, during his residence at Antioch, the emperor made several important decisions regarding Judaean affairs.

The first decision arose out of a stroke of luck for Herod. The Lebanese prince, Zenodorus, who three years earlier had been obliged to cede the Jews three large regions east of the Sea of Galilee, had just died of a ruptured intestine. Consequently Herod was now granted two further regions north of the Sea as well, and this meant a considerable extension of his kingdom. One of these territories was Ulatha, situated at the northern extremity of modern Israeli territory; the name of the region is preserved today in the drained Lake Huleh. The other newly acquired region was Panias beneath Mount Hermon, including the city of the same name, now Banyas, just inside the tract of Syria occupied by Israel in 1967. Augustus was always ready to dilute Herod's kingdom with non-Jewish lands, and he was very content to have so trustworthy a client monarch on the frontiers of the Syrian province, instead of the unreliable dynasty of Zenodorus.

As for Herod, he had the satisfaction of acquiring the important non-Jewish shrine after which Panias was named, the Panion or Sanctuary of Pan on the lower rises of Mount Hermon. Here above the cave containing one of the principal sources of the Jordan[12] stood the shrine of Pan. It is shown on coins of Caesarea.Philippi (as Panias was to be renamed by Herod's son), and its remains are still to be seen today.[13] In front of the grotto, Herod built a temple to Rome and Augustus, a counterpart of the temple he had erected at Sebaste. It was made of white marble, but broken columns strewn round about suggest that its portico consisted of Egyptian granite. If so, it was an ironic choice of provenance – perhaps designed as a malicious stab at the memory of Cleopatra. For Panion was the site of a battle where, in 200 BC, the Egyptians had lost control of Palestine for ever.[14] They had lost it to the Seleucids, but now the Seleucids, too, had long since gone; and the Hasmonaeans, who freed Judaea from them, had never come as far as Panion. But now Herod had annexed it, and his acquisition of these northern territories meant that the whole of traditional, historic Israel was his, from Dan to Beersheba – Dan which was only a few miles from Panion, and Beersheba in his native Idumaea. No Jew since Solomon had ruled over so great a kingdom.

The Hasmonaean whose territories had come nearest to Herod's in size was Alexander Jannaeus. And the most permanent of his achievements had been the conquest, and conversion to Judaism, of the land of Peraea across the Jordan. This long, narrow territory extended from twenty miles south of the Sea of Galilee down to the middle shores of the Dead Sea – from the breezy, fragrant woods, orchards, vineyards and grainlands of Gilead to the blasted, stony steppes of Moab. In the north there were Greek city-states (the Decapolis) beyond the Peraean border. But for the most part Peraea had a frontier that needed guarding against the Arabs of Syllaeus: and this was the purpose that Herod's formidable Peraean fortresses of Machaerus and Eastern Herodium chiefly served.

And now in 20 BC, when Herod visited Augustus in Syria, he told the emperor that he wanted to lighten his own burden by installing his brother Pheroras as tetrarch (prince) of Peraea. Some modern scholars have believed that this was a measure forced upon him by Augustus, who meant Pheroras to be largely independent of Herod. But surely the idea was Herod's own, and it was intended to strengthen his power, not to fragment it. It is true that Pheroras was by no means easy to control, but Herod believed he could manage him. Pheroras was a curious mixture of weakness and obstinacy. The weakness often made him a tool of ambitious members of the family, particularly women, who more than once led him into courses of action which might have got him into fatal trouble with his brother. Women were also responsible for the obstinate streak in his character, for he had rejected, in turn, two royal brides pressed upon him by Herod – Herod's own sister-in-law and daughter. Pheroras refused them both because he loved a slave-girl, whom he subsequently married. In this age of grimly loveless dynastic matches such romantic pertinacity strikes an unfamiliar note.

And Herod, too, was undeterred by it, for now, with Augustus' permission, he made Pheroras tetrarch of Peraea, with a substantial salary in addition to the income from the territory he was to control. In a sense it was just a glorified provincial governorship like similar posts held by other personages in Idumaea or Galilee or Samaritis; but it was something more than that. As always, Herod was safeguarding his own Idumaean family in case something should happen to himself. But the immediate effect of the conferment was small, since for the time being Pheroras preferred to maintain his court in Jerusalem, in order to be near the royal palace and its intrigues.

Augustus' visit to Syria was also the occasion of a mild embarrassment for Herod. Between Peraea and Herod's acquisitions further north were sandwiched two cities of the Greek Decapolis, Gadara and Hippos, which had been allocated to Judaea ten years earlier. Although they possessed the self-governing constitutions common to all such Greek communities, Gadara, a place of considerable cultural pretensions, had for some time been complaining that Herod interfered unduly and exercised a heavy hand. The Gadarene leaders had been encouraged in this agitation by Herod's northern neighbour Zenodorus, whose indignation, because of the territories he had been forced to cede to Judaea, caused him to seize every opportunity to make trouble for Herod.

Now that Zenodorus was dead – or perhaps before – the Gadarenes utilised the opportunity of Augustus' eastern visit to lodge their complaint with him in person. They urged strongly that their city should be transferred from Herod's kingdom and reintegrated in the Roman province of Syria, whose control they would find less oppressive. The emperor listened to their case in Herod's presence. Their charges against him included wild accusations of violence and pillage and the destruction of temples. All this was evidently exaggerated; but whether there was any truth in their general assertion that Herod had treated them harshly we cannot be sure. On the whole it seems unlikely, because the king, although not too keen on decentralisation, made a practice of behaving tactfully and generously to non-Jews. However, Gadara may, for religious and racial reasons, have found the interventions of his Jewish officials more offensive than similar action by a Roman would have been. And Herod's governors no doubt did intervene, to some extent, in the affairs of the Greek cities, and were entitled to; for example the governor of Idumaea described his province as Idumaea *and Gaza* – although Gaza was another ostensibly autonomous city-state like Gadara.

Nevertheless, it soon became clear that Augustus and his advisers were likely to take Herod's side against the Gadarene delegation. Whereupon the delegates decided that further prospects of good treatment by the king they had spoken about so severely were poor indeed; and so the entire mission committed suicide. The emperor's verdict then went in favour of Herod, and a coin issued by Gadara, that is to say by the pro-Herodian faction there, seems to commemorate the occasion. At the same time Augustus entrusted Herod with some sort of an appointment in connection with the province of Syria. Probably he was made financial adviser to the imperial agent (procurator) who stood second only to the provincial governor in a quasi-independent position; and his function may have included lucrative duties relating to the collection of taxes.

The Temple

It was also in this same year, 20 BC, that work was begun on the task which Herod regarded as the culmination of his life's work, the achievement which would brush aside all misunderstandings among his own Jewish people and win him their eternal gratitude. This task was the rebuilding of the Temple of Jerusalem.

It was on the north-east side of the city, at the place called Mount Moriah, immediately opposite the Mount of Olives, that Solomon had built the Temple which is described with such a wealth of picturesque and loving detail, and such a lack of concern for helpful topography, in the Hebrew scriptures. After Judah had fallen to Nebuchadnezzar the Babylonian, a subsequent attempted revolt caused him to raze the Temple to the ground (586), sending many thousands of people into exile. But seventy years later the Persians who had taken over Babylon's empire allowed a Jewish population to return to a small area round Jerusalem, and at that juncture a second temple, on a more modest scale, was reconstructed under the governorship of Zerubbabel.

It was this building that the Seleucid Antiochus IV Epiphanes plundered, desecrated and paganised in 168 BC; and the crowning

Limestone tomb (ossuary) in Jerusalem inscribed in Aramaic 'Simon builder of the temple': probably one of Herod's architects or masons.

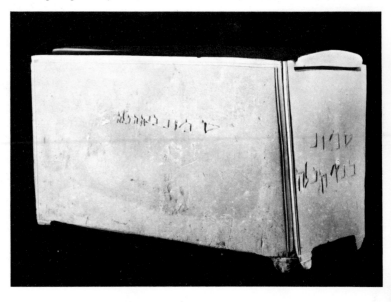

triumph of the nationalistic Hasmonaean revolt came when its leader, Judas Maccabaeus, rededicated the Temple in December 164 to the service of the Lord. The Festival of the Dedication (*Hanuka*) has been observed in honour of the occasion ever since.

Rock face showing Herod's excavations to level the Temple area. Now a school, on the site of the Antonia fortress.

And yet the building of Zerubbabel, which had already been recognised as somewhat makeshift when it was constructed nearly five centuries previously, now seemed increasingly inadequate as a symbol of Israel's renewed greatness. And so Herod announced he was going to rebuild it.

He announced his decision to a special gathering of the people, held in about the year 22 BC. Not everyone received his declaration favourably, because it was feared that he would pull down the old building and never construct a new one. To reassure such suspicions, he made and published all his plans for the reconstruction before starting on the work of demolition. The soft white stone was to be the stone that had been used for Solomon's Temple, and would be taken from Solomon's quarries a few hundred yards to the north; and it was to be hewn and shaped before it reached the Temple site, so that the holy place should not be disfigured by noise. There were to be ten thousand workmen, and a thousand of them would be priests trained as masons and carpenters, since the Law prohibited laymen from entering the Temple building itself.

The work of rebuilding started about two years after the initial announcement, and, once started, it progressed with great speed; and with a good deal of difficulty we can obtain some idea of what Herod's Temple looked like, by comparing Josephus with a considerably divergent Hebrew account.[1] (See plan 10.)

The entire complex was enclosed in the Court of the Gentiles, represented today by the great platform of the Haram al-Sherif. This

Reconstruction of Herod's Temple, seen from the south-east, by Comte De Vogüé in *Le Temple de Jérusalem* (1864).

was the courtyard the Jews called 'the mountain of the house'. A vast precinct of this kind, surrounding an inner shrine, was quite a common formula in the Levant, where it can best be appreciated today by visitors to Palmyra and Gerasa (Jerash). At Jerusalem the courtyard, covering about thirty-five acres, was much larger than the court of the previous temple, indeed almost twice its size. For if Herod, for religious reasons, was obliged to adhere to the supposed Solomonian dimensions for the actual Sanctuary itself, nothing debarred him from enlarging and enriching this more secular outer court: and he was particularly disposed to do so because he himself was able to enter it, whereas, not being a priest, he could not set foot in the Sanctuary.

The Court of the Gentiles, then, was extended from its former square shape and made into a huge oblong space, brilliantly paved and enclosed by a wall on all four sides. To the north, where the extension was made possible by filling in a deep valley between the Temple area and the Antonia castle, a second tower was added at the north-east corner, which partially balanced the Antonia to the north-west. 'Master,' cried one of the disciples to Jesus, 'see what manner of stones and buildings are here!'[2] And although Jesus knew that the Temple itself would not last for ever, on the west side of the precinct parts of the enclosure wall still survive, forming the nine lowest courses of the Wailing Wall beside which Jews come to offer their prayers. On this same side, too, there are extensive remains of viaducts[3] leading over the Tyropoeon (Cheesemakers') Valley which at that time extended below, but has now been largely filled in.

The temple of Bel at Palmyra (Tadmor) in the Syrian desert. Like Herod's slightly earlier temple at Jerusalem, it was surrounded by a huge precinct.

All that remains of 'Robinson's Arch', Herod's bridge at the south-western corner of the Temple area, linking it with the Upper City.

Jesus was also invited by the devil, according to Matthew's Gospel, to cast himself down miraculously from the Pinnacle or parapet of the Temple[4]. This was the summit of the enclosure wall at its south-eastern corner, where it soared four hundred and fifty feet above the level of the Kidron valley beneath. The vaults known as Solomon's Stables can be seen below the point where the Pinnacle stood. All this southern side of the precinct was artificially shored up by a massive substructure built into the hill. The largest of its stone blocks, cut with the utmost precision, is more than sixteen feet long, and can easily be discerned from the opposite side of the valley.

This southern end of the enclosure was reached by vaulted ramps leading upwards from the two Gates of Huldah or 'Triple' and 'Double' Gates. Of the Triple Gate all that remains is part of the door-frame of the western bay.[5] But the remains of the Double Gate (below the El Aqsa mosque) are quite substantial, and comprise the only considerable surviving portion of Herod's Temple. Behind its twin bays, which originally contained the doors, stands a square forecourt with a powerful monolithic column in the centre.

Top: Viaduct leading westwards from the Temple precinct, known as Wilson's Arch, after its discoverer. *Below:* The Double Gate on the south side of the Temple enclosure, from a sketch by De Vogüé (1864).

'Solomon's Stables' at the south-east corner of the Temple precinct. In fact, though the vaulting is medieval, the columns belonged to Herod's substructure.

The capital of the column has the form of a basket, from which emerge patterns of leaves. Other features include shallow pilasters, lintels made of a single stone, and a ceiling of elliptical domes with stucco decoration. These gates, each flanked by a series of small chambers, projected inwards into the courts like towers.

The Court of the Gentiles was entered by other gates as well, the total number being variously counted as seven and thirteen. Unlike the monumental, axially-placed propylaea of pagan temple precincts, they were irregularly located, but were fairly uniform in construction, generally resembling the Double Gate. The four openings on the western side included the Gate of the Chain or Coponius, of which Herodian paving stones survive; it was the terminal point of one of the viaducts which led across the valley. Next above it came a gate leading to the Upper City or north-western part of Jerusalem, but of this, too, only a very little can now be seen (the remains of a lintel). In the eastern wall of the enclosure was the Gate Shushan, identified since early Christian times with the Golden Gate by which Jesus rode into Jerusalem on Palm Sunday.

The interior of Herod's Court of the Gentiles was surrounded by colonnades of Graeco-Roman Corinthian columns, which apparently extended right round the periphery. On three of the four sides there was a double row of columns. The most famous of these colonnades, on the east side, bore the name of Solomon's Portico, because it was a greatly enlarged and altered version of a portico dating from the first Temple. But within the south side of the enclosure Herod erected a triple colonnade, a resplendent affair comprising a hundred and sixty-two columns and extending to a length of more than eight hundred feet. It was called the Royal Porch,

Naturalistic frieze from the 'Tomb of the Kings' - family burial place of Queen Helena of Adiabene (Assyria), converted to Judaism. Mid-first century AD.

because it was the place where according to tradition Solomon himself had been crowned. But it resembled an open-ended version of a Graeco-Roman basilica. Flanked by an aisle on either side stood a central nave much wider and twice as high. The additional height was obtained by a second, superimposed tier of columns which rested on the architraves of the aisle-columns below and were no doubt punctuated by clerestory windows. The ceiling was coffered with cedar-wood, covered with gold leaf, and embellished with rich carvings in high relief.

Josephus declares that these reliefs included all manner of different designs.[6] His words have sometimes been believed to indicate that Herod was ignoring the strict current interpretation of the

Herodian naturalistic and geometrical decoration: drawing by De Vogüé of the cupola of the Double Gate of the Temple.

Second Commandment vetoing the representation of animal life. But this seems doubtful; at all events the decoration of the domes of the Double Gate was strictly limited to inanimate objects. Wreaths, clusters of grapes, chaplets and rosettes alternate gracefully with geometrical designs.

On the whole the motifs are Hellenistic. Yet these Palestinian buildings of the second and first centuries B C – and there are parallels and variants in other regions of the Levant[7] – also display an oriental tendency towards sharply cut planes, in which the Greek plant designs forfeit their organic features and assume a flat appearance on geometrically stylised surfaces. The plastic classical values tend to be replaced by optic values based on contrasts between bright light and shadow. Herod's Temple, owing to the need to conform with Solomon's tradition, was non-Greek in most of its architectural framework – there are similar curious mixtures of west and east in tombs in the Kidron valley[8] – and its special traditional environment, together with the special exigencies of the Second Commandment, encouraged a certain deviation from classicism in its sculpture and relief work as well. Its disappearance has meant the loss of a vital link between Hellenistic art and the late Roman styles, in which these eastern features became accentuated.

Inside the Court of the Gentiles was the Court of Women, thus named because it represented the limit beyond which women could not go. Surrounded by a fence or grating, it was entered by three gates of which the largest was on the eastern side.[9] This was the place where, shortly after Herod's death, Joseph and Mary presented their infant son Jesus.[10]

The Court of Women led into the Court of Israel (or Court of Men) which was accessible to every male Jew; but, as surviving inscriptions confirm, any Gentile who penetrated thus far was liable

A prototype for the mausoleum Herod built for his family at Jerusalem? The
so-called 'Tomb of Absalom' in the Kidron valley.

to the penalty of death. The magnificent gate which led into the
court at its east end was approached by fifteen semi-circular steps.[11]
In its turn, the Court of Israel was adjoined on its west side by the
Court of the Priests, though the line and method of their demarca-
tion are not clearly stated.

In the middle of the Court of the Priests, in front of the Sanctuary
itself, stood the sacrificial Altar, approached by a ramp. The place
is now called the Qubbet es Sakhra, and here within the Omar
Mosque, or Dome of the Rock, stands the bare rock of Mount
Moriah, believed by the ancients to be the place where Abraham
planned to sacrifice Isaac his son. It was here, too, that King David
was commanded to build an altar to the Lord, upon the threshing
floor of Araunah of the Jebusites,[12] the people who had lived in

Jerusalem before the coming of the Jews. Upon the sacred rock, then, or just in front of it, stood the Altar of Burnt-Offering, a great cubical structure of unhewn stone. It had been the supreme desecration when the Seleucid Antiochus IV, in 167 BC, set up in its place a new altar dedicated to Olympian Zeus, and it was the supreme achievement of the Hasmonaeans to obliterate this abomination.

The Altar, it is true, stood for an archaic conception of Judaism which the spiritual religion of the Prophets, and now the expositions of the Law in the synagogues, had tended to supersede. The sacrificial scenes presented a bloodthirsty appearance. But they helped

The Court of Women, with gate leading into the Court of Israel; the sanctuary rises behind. Reconstruction by Michael Avi-Yonah.

the Temple to maintain its role as an economic asset of the first importance.[13]

There were dealers of many kinds – including vendors of pigeons – within the colonnades of the Court of the Gentiles. There were also money-changers, and one of the most startling stories about Jesus, repeated in all four Gospels, describes how he forcibly turned them out. In addition, there were store-rooms, a bakehouse for the twelve loaves of shewbread that were placed every Sabbath 'before the Lord', treasures and money-chests for offerings, administrative offices and the chamber where the Jewish council of state held its

'The Pools of Solomon', reservoirs south of Bethlehem which provided water for Jerusalem; mentioned in the Talmud.

meetings. And this whole seething population of the Temple area was provided with water by a new aqueduct which remained in partial use until after the present century had begun.[14]

A few paces beyond the Altar, twelve steps led up to the Sanctuary itself, a structure of massively thick white walls. Divergent ideas of what it looked like, based on the tantalisingly enigmatic ancient descriptions, can be obtained from various modern attempts at reconstruction. It was evidently a very high building – twice as high as the second Temple which it superseded. This was because it aimed to reproduce Solomon's first Temple, for which the *Book of Chronicles* (which had probably been handed down in an inaccurate, corrupt

161

form) gave an extravagant height.[15] Herod's building, made to follow these same lofty dimensions, must have presented a fantastic appearance, visible far and wide in every direction, 'like a mountain covered by snow'.[16]

The Sanctuary was preceded by a great porch. This, again, was extremely high; and in order to provide reasonable proportions it was made very broad as well, perhaps extending beyond the width of the building behind it so that the whole edifice was in the shape of a T, with the porch as its broad crossbar.

At the back of the porch the Sanctuary itself was entered through gigantic doors encrusted with precious metals. But across them was drawn a Babylonian tapestry embroidered with a sacred map of the heavens, its four colours denoting the four elements. Above the doors was sculpted a giant golden vine, each of its clusters as large as a human being – the replacement of a previous work which had been presented to Pompey as a bribe by one of the unsuccessful Jewish contestants for his favour.[17] The vine symbolised triumphant Israel.

Thou didst bring a vine out of Egypt;
Thou didst drive out nations and plant it;
Thou didst clear the ground before it,
So that it made good roots and filled the land.
The mountains were covered with its shade,
And its branches were like those of mighty cedars.[18]

As in Solomon's Temple, the Sanctuary was surrounded by thirteen store-rooms in three storeys. Inside the Sanctuary itself were two successive chambers. The first was the Holy Place, which housed the table of shewbread and the Menorah or seven-branched 'candlestick', a lampstand supporting seven lamps of olive-oil. Both these revered treasures were later depicted by the Romans on their Arch of Titus, who took them away when he plundered Jerusalem in AD 70.[19] Among the Jews, the depiction of the Menorah in sculptures and paintings was said to be forbidden. Yet it appears not only on graffiti upon a Jerusalem tomb,[20] but on the coinage of the last Hasmonaean monarch, Antigonus, from whom Herod had seized the city in 37 BC; it is the only Jewish symbol to be found on any Hasmonaean coin. As for Herod's own monetary issues, they show an altar which may well be the Altar of Incense, another of the objects that was lodged within the Holy Place.[21]

Between the Holy Place and the second chamber of the Sanctuary, the Holy of Holies, there had been a wall and door in Solomon's Temple; but Herod does not seem to have reproduced this feature. Instead, there were two curtains extending from side to side of the building. They constituted the Veil of the Temple which, at the moment of Jesus' death, was said to have been rent in twain.[22] The Holy of Holies could be entered by no one but the high priest, and even he could enter it only once a year, on Yom Kippur, the Day of Atonement or God's Great Pardon. Pompey, who walked into this

The Hasmonaean Antigonus, overcome by the Romans and Herod in 37 BC, had displayed a unique representation of the Menorah on his coins.

The spoils taken by Titus from the Temple (AD 70): golden candlestick (Menorah), golden table of the Shewbread, and silver trumpets.

inmost shrine, had earned undying Jewish hatred.

After eighteen months' work, the construction of the Sanctuary was completed in 18 BC, amid mighty celebrations and thanksgivings. The completion of the courtyards, which formed the remaining part of the precinct, was a less urgent matter, and work on them continued for ten years.

Indeed, there was really never any end to the task of reconstruction. In the riots after Herod's death the fabric was severely damaged. Later, when Jesus cryptically declared that he would raise the Temple again in three days, the Jews indicated, in their reply, that it had taken forty-six years to build.[23] That was said, if it is historic, in *c.* AD 28–30. And the final stages of building do not appear to have taken place until AD 63 when the eastern retaining wall was finished. Meanwhile, another portion of the wall had collapsed, and further attention to Solomon's Portico was also felt to be required. However, these repairs were never undertaken; and seven years later the Temple was destroyed by the Romans.

It remained only as a remarkable memory. And it was, or should have been, a memory entirely associated with the name of Herod. For whatever clearing-up operations later needed to be done, it was he who had virtually completed the reconstruction between 20 and 10 BC. Yet the later Hebrew lawyers and theologians tended to express admiration of the Temple while ignoring its association with Herod: or it was suggested that such reconstruction as he undertook was not his own idea.[24]

As for Herod himself, he was deeply proud of what he had achieved, and he never got tired of pointing out that the Hasmonaean liberators had never even begun to undertake this mighty task during the whole hundred and twenty-five years of their regime.[25] Even Solomon, though studiously (if inaccurately) imitated in regard to the sacrosanct dimensions, had been totally surpassed. Herod's secretary Nicolaus of Damascus could reasonably assert that the king was a generous man – and that the greatest part of his munificence was devoted to works of piety.

And yet Herod was also a Roman client. The Romans were tolerant of the national gods of their client peoples, and, as we shall see, when Marcus Agrippa visited Jerusalem, he made a point of coming to the Temple to do it honour. But Augustus himself seems to have felt certain reservations. Was not the gigantic scale of this commemoration of a national deity perhaps a little disproportionate, amid a community of nations who more tolerantly shared their gods with one another? At all events, after Herod's death Augustus publicly commended one of his grandsons for not stopping to see the Temple when he passed through Judaea.

How Herod paid for it all

What resources did Herod possess to enable him to shoulder gigantic expenditure such as this?

Judaea was a poor country, a stony and waterless moorland plateau on the road to nowhere, interspersed with only a few small fertile places, though these were significant enough to inspire covetousness among its neighbours.[1] And the population was uncomfortably high for its size; at a rough guess there may have been three million Jews in Palestine. Moreover, numbers were increasing, at a rate as high as anywhere else in the Roman world. Why this was so is disputed, but reasons that have been given include the absence of the Graeco-Roman practice of infanticide (which Moses had been commanded to shun), the Jewish abhorrence of homosexuality, and a patriotic desire to increase the national population.

Very many of the communities of this part of the world hopefully placed the horn of plenty, the *cornucopiae,* upon their coins. The Ptolemies, Seleucids and Hasmonaeans all portrayed it; and so did Herod. But in Judaea the hope was not always fulfilled. For one

Lamps for burning the oil in which parts of Judaea were so rich.

thing its rains are the least reliable and predictable in the entire Mediterranean area. The Bible is full of reference to God's displeasure in withholding rains, especially the 'later rains' of spring; and Herod's reign had already witnessed serious droughts.

Yet by hard work a livelihood could be won. The Gospels depict Palestine as a rustic land, a land of peasants, very different from the cultured, Hellenised cities on the periphery. There were rich Palestinian Jews, it is true, but they were usually the wealthy owners of land and cattle. Cattle-raising appears in the rabbinical writings of the Talmud as the backbone of agriculture; and outside Judaea proper the sheep-runs of the newly acquired territories in Transjordan were lucrative. In Galilee, Judaea and Gadara there were good wheat and barley districts, though they were small, too small to allow the country to export grain. The well-wooded, spacious uplands of Galilee were studded with hundreds of peasant villages. Its lakes abounded in fish, and their shores were rich in walnuts, palms, olives and figs. 'It is easier,' says the Talmud, 'to raise a legion of olives in Galilee than to bring up a child in Palestine'; and there was a modest exportation of oil to neighbouring countries. Galilee, too, produced the best and most wine, though it was cheaper across the frontier in Tyre. The wines of Ascalon and Gaza were also very popular, and the former still produces a smooth wine today. The other products of Ascalon included lilies and onions – the shallots (scallions) that derive their name from the town.

Excellent fruit was grown near the Sea of Galilee and round Sebaste (Samaria), while Geba north of Jerusalem, like a number of plainland regions, was famous for its pomegranates. As a natural symbol of fertility, and of the Jewish people's ever-lasting life, pomegranates were sculpted on the pillars before Solomon's temple, and depicted on the hem of the high priest's robe; they are also to be seen on Herod's coins with a bunch of three fruits on a stem as described in rabbinical literature. It was customary to hang up sprigs of pomegranate at the Feast of Succoth or Tabernacles;[2] and now again in our own day, on Tu Bishvat the New Year of the Trees, pomegranates have been planted at desolate Masada. There was cultivation of figs behind Joppa, truffles were dug up at Jerusalem, and high-quality Palestine flax was exported to other countries. As for the date-palms and balsam groves of the Jericho oasis, which Herod had got back from Cleopatra, the exportation of date syrup was resumed; and he depicted the palm-branch, favourite symbol of Jewish art and cult, upon his coins.

The Palestinian Jews were content for the most part to leave commerce to the more urbanised Jews of other countries: they were not great traders themselves. Indeed, *Ecclesiasticus* regards commercial activity as almost synonymous with crookedness: 'As a peg is held fast in the joint between stones, so dishonesty squeezes in between selling and buying.'[3] Yet craftsmanship was respected unless there seemed special reason to view it with moral suspicion. People also felt an objection to crafts that soiled the hands, such as pottery and dyeing. The prejudice is still found in the Near East today. Evidently, however, it was possible to get over it then as now, since there were whole villages of ancient potters.

The southern, Idumaean region of the country came into a good deal of indirect contact with long-distance trade, because of the adjacent port of Gaza. For one thing this was an important slave-market. The supply of slaves from the southern Levant was nothing new. The chief minister of Ptolemy II of Egypt had received a consignment of exquisite and aristocratic boy and girl slaves from a Transjordanian sheikh, and Pompey's capture of Jerusalem had filled the markets of Rome and other centres of this traffic with Jewish slaves. Herod made use of the institution in the interests of internal security by permitting thieves to be sold into slavery and deported from the kingdom: an abominable ruling in the eyes of orthodox Jews, because, although slavery as such was universal the Jewish Law did not permit the sale of slaves to any Gentile.

Idumaeans could also observe the passage of another sort of trade through Gaza, because that city was the terminal for the camel caravans of incense which came all the way from south Arabia. No doubt there were profits here for Herod, to whom Gaza belonged. However, as a trading activity this was nothing like enough to satisfy his ambitions. The whole Mediterranean, with all its vast opportunities, lay before his eyes, and he possessed an extensive sea-coast. Yet the maritime trade of Judaea, at the time of his accession, was irritatingly insignificant.

The main reason, or one of the main reasons, for its insignificance was the total absence of good ports. Gaza and Ascalon were inadequate, and situated too far to the south. Joppa was much nearer to Jerusalem, and Herod had been glad enough to get it back; yet Joppa, too, possessed an extremely unsatisfactory open harbour, endangered by wind-swept reefs and shoals. There was not one reliable harbour along the whole fifty miles of Judaea's rocky, sandy strip of coast. Consequently the country was in the humiliating position of having to depend, as far as ships of any size were concerned, upon the harbour-city of Ptolemais Ace (Acre, Akko), which lay outside the borders of Judaea altogether.

Herod was determined to change all that; and the port that he created was an outstanding achievement of his reign, one of his greatest contributions to the prosperity of his country. He selected for the purpose a little place known as Stratonis Turris. This town, named after a circular stone tower that has recently been excavated, was ancient, dating at least from the fourth century BC – or possibly from a thousand years earlier.[4] But it had always been unimportant. Yet this was the site Herod chose. He started to build on it in 22 BC, and finished the work twelve years later.

No doubt his engineers had advised him that this part of the coastline had potentialities, but a further, special factor which weighed with him was its geographical relation to the interior of the country. Standing at the northernmost point on his seacoast, adjacent to the Roman province of Syria, it was the maritime outlet for Samaritis rather than Judaea; and he had always found more loyalty in the former than the latter. Moreover, Stratonis Turris

Ruins of the sea wall at Caesarea Maritima. The porphyry and syenite columns, imported from Egypt, were re-employed in Crusading times.

was conveniently close to his own Samaritan foundation of Sebaste. It was not fortuitous that some of the inhabitants of the new harbour-town, when it was built, were united with the Sebasteans in a single unit of the army. The link was also stressed by the name of the new port, which was Caesarea: for the emperor's name was Caesar Augustus, and just as Sebaste was the Greek for Augustus, so this second major foundation of Herod would bear his other name – a name, moreover, inherited from Julius, who had established the fortunes of Herod's house. Indeed, the formal name of Caesarea, as can be seen from a later coin, was 'Caesarea beside the Augustan Harbour'. Herod could scarcely show more clearly his conviction that the prosperity of Judaea, which the new port would so greatly enhance, depended wholly, in the last resort, on his policy of collaboration with Rome.

The great new harbour, twenty fathoms deep, was going to be as large as the Piraeus, or larger. It was entered from the north, like the modern port of Haifa nearby, because the wind blows most gently from that quarter. The harbour was protected by a stone mole two hundred feet long; for half its length it formed a break-

The remains of the theatre at Caesarea are mainly post-Herodian, but there are also traces of Herod's theatre, built on concrete with stone seating.

water, and the other half supported a sea-wall encircling the harbour. As a vessel sailed in, ten towers came into its view, the largest named Drusion after the emperor's stepson Drusus, and six colossal statues also became visible, three on either side. The statues on the left stood on top of a tower, and those on the right rested on two enormous stone blocks. Recent dredging at the entrance to the harbour has revealed blocks weighing twenty or thirty tons each, and these could be the bases on which the flanking colossi stood. The sea-wall which protected the wharf buildings was fitted with an elaborate series of vaulted recesses, and the place is a vast honeycomb of underground passages.

South of the harbour, close to the modern village of Sdot Yam which played so prominent a part in the illegal immigrations after the Second World War, excavations have revealed the outlines of an immense public building.

It may very well be the Temple of Rome and Augustus, which Herod built here at Caesarea as a counterpart to the shrine he had recently erected at Sebaste. Air photographs have also detected a road running from the shore, and at the end of it a large theatre, reconstructed in later antiquity. Towards the north there was an amphitheatre – with which Josephus confuses the theatre – and Caesarea possessed its own hippodrome as well. If a Herodian city wall existed, it still remains to be discovered. Portions of an aqueduct are attributable to the foundation period.

The initial population of Caesarea may have totalled about fifty thousand, of whom perhaps half were Jews. At a later date, in the 60s AD, they claimed citizenship of the place on the grounds that the city-founder had been a Jew, but their appeal did not meet with success. For this had always been a township of the Hellenised kind, with its municipal offices in the hands of 'Greeks' – who were in fact, no doubt, mostly Syrians, or other orientals possessing a Hellenic veneer. Ten years after Herod's death, Caesarea became the capital of the new Roman province, and the Jews called it 'the daughter of Edom', which was not only a sneer at Herod but their symbolical name for Rome.[5] An inscription put up by the most famous or infamous of all the province's governors, Pontius Pilatus, has lately been found at Caesarea; and it was here also that St Peter baptised a Roman centurion, and St Paul was imprisoned for two years. The rapidity with which the city grew shows how well Herod had chosen the site. It was an important customs station, and it revolutionised the trading position of Judaea. Yet history has treated it very badly, for depredations had already begun in late Roman times, and the Crusaders used many of the remains as building materials. Even then, a good deal was still left; but much of it has been lost during the past hundred years.

Because Caesarea was so far from Jerusalem, Herod established a settlement at the half-way point between the two cities, on the edge of the coastal plain. The place is now named Afek or Ras al Ain, near Petah Tikvah. In ancient times it had been called Capharsaba, but was also known as Pegae, 'the Springs', because it was adjacent to the sources of the one perpetual stream that flows from the Judaean hills into the Mediterranean, Aujeh 'the Crooked'. But Herod piously named his new settlement Antipatris, after his father, just as he had called another foundation Phasaelis after his brother. And indeed the two places seem to have been similar in purpose, serving as agricultural settlements and model farms. Antipatris attained biblical fame because St Paul was brought here on one occasion, and guarded by an escort of four hundred and seventy soldiers.

Caesarea brought in trade and money. But first its construction had to be paid for. How did Herod raise all the funds that were needed for projects of this magnitude?

His total revenue at the time of his death was 1,050 Jewish talents, or 1,050,000 *drachmae*. But the figure is meaningless to us, since we have no way to estimate the purchasing power of these denominations, or to convert them into modern currency. Perhaps it would not be too completely far out to compare this total income with something over a million pounds, or with three million dollars. It was not really very much – enormously less than the revenue of Egypt, and less than what Herod's own grandson later derived from a Judaean kingdom of approximately the same extent.

Herod had to pay a fixed tribute to Rome, and the best way to raise this was by levying a poll-tax, which he did. There was also a land tax, collected for the most part in grain which was stored in public granaries.[6] Customs duties, too, were collected, as we have seen; this had likewise been the practice in the older Hellenistic monarchies. Herod also introduced a tax on house-property, and there was another (possibly though not certainly new) on purchases and sales – probably a stamp duty on contracts of sale, with special application to real estate. Salt was a government monopoly. And

Pontius Pilatus, prefect of Judaea at the time of Jesus' crucifixion, commemorates the erection of a building at Caesarea in honour of Tiberius.

in pursuance of eastern as well as Roman custom, people of sub-
stance were from time to time expected, perhaps ostensibly on a
voluntary basis, to contribute gifts in the form of gold crowns, for
which they in their turn no doubt exacted contributions from their
own dependents.

The collection of most taxes was probably farmed out to private
corporations, as had long been the case with certain revenues of

A limestone measuring cup of the Herodian period from the Jerusalem region.

Rome itself. The tax-gatherer (*publicanus,* 'publican') is one of the
New Testament's most familiar and hated figures. But the governments of the ancient world did not possess large enough civil
services to collect taxes direct.

Nevertheless there were some fairly elaborate bureaucracies in
antiquity, and Herod's was one of them. Ptolemaic Egypt had
collected its poll-tax on the basis of annual returns by village clerks,
listing the whole of the male population from the ages of fourteen
to sixty, and Herod may have done the same. The great Hellenistic
kingdoms had also organised periodical censuses. In Egypt these
had been held every fourteen years, and in Rome a five-year interval
was customary. Perhaps Herod organised some kind of a census
every six years.[7]

The evidence, in so far as it exists, adds up to a picture of
efficiency, but by no means of oppression. After Herod was dead,

delegations complained to Rome that his administration had been financially ruinous. But as his minister Nicolaus of Damascus pointed out, no such complaints had been heard during his lifetime; and when there was drought or famine or other emergency or special occasion, his generosity proved to be spectacular (see Chapter 8).

And yet, in spite of his relatively small revenue and unoppressive government, and an extremely ambitious public works programme, Herod left enormous sums of money in his will. For example, he bequeathed fifteen hundred talents to Augustus and the imperial family alone. All this was possible because the 1,050 talents which were estimated as his revenue by no means comprised the whole story. Probably the sum in question only signifies his revenue from taxes; whereas he had other, very substantial sources of income as well. A large proportion of it came from land that was his personal possession. The family owned a lot of territory in Idumaea, and Herod's father Antipater, in the course of his astute career, had no doubt acquired a great deal in other parts of the country as well. Herod inherited all this (including the famous Jericho plantations) and added to it on a vast scale by confiscations. An enormous amount of property, in addition to gold and silver, came into his hands through the seizure of the estates that had belonged to the Hasmonaean family, as well as those of its supporters who were executed or driven out when Herod took over the kingdom in 37 BC.[8] It may well be the case that half or even two-thirds of the entire Judaean state was his private domain.[9] He also owned land in other countries, for instance in the Arab kingdom from which his mother had come; and his father may have owned property there as well.

In addition – and here again he was following in the footsteps of his father – Herod made substantial loans to the Arabs. No doubt he charged the elevated rates of interest which generally prevailed in the ancient world, and these loans formed part of the troubles which sprang up at frequent intervals between the two countries. The loans also recall the fact that Herod took after his father in yet another respect as well: like Antipater he was a business man, speculator and entrepreneur on a monumental scale. If most of the Jews of the homeland (though not elsewhere) preferred to keep out of trade, Herod was extremely far from sharing this view. In addition to the Temple at Jerusalem, which was the national bank for the government and its officials, he founded royal banks at each of his administrative centres. He also possessed business contacts all over the east and no doubt at Rome as well. In 12 BC he did a highly lucrative deal with Augustus himself, according to which he paid the emperor three hundred talents and in return received half the revenue of the copper mines of Cyprus – mines which were so extensive that they even supplied the Indian market.

The massive scale of these operations is only feebly mirrored in Herod's coinage, which has a rather shabby appearance. Although its designs were suitably edifying, Herod evidently did not fully share Augustus' view that coinage could be made an attractive vehicle for propaganda.[10] For one thing, his issues were limited to token currency in base metal (bronze). Most client kings were restricted by Rome to base metal issues, and the small-scale internal economy of Judaea did not warrant an exception in Herod's case (though an exception was made for the Arabs). Nor did his four bronze denominations include the large pieces of which the emperors made such imposing use. At the bottom of the scale was the wholly insignificant 'mite' or *prutah*, of which Hillel's disciples said, in disparagement of the female sex, 'one can trust a woman with a prutah or with an object worth a prutah'.[11]

Nevertheless, this royal coinage was abundant enough to supply most of south-west Palestine with small change. It was augmented by a few bronze issues of towns such as Ascalon and Gadara. Use was also made, especially in Galilee and Caesarea, of the bronze currencies of Syrian and Phoenician cities. Moreover, those cities, unlike most client kings, were sometimes allowed to coin silver, which likewise found its way to Judaea. And along with these Greek denominations the imperial gold and silver, on the Roman standard, was also theoretically valid, though our knowledge of such coin circulation in Judaea, as in other parts of the east, is still extremely limited.

Marcus Agrippa
and the Jews outside Judaea

And now this kingdom of Herod's, which he had taken so much trouble to develop, was about to receive an imperial visitation. The visitor was to be Marcus Agrippa, whom Herod had already met in the east only seven years previously; and on that occasion, if not earlier, the two men had apparently made friends.

Posthumous copper coin in honour of Marcus Agrippa with figure of Neptune, commemorating his naval victories. sc = *senatus consulto*, by senatorial decree.

Agrippa was the second greatest man in the Graeco-Roman world. He was not, it is true, the heir to the imperial throne. For there was no question, as yet, of anyone inheriting the special position which Augustus had invented for himself; his powers as *princeps* were regarded as personal and not heritable. Nevertheless, he had given his daughter Julia to Agrippa in marriage and she had just borne him a second son. Whereupon the emperor had immediately adopted both infants, encouraging the inference that these two boys, or one of them, might be chosen in due course to succeed to his own position. In a sense, this condemned Agrippa to the permanent status of a subordinate.[1] But the second man in the Roman empire was a hundred times greater than the first man anywhere else, and his importance was confirmed and enhanced by the outstanding honours conferred upon his sons. When, therefore, in 17 or 16 BC Augustus once more felt it necessary to send a viceroy to represent him in the east, it was Marcus Agrippa again whom he decided to send. Agrippa was accompanied by his wife, Julia, a lively woman of questionable morals whom he or his chief may have thought it imprudent, after the enactment of Augustus' law penalising adultery, to leave at home.[2]

Then, in 15 BC, Agrippa visited Herod in Judaea. Escorted by the king, he made an extensive tour of the royal foundations and fortresses, visiting Caesarea, Sebaste, Alexandrium, Herodium and Hyrcania. Finally he came to Jerusalem where he was lodged in the apartments of the new palace that had been given his name. Agrippa gave banquets, and, in the Temple where the Court of the Gentiles was still under construction, he sacrificed a hundred oxen (the offering of sacrifices by non-Jews was an accepted and regulated practice[3]). One of the Temple gates was called after him, and a Jewish writer, Philo, enlarges at length upon the widespread enthusiasm inspired by his diplomatic actions and the tactful utterances accompanying them. 'He conferred all such benefits as he could grant without doing harm', judiciously estimated Philo. 'He and Herod then exchanged innumerable compliments, and finally he was escorted as far as the harbour, not just by a single city

Portrait-bust of Marcus Agrippa, who toured Herod's kingdom in his company in 15 BC.

but by the whole country, while branches were strewn in his path and his piety was a subject for admiration.'4

Augustus himself, it was suggested earlier, did not feel too sure that national cults ought to receive quite such fulsome treatment (see Chapter 10). Nevertheless, Agrippa's attentiveness evidently went down exceedingly well with the Jews, and Herod must have felt that they were really beginning to appreciate the advantages of

Part of a tablet in the Court of Gentiles in Herod's Temple warning non-Jews against entering the inner courts on pain of death.

his pro-Roman policy. Moreover, his own personal success with Agrippa reached new heights. It was said by Herod's admirers that he was loved by Augustus next only to Agrippa, and by Agrippa next only to Augustus. This was no mean achievement. Obviously, everyone flattered these Romans. But hardly anybody gained their friendship and confidence to the extent that Herod did.

Agrippa spent the winter on the Aegean coast of Asia Minor. There, before long, it became known he was planning an expedition against another eastern client kingdom of Rome, the Cimmerian Bosphorus (Crimea), where a usurper had seized power as viceroy to the local queen, claiming, wrongly, that his action was sanctioned by the emperor. The Bosphorus was extremely important to Rome, because of its immense grain exports; and Augustus, feeling unable to turn a blind eye, started to plan punitive action. At this point Herod decided that it would be to his own advantage, as well as useful to Rome, if he himself joined the expedition. The development of Caesarea, though incomplete, had enabled him by now to develop a navy, built of timber from trees near the port. And his interest in naval affairs is shown by the nautical designs he engraved on his coins. Here he was following the Hasmonaeans. In addition to decorating the monument for the liberating hero Judas Macca-baeus, at his home town Modin, with the prows of ships, they had depicted an anchor on their coins; and Herod now did the same. He also displayed representations of the decorative stern ornament (*aphlaston*) which had figured on the coinage of Phoenician towns and later became a favourite coin-type of Ascalon. And now a further issue of Herod showed a picture of a war-galley.

An anchor on a coin of Herod, to show his maritime pretensions. Reverse: double cornucopiae and herald's staff, Graeco-Roman emblems of prosperity.

These were symbols of the fleet with which, as soon as spring came, Herod hastened northwards to reinforce Marcus Agrippa. He hoped to join him at Lesbos but he was delayed at Chios by a contrary wind, and arrived too late. He missed Agrippa for a second time at Byzantium, but finally caught up with him at Sinope (Sinop) on the north coast of Asia Minor: it was the nearest point of approach to the Crimea. At this juncture, however, it became clear that the Crimean expedition was not going to take place after all. Frightened by Agrippa's preparations, the Crimeans themselves had killed their usurper. Having done so they still held out for a while against Rome's intentions regarding his successor; but finally they submitted, and Agrippa did not have to proceed against them.

Thereupon, he turned back through Asia Minor instead (14 BC), passing right through the peninsula all the way to Ephesus (Selçuk) and Samos. And he took Herod with him. Agrippa had been grateful for the king's willingness to help, and Josephus stresses that he invariably found Herod's advice and hard work very useful. Agrippa also enjoyed his company. Apparently Herod had a knack of being an entertaining companion without ever forgetting that the Roman represented the majesty of the imperial power; or, as the historian (rather unattractively) puts it, the Jewish monarch showed not only 'loyalty in times of trouble but deferential behaviour at times of relaxation'.[5]

The long journey to reach Agrippa, and the long return journey in his company, enabled Herod to carry out two important plans. The first consisted of an extraordinarily lavish campaign of munificence to the numerous Greek city-states through whose territory he passed. He had already shown his interest in this sort of activity twenty-six years earlier, *en route* to see Antony in Rome; for he had paused on the way at Rhodes, and had showered generous benefactions on the city. On the present occasion, too, Rhodes got further contributions, to assist it in building a temple and ships, and Chios, while Herod was storm-bound on the outward voyage, was presented with a colonnade, supplemented by a gift of the

Burial cave in Jerusalem of about the time of Judas Maccabaeus, known as 'Jason's tomb' because his name was found carved in it.

179

funds the islanders needed to repay a debt to Augustus. Samos, too, received help, and Cos was endowed with the revenues to pay the salary of its athletics director for evermore. Towns along the south coast of Asia Minor, where Herod had called on his way up to the Black Sea, also received presents. And so, probably, did others in the interior which he visited on the way back with Agrippa; unless he thought it more tactful, at a time when he was necessarily playing second fiddle, not to seem to be too free with his money. This was also the occasion when his secretary Nicolaus of Damascus, who was travelling with the party and tutoring Herod in philosophy, interceded with Agrippa on behalf of Ilium (Troy) when it was in peril for nearly allowing the Roman's imperial wife Julia to get drowned in the local stream.

Nicolaus also took the opportunity of addressing Agrippa in support of an appeal by the Jews of western Asia Minor. And it becomes clear, at this point, that one of the reasons why Herod was so generous to the Greek cities of the peninsula was that he hoped to persuade them to give better treatment to their Jewish colonies. He liked being generous, it is true, just in order to create an impression and cut a dash; but it was also useful because it helped the local Jewish residents.

Almost every city in the Graeco-Roman world had its community of Jews. Over a period of many centuries, ever since the destruction of Jerusalem by Nebuchadnezzar in 586 BC, the various processes of war, deportation, enslavement, persecution, overpopulation at home, proselytism and a growing taste for trade had all contributed to the creation and growth of this Dispersion. When Rome was backing the nationalist movement of the Hasmonaeans in the second century BC the anonymous Jewish author of a prophecy boasted that his compatriots and co-religionists were already scattered all over the world.[6]

In Egypt there was a particularly large and important settlement, especially at the capital Alexandria where it may have amounted to as much as one-third of the population. It is only now that this community has been blotted out, since a final group of ninety families left in 1970, leaving only four behind. At Rome, too, the number of Jews may by Herod's time have totalled eight thousand. Many of them belonged to families which had been deported to the capital by Pompey but subsequently freed; Cicero complained of the influence they were able to mobilise.[7] This Roman community was grouped in thirteen synagogues. Two of them were named after Augustus and Agrippa as a symbol of the recognition of these Jewish institutions by Roman law. For both in the capital and in the provinces the Jews were exempted from the general ban on associations. Moreover, outside Rome and Italy, as Josephus is proud to declare, repeated attempts were made by the Roman government to protect them from the authorities and inhabitants of the city-states in which they lived.[8] This tolerance was partly a matter of principle because the Romans were prepared to tolerate and protect all cults unless they were politically or morally objectionable, or engaged in proselytism. But another reason for Roman toleration was the existence of a great many Jews in the Parthian empire and along the frontier zones; Rome did not want these to infect its own Jewish communities with disloyalty.

Now these protective edicts, as their very frequency suggests, were clearly necessary. For the Jews had been tending for several hundred years to become extremely unpopular with the communities in which they lived.[9] Sometimes this was sheer ignorant prejudice on the part of the latter – the utter ignorance which annoys Josephus so much. His fellow-historian Tacitus, for example, describes some of their practices as sinister and revolting.[10] But Tacitus is much nearer the mark when, in the same passage, he complains about all the Jews dispersed throughout many countries who were accustomed to send offerings to the Temple of Jerusalem. For it is true that every male Jew, from the age of twenty upwards, wherever he might be, was expected to make an annual contribution of half a shekel (two silver *denarii* or *drachmae*) to the Temple.[11] This was over and above various tithes in kind, and such supplementary contributions as people wished to make. The money was collected by local Jewish bankers, who charged a commission and sent the proceeds to Jerusalem, where they were allocated to carefully laid down purposes relating to the upkeep, personnel and sacrifices of the Temple.[12]

It is often pointed out today that modern Israel is dependent on world Jewry; and, at least as far as the Temple was concerned, the same was true in antiquity. But it seemed extremely irritating to the non-Jewish populations in various parts of the world that so much money which, in their view, ought to contribute to the general welfare of their own communities should instead have to go to Jerusalem, belonging to quite another region and province and race.[13]

All this seemed part and parcel of the general separateness symbolised by the uncompromising monotheism of the Jews. It was in the same spirit that they recognised the high priest rather than the emperor as their religious head, and such feelings could easily, it was felt by their non-Jewish neighbours, turn into rank disloyalty. Moreover, the toleration of the Jews by the central government meant that they were exempted from ordinary Graeco-Roman cults; and this in turn signified that they did not have to join in the patriotic procedures of ruler-worship. Furthermore, their inability to work on the Sabbath got them excused service or appearance in the law courts on those days, and, sometimes, at least, they were actually exempted from military service for the same reason.

But their enemies in the cities, especially in Asia Minor, set themselves to encroach on these privileges in every way, taking advantage of the fact that the Jews did not possess local citizen rights; and when Marcus Agrippa and Herod came to Ionia on the west coast of the peninsula, the Jewish population there, which was substantial, poured forth a mass of grievances about the persecutions of this kind from which they were suffering. Agrippa convened a council of Roman officials and Asian princes to hear their case, and at Herod's wish Nicolaus of Damascus, though a pagan himself, acted as the spokesman for the Jews. His speech is reproduced by Josephus. Most of the orations in Josephus, as in other ancient historians, are more or less fictitious: they indicate what such-and-such a person, for or against the Herodian interest, should or might have said. But since Nicolaus was Josephus' principal source, and is specifically stated by him to have written about this whole occasion at length, the speech is probably authentic.

Nicolaus provided a very thorough statement of the Jewish case; indeed, for modern taste he was positively verbose. He pointed out to Marcus Agrippa not only the excellence of the Hebrew Law but its antiquity; the Jews were accustomed to taking every opportunity to point out that their institutions were senior to those of the Greeks and Romans. Nevertheless, he went on to emphasise his political support for Rome, that support which was the keynote of Herod's whole policy. And Nicolaus concluded by pointing out that those members of the Greek and Hellenised city-states who sought to undermine the privileges conferred by the Romans upon others (namely the Jews) were damaging the general security of the population by creating a situation in which their own privileges, too, might later on be at hazard.

Agrippa ruled in favour of the Jews. According to Josephus' first version, he merely stated that it would not be proper for him to change the rules – in other words that he must adhere to the pro-Jewish decrees already issued by his government on a number of previous occasions. But when Josephus returned to these events at a later date (see Chapter 17), he made Agrippa speak more graciously, if somewhat contradictorily: first, he was reported as saying, the Jewish cause was just – and so they must be allowed to maintain their own customs without ill-treatment; and secondly, he was deciding in their favour because of his friendship with Herod.

The king then went up to Agrippa and embraced him; and Agrippa returned his embrace 'like an equal'. Soon afterwards, in spring 13 BC, he departed from Mytilene and went back to Rome. As for Herod, he set sail for his own new port of Caesarea, and from there he went up to Jerusalem, where he announced to an enormous crowd of city-dwellers and countrymen the success of his efforts for the Jews of the Dispersion. And he had not failed, he added, to speak to Agrippa about the needs of Judaea itself: 'He had neglected nothing that might be to their advantage.' One quarter of the country's taxes was remitted for the past year in order to celebrate his success; and he enjoyed widespread popularity.

III

ANTI-
CLIMAX

Changed plans for the succession

Everything seemed to be going well for Herod. But he was sixty years old – quite an age in the Near East at that time – and his life had been a hard and exacting one. It was inevitable that there should be speculation about his eventual successor or successors.

Something has been said about the obscurities of the succession at imperial Rome. But it was even more obscure in a kingdom such as Judaea where the monarch possessed a whole series of wives, successively and simultaneously. For Herod, as time went on, increased the total from the four who have been mentioned in these pages to at least ten (see Genealogical Table). And he had at least fifteen children, and very probably more: so which of them was going to succeed him? It is true that, in theory, client kings were obliged to leave it to the emperor to decide who their successor was going to be – if, that is to say, it was going to be anyone at all, since after the death of a king Rome might well decide upon annexation. But no one doubted that Herod would have a large say in the matter.

Already in about 17 BC the question had begun to come to a head. The oldest of Herod's sons was Antipater (II), the son of his first wife Doris. But both had been away from court for twenty years and Herod still had no plans for them. Nor was he taking any very decisive interest in the offspring of his Samaritan wife Malthace, or in the son of the second Mariamme whose father had been made high priest. The boys he was much more interested in were the sons of the *first* Mariamme, whom Herod had so tragically loved and executed twelve years earlier; she had been a Hasmonaean, and, despite all his trouble with the Hasmonaean house, it was his sons containing this royal blood whom he had chosen to push forward. These young men, Alexander (III) and Aristobulus (IV), had been sent to Rome for their higher education, and now that it was complete, Herod went to Rome himself to fetch them back. Perhaps he was there for the immensely elaborate Secular Games of 17 BC with which Augustus glorified the eternal city and his own regime.

At all events, Herod and the two youths returned together to Judaea, and very soon afterwards he arranged distinguished marriages for them. Alexander married Glaphyra, daughter of Archelaus Sisinnes king of Cappadocia, a large client state in eastern Asia Minor which played a vitally important part in Rome's eastern frontier system. Named after her grandmother, a famous seductress who once may have attracted the interest of Antony, Glaphyra enjoyed making fun of Herod because he chose his wives for beauty rather than breeding. But the king quite liked her all the same. His other son, Aristobulus, was married to his own cousin Berenice, the daughter of Herod's sister Salome (II). There was no doubt in anyone's mind that these young men were being groomed to succeed Herod. And they were popular because, on their mother's side, they were the last surviving representatives of the Hasmonaean house which had once liberated Judaea; and they had the appropriate aristocratic good looks and panache to enable them to play the part. Unfortunately, however, they were also arrogant and tactless, particularly to their aunt Salome whose social origins they manifestly regarded as inferior to their own. And the situation was not at all helped by their young wives. If Alexander was a snob, Glaphyra was a worse one and never stopped reminding people that she claimed the most regal of regal blood on both sides of her family, and indeed the blood of gods on the maternal side.[1] As for Aristobulus' wife Berenice, she was treated with contempt by her husband, so that she felt no hesitation in telling her mother Salome all the many imprudent remarks he used to utter. For he was accustomed to complaining that he had only been allowed to marry a commoner, whereas his brother Alexander had got a princess. But he agreed heartily with Alexander in proposing that when they ultimately reached the throne, they would make their stepmothers work at the loom with the slaves, and degrade their half-brothers to the status of village clerks. They were also heard lamenting the loss of their own mother, Mariamme (I).[2]

Salome, backed by Pheroras, passed on these indiscretions to Herod, in the hope that this would plunge the two young couples into disgrace and lead to their destruction. The atmosphere at court was now thoroughly painful. Not a single day or hour passed, says Josephus, in which the king was able to relax; for there was always some new squabble among his relatives and closest friends.[3] And Herod, who was not only a suspicious man but always wanted to protect his Idumaean relations, became gradually convinced that some of the charges against Alexander and Aristobulus were justified. This caused him to revise his idea that they were going to be his successors. Instead, he brought their half-brother, his eldest son Antipater, out of retirement and began to show him some favour. So when Marcus Agrippa left for Rome in spring 13 BC, Herod asked him to take Antipater with him; and Agrippa agreed, and did so. The young man was bearer of an important document, for approval by the emperor. It was Herod's first will and it declared that Antipater himself was to be the king's heir, in conformity with the Jewish Law's insistence upon primogeniture.[4] At the same time Antipater's mother Doris was allowed to return to Jerusalem.

The promotion of Antipater was a violent *volte-face,* and the father who brought about such abrupt ups and downs in the prospects of members of his family could hardly expect to avoid repercussions. Moreover, whatever faults Alexander and Aristobulus might possess, the desirability of favouring Antipater as the oldest son was more than counterbalanced by his malignant and extremely cunning character, his great capacity for deceit and espionage, and his extraordinary talent for making others do his dirty work. Herod had evidently underestimated the immense, ingrained and incurable bitterness which had infected both Antipater and his mother owing to their prolonged relegation to the wilderness. From the moment that she arrived back in Jerusalem, Doris did nothing but intrigue against her stepsons Alexander and Aristobulus, while Antipater, from the vantage-point of the imperial capital, did just the same. He and his mother felt none too sure of the dizzy pre-eminence they had suddenly achieved, and their one aim was to bring the two young men, who still seemed dangerous potential rivals, to utter ruin.

Again Herod was impressed, and more than half persuaded that Alexander and Aristobulus were disloyal; and after a bit he felt the urge to take them to Italy, so that Augustus should see what they were like and adjudicate on the issue. This was, surely, a mistake. The emperor wanted client kings who would get on with the job and contribute to imperial security, and the last thing he desired was to have to clear up their domestic messes. But probably Herod felt that he could not avoid consulting Augustus, because events had affected the succession to his kingdom: a matter on which the emperor had the last word but was sure to want Herod's guidance. And Herod's wishes had now drastically changed – in place of a more or less vague understanding that Alexander and Aristobulus were to be his successors, his first will specifically named Antipater instead. The king probably felt that Augustus would agree to these proposals readily enough if he could learn about the deficiencies of the other two youths at first hand. But in any case Herod needed the support of a more powerful man: the combined plagues of polygamy, his own suspicious nature and a growing tendency towards indecision were taking their toll, and he was beginning to doubt his own judgment.

So, without forgetting popular gestures en route, including gifts to Athens[5] and the acceptance of the honorific presidency of the Olympic Games, Herod now set off with Alexander and Aristobulus to meet Augustus in Aquileia at the head of the Adriatic. When the emperor heard the accusation against the young men, he did not feel this amounted to very much; a suggestion that they had actually intended to murder Herod was obviously groundless, and Alexander's anxious assurance of their loyalty appeared convincing enough. So Augustus cleared them of the charges, diplomatically conceding, at the same time, that they had been at fault in making it possible for such reports to arise. He then got Herod to put aside his grudges and reconcile himself with the two youths, and Herod duly forgave them. As a special compliment Herod was also assured that, when the time came, he would be permitted to

186

nominate his heir himself – a unique concession to a client monarch which shows that, in spite of all the scandals, Augustus' confidence in the efficiency of his government was still not shaken. So Herod, after presenting the emperor with three hundred talents as a contribution to the entertainments and free hand-outs provided for the Roman population, returned home with the sons he had forgiven. And their elder stepbrother Antipater went with them, pretending to be delighted with the reconciliation.

When they had all returned to Jerusalem Herod proceeded to the Temple and addressed the people. After giving thanks to God and the emperor for restoring harmony in his family, he made an announcement about the succession. He himself, he said, did not propose to relinquish power in his lifetime – he declared that Augustus had insisted that he should not – but Antipater, Alexander and Aristobulus were all three going to be elevated in rank forthwith, since they would be sharing the kingdom between one another after he had gone. That is to say, Herod had abandoned the idea of handing over the kingdom as a single, undivided unit to Antipater or anyone else. Yet Antipater was still given first place; the practical meaning of the priority was left vague, but its existence was undeniable.[6] And at some stage, to emphasise the point, it was arranged that Antipater should marry the daughter of Antigonus, the last of the Hasmonaean kings.

Nevertheless, Antipater was far from satisfied with the new arrangement, which involved from his point of view a distinct retrogression from the progress he had achieved when he took Herod's first will to Augustus such a short time ago. For the new plan meant that his stepbrothers, even if they ranked below him, were destined to have a share of the power and thus to diminish his own position. They, on the other hand, were furious that, in spite of their acquittal on all charges of disloyalty, Antipater was still intended to have the first place. Moreover, unlike Antipater, they had a habit of putting their feeling into words: the sort of words which could be reported back to Herod. And so Antipater and his mother Doris resumed their efforts to discredit the two young men, and they made sure also that Salome and Pheroras should each lose no opportunity to breathe poison about them into the king's ear.

So the reconciliation in Herod's family arranged by Augustus had not proved effective for very long. Now, however, another mediator tried his hand. This was the client monarch Archelaus of Cappadocia, who was the father of the young Alexander's wife Glaphyra. On the way back from Aquileia, Herod and his sons had called in to see Archelaus at his new southern island capital of Elaeussa Sebaste (Ayaş) in order to reassure him that concord in the family had been re-established. Now that trouble had broken out once again, Archelaus decided to visit Jerusalem for himself to see what he could do.

He found that his son-in-law, and therefore his daughter as well, were in real trouble and danger. The young Alexander, as if eager to demonstrate that Sodom formed part of Idumaean territory, was accused of the remarkable feat of seducing all three of Herod's favourite eunuchs. This, if true, created a real security risk for the king; and his investigators elicited a good deal of damning information. For example it was revealed that Alexander had made wounding remarks about his father's vanity. He had declared that Herod dyed his hair in order to look younger than he was. Moreover, Alexander was quoted as saying, he himself always took care to stoop when he was standing with his father so as not to look the taller of the two, which would have upset Herod's vanity, and when they were out hunting together, he added, he used to miss his own aim deliberately so as to conceal the fact that he was the better shot. And then a youth declared, under torture, that Alexander was planning a future hunting expedition on which he was going to kill his father; and that in case this did not work Alexander also had poison ready at Ascalon.

Were these last disclosures true? Perhaps they were, and perhaps not. But in any case Alexander now proceeded to draw up a document confessing his guilt. It was at this point that Archelaus arrived. With an astonishing display of insight into Herod's worsening psychological condition he succeeded in effecting a reconciliation all round.[7] Herod, for his part, shared so profoundly in the general relief and euphoria that he presented his fellow-monarch with a concubine named Pannychis ('All-Night-Long') and accompanied him back as far as Antioch. And there he repaid the mediator's valuable service by patching up differences that had arisen between Archelaus and the Roman governor of Syria, Marcus Titius, a wealthy and powerful henchman of Augustus.

The second Arab war

When Herod's son Alexander, terrified by the anger of his father, had produced a panic-stricken admission of his own guilt, he had added, for good measure, that his aunt Salome and his uncle Pheroras had likewise been disloyal to the king. In the case of Pheroras the truth is difficult to discern, but the charge against Salome was improbable. For that disagreeable woman had always, in her way, been faithful to her brother. Long ago, Herod had prevented her from marrying the Arab chief minister Syllaeus; and what Alexander now declared was that she had been passing Syllaeus Jewish state secrets. The charge was almost certainly untrue, and left Herod quite unmoved.

But it was a fact that relations between the Jews and Arabs had now become very bad once again. Syllaeus had never been able to forget the insult he had received over the match with Salome; and since then he had received a further rebuff, when Augustus refused to allow him to purchase Auranitis (south-west Syria) and gave it to Herod instead. Now, Syllaeus had begun to get his own back, in two ways. First, his government showed no signs of repaying a debt it owed to Herod, although there was a clause in the original agreement authorising him, in the event of such failure, to recompense himself forcibly on their territory. Secondly, when Herod was at Aquileia in 12 BC, another of the Syrian territories acquired by him eleven years earlier, the mountainous land of Trachonitis, had revolted against his rule: and when the rebellion was put down, forty of its leaders escaped into Arab territory. There Syllaeus gave them a refuge and a fortress from which they could safely conduct raids across the Judaean frontier. Herod massacred all their relatives he could lay hands upon but could not get at the rebels themselves, who were meanwhile enticing a good many of his subjects to cross the border and join them.

The matter came to a head in 10 BC, when Herod formally cited Syllaeus before the new governor of Syria, Gaius Sentius Saturninus, and the imperial agent in the province. Saturninus was a trusty and competent commander with a reputation for old-fashioned severity, and he and his colleague gave Syllaeus thirty days to restore Herod's subjects and to pay back his loan. Syllaeus failed to do either and so Herod received authority from 'those around' Saturninus and the agent, that is to say presumably from their staffs, to take some sort of action against the defaulters.[1]

Thereupon he proceeded to march into Arab territory, where he

Aqueduct bringing water to Herod's new harbour-town at Caesarea. Parts of the surviving masonry go back to his time.

captured the principal rebel fort at Raepta (probably Qalaat er-Rabad in Ajlun, north-west Jordan). An Arab force which tried to relieve the place was beaten off, and its commander Nacebus (Naguib), a relative of Syllaeus, was killed. Herod returned home in triumph, bringing prisoners and loot, and gave orders that Trachonitis should be reinforced by a settlement of three thousand Idumaeans, whom he supplemented at a later date by dispatching five hundred Babylonian Jewish horse-archers to neighbouring Batanea.

But there must have been some confusion about the instructions Herod had received from Syria. Or perhaps he had received permission to attack, but had interpreted it far too liberally; his expedition against the Arabs seems to have been on a much larger and more destructive scale than was expected or seemed tolerable. At all events Augustus, when he learnt at Rome what had happened, was angered beyond measure. It was most unfortunate for Herod that Syllaeus himself was in the imperial capital at this very time. He had hastened there as soon as trouble began to blow up, pausing only at Miletus (western Asia Minor) to dedicate to his national deity Jupiter Dusares a votive tablet inscribed in Latin and Greek with a prayer for the safety of his 'brother' King Obodas III.

When Syllaeus had first arrived in Rome, he rapidly managed to exercise considerable pressure on the government; and it was because of this that, before his punitive expedition, Herod had failed to gain much Roman backing against his rebels. It must have been at some point in 10 or 9 BC that Augustus turned against him. In the earlier stages of that period the emperor had still been well-disposed, for he and his wife Livia sent generous gifts amounting to five hundred talents to celebrate the dedication of the new city of Caesarea and defray popular entertainments to mark the occasion. Soon afterwards, however, came the shocking news of Herod's invasion of Arab territory. It lost nothing in the personal account given to Augustus by Syllaeus, who declared that the death-roll of the Arabs at Herod's hands amounted to twenty-five hundred. And he himself, he pointedly commented, 'would never have left his country unless he had known very well that the *princeps* was concerned that they should all be at peace with one another'.[2] The malice was very much to the point, because it seemed to Augustus quite outrageous that one client monarchy of Rome should make war upon another. Moreover, in spite of every effort by Herod's friends in Rome to present his case the emperor did not seem at all disposed to concede that the king had acted on clear Roman authority from Syria.

The outcome was sensational. Augustus wrote to Herod in very harsh terms, indicating that whereas up to now he had treated him as a friend, he would henceforward treat him as a subject. The polite aura which surrounded the relations between imperial nation and client monarchy was dispelled, and the emperor's confidence, which Herod had done so much to win and cherish over a period of twenty years, was completely lost. It also appears probable that, in the same letter, Augustus withdrew Herod's unique privilege of nominating his own successor.

It was only to be expected that when Herod's loss of favour with Augustus became known in the Levant, he would find it difficult to maintain internal control of his own kingdom. And so when the hillsmen of Trachonitis learnt the good news, they duly renewed their rebellion, massacring many of Herod's three thousand Idumaean settlers. They were, of course, encouraged in this action by the Arabs.

But at this stage a decisive change occurred in Arab affairs. The old, weak King Obodas III, who had been dominated by Syllaeus, died (9 BC), and an enemy of Syllaeus seized the throne, assuming the royal name of Aretas (Harith) IV. This was an even more outrageous action, in Rome's eyes, than Herod's military adventure, since the succession to a client kingdom was a matter for decision

by the emperor. Moreover, in this case Augustus may well not
have intended to maintain the rather unsatisfactory kingship after
Obodas' death. It is probable that he was considering outright
annexation, and not for the first time either. But this would not be
very convenient, since it would greatly lengthen the eastern
frontier. An alternative course, therefore, which must have recommended itself was the transference of the kingdom to a more reliable

Aretas IV Philopatris, king of the Nabataean Arabs (9 BC–AD 40), places his
own head and his wife's on this bronze coin.

royal line. At an earlier stage, the emperor may have thought of
presenting the entire Arab state to Herod. But he certainly cannot
have continued to cherish any such intentions now that Herod was
out of favour. Another possible candidate for the Arab throne was
Syllaeus: it seems very likely that while he had been at Rome he
discussed the possibility of securing the *de iure* royal power for himself, in addition to the *de facto* power which he already possessed. In
any case he was just as taken aback as Augustus by the *coup d'état*
which had now occurred at Petra, and when the envoys of Aretas
arrived in Rome Syllaeus found it easy to persuade the emperor not
to receive them.

So the Arab and Jewish kings were both in disgrace with the
western power, and both because of the same man Syllaeus. This
had the natural effect of bringing the two monarchs together, and,
forgetting Arab-Jewish enmities, they collaborated in the task of
destroying their mutual enemy Syllaeus. The selected agent was
Herod's indefatigable and eloquent secretary Nicolaus of Damascus. In 7 BC he proceeded to Rome and, in collusion with the envoys
of Aretas, assailed Syllaeus before the emperor with a formidable
array of charges.

The charge which interested Augustus most was that he had
grossly exaggerated the Arab casualties caused by the Jewish raid,
declaring that they totalled two thousand five hundred whereas the
real figure was only twenty-five. Whereupon the emperor, who did

not like being deliberately misled, drastically revised his views on all concerned. The only penalty that Aretas received was a lecture regarding the impropriety of seizing the throne without authorisa-

Top: The mausoleum of Ed-Deir (second century) cut out of the pink rock in the Siq valley leading to Petra, capital of the Nabataean Arabs.

Bottom: Oboda (Avdat), the city foundation of Aretas IV in honour of his predecessor Obodas III, who was buried there and deified.

Silver *drachma* of Aretas IV, shown with his wife. On the reverse is the eagle depicted by many Hellenistic monarchs.

tion. But then his accession was formally confirmed.[3] Syllaeus was sent back home under a heavy cloud, with orders that he must repay Herod all he owed to him. A little later, after he had caused further trouble and had tried to arrange the assassination of Herod,[4] Augustus had him executed.

Herod, on the other hand, was received back into the imperial favour; not, evidently, the complete favour in which he had basked before, but a sufficient degree of favour to prevent rebellion and chaos in his own country and on its frontiers.

The downfall of
Herod's sons

Meanwhile, the squalid intrigues centring upon Herod's sons had broken out again with full force. The mediation of King Archelaus of Cappadocia, who had attempted in 9 BC to reconcile the members of the royal house, proved even more short-lived than that of Augustus a few years before.

15

This time, the trouble was stirred up by the visit to the Judaean kingdom of another client ruler and a very unpleasant one too, Eurycles of Sparta (*c*. 7 BC). Gaius Julius Eurycles, the son of a pirate, was the greatest man in Greece. As a result of services to Augustus' family, followed by outstanding support during the Actium campaign, he had been virtually made the dictator of the 'free' city-state of Sparta and other regions of the Peloponnese.[1] Now, however, he was short of money, and it occurred to him, rightly as it turned out, that a good way of rectifying this was to immerse himself in the domestic intrigues of Herod's family, which perhaps owed him a debt of hospitality.

So Eurycles arrived, and carefully ingratiated himself not only with Herod but with his two mutually hostile sons Antipater and Alexander, and with Alexander's wife Glaphyra as well. Alexander characteristically entrusted him with a whole lot of indiscreet complaints about his own position. Eurycles passed these on to Antipater and Herod, who were so grateful for the information that they both gave him presents – the king's was fifty talents. Then, on his homeward journey, Eurycles called in to see Archelaus of Cappadocia, whom he informed, quite inaccurately, that he had succeeded in reconciling Archelaus' son-in-law Alexander with Herod. This earned him a further monetary gift. It is gratifying to learn that before his death a few years later Eurycles was banished from Sparta by Augustus, though his family later returned to power and posthumously awarded him an honorific cult of worshippers.

Before these further developments, however, Eurycles had done great damage to the cause of Alexander and Aristobulus. No wonder Augustus made the remark, with an untranslatable play upon words: 'I would rather be Herod's pig than his son.'[2] For at least the pig was safe from the onslaught of a professing Jew, whereas the situation of his sons Alexander and Aristobulus was now desperate. Very soon, a fresh series of tortures of members of their households, assisted by the discovery of a compromising letter, elicited evidence of a plot to assassinate Herod. The king,

The apsed walls of Herod's water garden at Jericho.

who was beginning to experience hallucinations in which he saw
Alexander advancing upon him or standing over him with a drawn
sword, haled him and his brother before a massed people's court at
Jericho: where they would have been lynched if the king had not
personally intervened. Then they were cast into prison. However,
all they would admit was that they had planned to escape from the
kingdom in order to save their own lives. Herod, however, was
convinced that there was a plot to kill himself. He also believed that
Alexander's father-in-law Archelaus of Cappadocia was involved.
But from him, too, came the assurance that all he knew about
was a scheme to give sanctuary to the young men – not out of disloyalty to Herod, but to protect the king from himself.

Herod also wrote to Augustus. But he had lost the knack of

enlisting the emperor's interest and favour. On top of the tiresome
Arab business – in which he had admittedly misjudged Herod to
begin with – Augustus must have found it deeply depressing to be
confronted, for the second time, with the appalling domestic
affairs of the Judaean court. Furthermore, Herod's envoys chose
an unfortunate moment to present his letter to the emperor. When
he was handed it, he was just trying to decide what to do about the
Arab kingdom. If the idea of Herod taking it over had ever begun to
revive in Augustus' mind, the lamentable domestic disturbances
revealed by the letter certainly put an end to any such thought.[3]

Nevertheless, Augustus answered with the patience and dip-
lomacy of a first-class administrator. The whole situation, he said,
distressed him very much, and if the young men had really plotted
to assassinate their father Herod must punish them accordingly;
this he was fully entitled to do. If, however, they had merely
planned to escape from Judaea, a reprimand would presumably be

Antioch honours Augustus as high priest (5–4 BC). The colonnaded street
built by Herod for the city is the earliest recorded anywhere.

sufficient. He advised, however, that Herod should not deal with
the whole matter on his own, but should convene a special court
at Berytus (Beirut), outside his kingdom. Its membership should
comprise not only his own advisers and other important personages
from various quarters, but the principal Roman officials of the
Syrian province and King Archelaus of Cappadocia. Since the
whole distressing matter could evidently not be kept quiet,
Augustus was determined that it must be handled in as open,
respectable and authoritative manner as possible.

In general, Herod acted upon this advice; as indeed he was
obliged to, for it was virtually an instruction. But he deviated from
it in regard to one single point: he did not invite Archelaus, whom
he now regarded as his enemy. With Archelaus out of the way, he

197

Bronze coin of
Sidon in Phoenicia
with head of
Augustus and
figure of Europa
riding a bull. Herod
built a theatre for
the Sidonians.

cannot have felt very much apprehension about the outcome of the proceedings. His reputation in the Syrian province stood very high. Its governor, Saturninus, was his personal friend, and had given him a residence near the provincial capital, Antioch;[4] while that city – which would be sending its notables to the hearing – had been presented by Herod in turn with a superb covered colonnade, marble-paved, along the main street.

The choice of Berytus for the trial also suited him very well. This ancient Phoenician harbour city had been made a Roman citizen 'colony' in 16 BC, with a draft of ex-soldier settlers. That was a visitation which Herod had not been asked to undergo at any city in his own territory, but it suited him to have this reinforcement of his pro-Roman policy so close outside his borders. Thus transformed in character, Berytus had been endowed by Augustus with extensive territories, including maybe the shrine of Heliopolis (Baalbek). It had also, by an act that now seemed prescient, been the object of important benefactions from Herod himself, including colonnades, temples and handsome market-places. So it provided a sympathetic atmosphere for the case he was now presenting. Indeed, so great was the confidence he felt that he did not even propose to produce his sons the defendants in court at all. Instead he lodged them in the neighbouring village of Platana (Aramain). This belonged to the city of Sidon, which once again was a community in which he felt full confidence, since he had presented the Sidonians with a theatre.[5]

The subsequent trial was a mockery. The court, in spite of its distinguished membership of one hundred and fifty persons, just gave in to Herod.

The governor of Syria, Saturninus, pronounced his condemnation, but urged clemency; he was a father himself and felt it horrible to put one's own sons to death. His three sons expressed the same view. The imperial agent more logically advocated the death penalty, and most of the other members of the court followed his lead. Herod was satisfied and started home, taking his sons with him.

At Tyre he was met by Nicolaus, who had just returned from Rome, and asked him what the feeling about the case was in Rome. Nicolaus replied that the general view was that, even if Alexander and Aristobulus were guilty, Herod would be well advised if he exercised moderation. The wisest course would be to pardon them. If he could not bring himself to that, he might keep them in prison. But to put them to death would be regarded as savage and vindictive. Herod was somewhat dashed at this news, and began to hesitate. He moved on to Caesarea, taking his sons with him.[6]

The proceedings had been deplorable, but were the young men guilty? Nicolaus, in his autobiography composed after Herod's death, felt he could not be sure.[7] It is probable enough that they had secretly planned to leave the kingdom, and that King Archelaus had been their accomplice. But it is also very possible that they had indeed planned to murder their father, since ten years of persistent slander had turned him completely against them and they now saw no other way to save their lives. Moreover, there is some evidence that they could command support in the army, which might be expected to contain pro-Hasmonaean elements: for two of the men compelled to produce disclosures were officers who had been dismissed by Herod and taken into Alexander's service.

Much depends on our estimate of the letter that was used in evidence against the two brothers. It was alleged to be a communication from Alexander to the governor of the fortress of Alexandrium, and it read: '*When with God's help we have achieved all that we set out to do, we will come to you. Only take it upon yourself to receive us into the fortress, as you promised.*'[8] Alexander insisted that the letter was a forgery by one of the king's secretaries, concocted by arrangement with Antipater. But it may equally well have been genuine.

And indeed, when Herod returned to Caesarea, a conversation he had with a retired senior officer Tiro, who was an old friend of his, lent some support to the idea that there were plans for a military revolt. Tiro, very courageously, had taken it upon himself to support Nicolaus' advice in favour of moderation. In the course of his appeal to Herod, he emphasised the sympathy felt for the young men not only among the population but in the army. The old soldier's words, containing far too blunt references to the deterioration of Herod's formerly excellent judgment, cost the lives of himself and of his son. One of the king's barbers, too, who had unwisely turned state informant against Tiro, brought the same fate upon himself. Then Herod turned against the whole corps of officers, which Tiro's words had brought under suspicion. Three hundred military leaders were arrested. After a travesty of a people's court, they were thrown to the crowd and lynched.

Then, Alexander and Aristobulus were taken to Sebaste and strangled (7 BC). Their bodies were removed by night to Alexandrium, and buried secretly beside their Hasmonaean ancestors.

Their deaths, the culmination of ten years of domestic quarrels centring round their persons, had left Antipater in what seemed outwardly to be the strongest of strong positions. Nevertheless, he still did not feel at all comfortable. He was always afraid that his endless criminal intrigues of the past would come to Herod's ears, and this particularly applied to the lethal part he had played in driving his two half-brothers to destruction. He had particular reason to fear the capacity of his aunt Salome to pick up inconvenient information about him. For example, she had lately reported to Herod that he was indulging in private stag parties with his uncle Pheroras. As will be seen in the next chapter, the king's relations with Pheroras were strained, and Antipater was now ordered to shun his company, while Antipater's mother Doris was also forbidden to associate with Pheroras' wife.

There was also another thing that never ceased to worry Antipater. Even if the number of his half-brothers had now been diminished by two, there were still far too many survivors – in fact no less than five, any of whom might, at some whim of their father's, be pushed forward as a rival to himself. It was also a source of anxiety that Herod was taking a great deal of trouble to give these boys a good education. In particular, he had sent three of them to Rome in 8 BC, lodging them with a Jew this time so as to avoid hostile Jewish comment. They were Archelaus (II) and Antipas (II), the sons of Malthace the Samaritan, and Philip the son of Herod's fifth wife, a Jewish woman with the uncomfortably reminiscent name of Cleopatra.

Antipater was further disturbed when in 6 BC the king summoned a gathering of his royal council of friends in order to parade a group of his grandchildren before them. The reason for Antipater's alarm was that they were the children of his recently executed half-brothers Alexander and Aristobulus. Although these boys and girls were still very young, Herod had formed impressive marriage plans for them within his own family, in the pathetic hope of healing the bloodstained feud between its Hasmonaean and Idumaean sides. And it was clear that there was popular affection and support for the children. This did not suit Antipater at all, and he summoned up the courage to beg his father to change their proposed marriage arrangements so that he himself, instead, should remain at the centre of the picture. And such, despite all his misgivings, was his dominant position at this stage of the proceedings, that his wishes prevailed, and the matrimonial plans for the younger generation were revised in favour of himself and his family.[9]

Antipater also scored a further success when, in spring 5 BC, he was sent to Rome with Herod's second will. For in this document, as in the first eight years earlier, he was unquestionably named as the heir. Nor did he have to worry about rivalry from his youthful half-brothers, Archelaus and Antipas, who were being educated in Rome. For although an heir presumptive was mentioned in the will, it was neither of them, but an even younger half-brother, Herod (II), who aroused little suspicion.[10]

However, Antipater, now at Rome, became aware that all was not going well for him in Judaea. He received a disquieting letter from Herod stating that his mother Doris was under suspicion and had been sent away from court (without being allowed to take her wardrobe with her). Antipater at once left the capital and set out for Jerusalem. But when he had got as far as Tarentum (Taranto) he received the further bad news that his uncle and ally Pheroras was dead (see Chapter 16). Antipater pressed on, and on reaching the port of Celenderis (Gilindire) in southern Asia Minor he received a further note from his father requesting him to get back as quickly as he could. Against the advice of certain of his friends he complied. But when he sailed into Caesarea he saw that something had really gone wrong, for the usual reception committee for important princes was not to be seen on the quay. Indeed, there was no one there to meet him at all. Nevertheless, he pressed on to Jerusalem. On arrival he proceeded at once to the palace in his

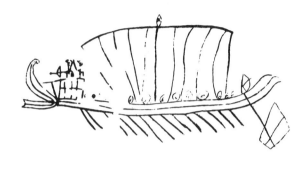

Graffiti of ships on the walls of a Jewish burial-place, 'Jason's tomb' in Jerusalem.

purple robe. The doorkeepers let him in, but refused to admit any of his companions.

When Antipater reached the royal presence, he found that the governor of Syria, at this time a famous lieutenant of Augustus named Varus, was with him. As Antipater moved forward to embrace Herod, the king pushed him away and denounced him as a father-murderer, declaring that he would have to answer for himself the very next day before Varus.

For after the death of Pheroras a number of appalling stories had come to the king's ears. He had been investigating a rumour that Pheroras had been poisoned by his wife's female relatives, who were already suspect on other grounds as well. The truth of the matter is unknown, but investigation and torture in Pheroras' household led to several unfortunate revelations about Antipater. He had disobeyed his father's instructions to keep clear of Pheroras. He had complained often and bitterly at Herod's slowness in dying. He had declared that the reason for his departure to Rome was his fear that his father would kill him. And it was disclosed that behind all this subversiveness was his mother Doris. That was the point at which Doris had been dismissed from court – the news which caused Antipater to cut short his visit to Rome.

With Salome's 'I told you so's ringing in his ears, Herod began to look more carefully still into the conduct of Antipater. For what

Bronze coin issued for Augustus by Publius Quinctilius Varus as governor of Syria. His name is inscribed round two legionary standards.

happened next, Josephus draws upon the personal reminiscences of Nicolaus, augmented perhaps by Herod's own memoirs.

The man who most aroused the king's wrath against his son was a Samaritan agent of the king's son Antipater. Among the other things that he revealed under torture was the fact that this Samaritan had prepared a fatal drug and had given it to Pheroras with instructions to give it to his father – during Antipater's absence from the country in order that Antipater might be removed as far as possible from any suspicion attaching thereto. The drug had been brought from Egypt by one of Antipater's friends, and had been sent to Pheroras through Antipater's maternal uncle.[11]

As investigation proceeded, strong suspicion fell on Herod's wife Mariamme (II). Herod divorced her, her father Simon lost his high priesthood, and her son Herod (II) was deprived of his position as heir-presumptive.

Herod also remembered that, during Antipater's absence in Rome, he himself had been receiving letters from friends in the imperial capital denouncing his other younger sons, who were being educated there, for allegedly declaring that Herod's domestic executions were the acts of a murderer. The king now formed the impression, no doubt accurately, that these letters were instigated by Antipater; although at the time, to disarm suspicion, Antipater had also been writing to Herod and begging him to excuse the boys on account of their youth.

That, then, is why Antipater, on his return to Jerusalem, received a horrifyingly bad reception from his father. While he tried to prepare himself for interrogation by Varus the governor of Syria on the following day, he was given the opportunity to talk to his mother and wife and hear just how bad the prospects were. The visitation of Varus was almost as serious as if the emperor himself were present. Historians later described him as torpid, rapacious and incompetent, but such reports only got around after he had suffered a fatal defeat in Germany fourteen years later; meanwhile in Syria, where he was now, he behaved with decisive competence. On the present occasion his verdict, or the recommendation he would make to Augustus, was likely to be decisive.

Herod started the proceedings by warning Varus against 'the little beast,' and his specious pleas and crocodile tears.

When I remember his cunning hypocrisy on every occasion, I can hardly believe I am alive! I only wonder how I escaped so deep a conspirator. But since some evil genius desolates my house and makes my dearest ones rise against me one by one, I shall indeed lament my cruel fate and inwardly grieve for my loneliness. But I will let no one escape who thirsts for my blood, not even if judgment finds *every one* of my children guilty![12]

In reply, Antipater delivered an impassioned plea. By this stage the king was too overcome by emotion to go on speaking and he handed over the case for the prosecution to Nicolaus. In spite of his mild nature, and in contrast to his unsuccessful attempt, on an earlier occasion, to dissuade Herod from executing Antipater's half-brothers, he now spoke with the utmost severity, backed by overwhelming, damning documentation.[13] Thereupon Antipater called for a sign from God to demonstrate his innocence. Varus, however, proposed a more practical test, indicating that he would like to see whether the drug which the defendant was supposed to have prepared for consumption by Herod was in fact poisonous or not. So a condemned criminal was brought into court, and ordered to drink it. Having done so, he immediately fell down and died.

So Varus left Jerusalem and returned to his province of Syria, and Herod wrote letters to Rome giving Augustus an account of what happened and requesting his own friends there to see the emperor and add verbal clarifications. And meanwhile, even more sinister evidence was coming to light. It included proof that Antipater had paid a Jewish slave of Augustus' wife Livia – the woman was called Acme – to forge letters incriminating the king's sister Salome of high treason. This new material, too, was dispatched to the emperor.

Meanwhile, without awaiting his reply, Herod proceeded to draw up a third will. In this, Antipater was replaced as his heir by Antipas (11), one of the Samaritan Malthace's sons who were still being educated at Rome.[14] To his sister Salome, who had been so tireless in passing on disagreeable information, Herod expressed his gratitude by enormous bequests. And indeed it must be admitted that her warnings against Antipater at least had been wholly justified all the time.

Repression of the Jews: the last days of Herod

16

While Herod was grappling with his unreliable sons, he was also trying to deal with a series of troubles and embryonic resistance movements in Jewish circles.

For a long time, in spite of his periodical infringements of their code, the leading Jews had remained on the whole docile. But matters had begun to come to a head in 7 or 6 BC, when he had ordered his people to swear a joint oath of loyalty to Augustus and himself. This was an attempt to restore his still somewhat damaged position with the emperor and to demonstrate once again the solid pro-Roman position of himself and his fellow Jews.

Already at a much earlier date he had revived the practice, which had been current under previous Persian and Seleucid suzerains, of twice-daily Temple sacrifices in honour of Augustus, who had volunteered to pay for these rites himself.[1] As for the oath, this too followed Seleucid models, and it was apparently regular practice in some or all of the client kingdoms, as well as in Roman provinces;[2] so that perhaps Herod had not really very much choice in the matter, apart from the timing.

In *c*. 17 BC, Herod had already instituted an oath to himself and his acts, and on that occasion two important Jewish religious groups, the Essenes and Pharisees, had asked to be excused, the former because they objected to oaths on principle and the latter because they disliked using the name of God in an oath. The obedience of these two groups to Herod had never been much more than lukewarm, being based on a tacit contract of mutual non-interference which could not be estimated quite as high as positive loyalty. Still they were generally obedient, and so on that earlier occasion Herod had excused them from the oath to himself. Now, however, ten or eleven years later, a much more serious situation would arise in the event of their refusal, since they were being asked to swear loyalty not only to Herod but to the emperor. How the Essenes dealt with this problem we do not know, but the Pharisees, by now more than six thousand in number, again refused to swear. Yet even now Herod punished them with nothing but a fine – a remarkable contrast to the savage treatment which he so often handed out to uncooperative subjects.

The reason why the Pharisees were treated so indulgently was because they possessed support within Herod's own family. For when Herod fined them, their fine was paid by the wife of his own brother Pheroras. It will be recalled that Pheroras had firmly refused two royal matches owing to his love for a slave-girl; and now, some years previously, he had married her. It is not surprising that this woman, whose name we do not know, lined up with the enemies of Herod who had twice tried to supersede her. She was particularly offensive to two of his younger daughters,[3] and now her payment of the Pharisees' fine was a vigorous public display of her rebellious feelings. But the king had no intention either that she or the recalcitrant Pharisees should escape retaliatory action. The extreme wing of their movement was very strongly involved with Messianic beliefs and hopes (see Chapter 4); and some of the holders of these extremist views, carried away by the support they were receiving from the king's sister-in-law, declared prophetically that, by God's decree, Herod's throne would be taken away and given to Pheroras and his wife and their offspring. And meanwhile further Messianic hopes, contradictory in content but equally seditious, were implanted by the same section of Pharisaic opinion in the heart of a certain eunuch Bagoas, who was evidently an important official of the royal household. Bagoas was assured that, in spite of his physical disability, he was destined to become the father and guide of the future Messianic king. For had not one of the writers of the *Book of Isaiah* declared: 'The eunuch must not say, "I am nothing but a barren tree"'?[4]

All this perilous talk came quickly to Herod's ears through the intelligence network of his indefatigable sister Salome. It created an extremely disagreeable impression in his mind. In the first place, he was against Messianic views altogether, except in so far as they identified himself with the Messiah. Just as the Augustan Age in Rome was the awaited Golden Age, he himself aimed to receive honour in Jewish lands as the King Messiah who, as large numbers of people imagined, would redeem God's people and establish the divine kingdom upon earth.[5] The world-ruler, it was believed, was to come from Judaea. Later, at least one of Herod's descendants was pronounced to be this very Messiah, and now he was facilitating his own claim to the title by allowing it to get around that he belonged to the house of David. The star that appeared on his coinage may refer to the star which the *Book of Numbers* declared would foreshadow the Messianic coming;[6] and the various legendary tales about Herod's destiny, and his miraculous escapes from death, all contributed to the same picture that he himself was the awaited Holy One, the Holy of the Holies.

It was clear therefore that Messianic beliefs, unless they centred upon himself, were likely to make no appeal to Herod. But his distaste for them was nothing compared to his disapproval of the idea that a specific Messiah was preparing to take his own place. His hand fell heavily upon those involved in spreading such doctrines. Bagoas was executed, and a number of Pharisees with him, and a group of his courtiers who showed them sympathy, including an exceptionally beautiful boy-friend of his own named

Coin of Herod with star (at top), which perhaps reflected his Messianic claims. The principal object may be a vessel for burning incense.

Carus ('Darling'). Nevertheless, Pheroras' wife was still spared for the moment. Pheroras was ordered to send her away. But he refused, and Herod did not insist.

All he did to Pheroras was to request him to retire to the Transjordanian principality of Peraea, from which he had drawn the revenue as an absentee governor for the past fifteen years. Pheroras duly left for Peraea, and when Herod had fallen gravely ill and wanted to see him he refused to come back. But when Pheroras in turn became sick, the king went to Peraea, uninvited, to visit him. Then Pheroras died, and was given a fine burial in Jerusalem (5 BC).

The troubles that followed his death, when enquiries in his household disclosed Antipater's plot to poison Herod (see Chapter 15), indicated the complicity of the wife of Pheroras, and this, finally, was the end of her. Her fate at Herod's hands no doubt alienated still further the powerful section of the Pharisees who were her friends. At all events in the following year (4 BC), the Jewish resistance to Herod broke into open violence. This took the form of serious student demonstrations, instigated by senior Pharisee professors. The reason for the upheaval was a large eagle, made of gold or gilt bronze, which Herod had erected over the great gate of the Temple.

A quarter of a century earlier, Herod had got into difficulties because he was suspected of breaking the Second Commandment, which, if interpreted strictly, forbade sculptural representations not only of human beings but of animals as well. He had demonstrated amid a certain amount of mirth that he was not breaking the Commandment at all (see Chapter 6). In those days, the early twenties, there had been a good deal of friction between Herod and the Jews, but since that time less had been heard of their strained relations. More recently, however, his apparent carelessness of orthodox opinion had caused religious feeling to harden against him, and the executions of Pharisees in 6 BC had inevitably caused a direct breach.

In earlier years, the more moderate Pharisees, led by the famous Hillel and Shammai, had led the movement which counselled obedience. But now matters had come to the point when even those who had hated the Hasmonaeans no longer praised Herod for supplanting them, but regarded him as just as bad. Hostile stories directed against him were going the rounds. For example, when he erected a monument to David and Solomon, this was said to be an act of expiation because he had rifled David's tomb. There were legends (which still persist) of the immense riches hidden in this tomb, beneath the hill of Ophel. And the story of Herod's ransacking these treasures was another legend, which the Pharisees had already told many years before in denigration of another Jewish monarch whom they hated, John Hyrcanus I.

As regards the eagle over the Temple, it is not by any means

certain that Herod had only erected it now in 4 BC. The eagle may
have been there ever since he had completed the reconstruction of
the Sanctuary (18 BC). Solomon himself had not hesitated to
ornament his temple with animal sculptures,[7] and eagles in
particular possessed important Jewish associations.

Stone urn of Herodian date from the hill of Ophel south-east of the Temple,
believed to be King David's treasure-filled tomb.

In *Deuteronomy,* the Lord himself had been compared to an eagle.
In later Hebrew theology, too, it was an eagle that told Jeremiah
to gather the peoples together; and the faithful were described as
rising to heaven on an eagle's wings.[8] Moreover, sculptured representations of eagles occur (admittedly at a later date) above the
doors of a number of synagogues and at the top of Jewish inscriptions.[9] However, if people wanted to make trouble, as they now
unmistakably did, the eagle was also the classic symbol of pagan

207

Eagle-destroying serpent from Nabataean Arabia. The eagle is also reproduced on the coins of its kings.

domination and pagan cult. This was a well-known fact to anyone who had seen the temples of Syria and Rome. For on the façades of these temples were displayed eagles soaring aloft with spreading wings – just like the eagle of Herod's Temple; and the same formula was to be seen on a number of coins. On the coinage issued by Ptolemaic Egypt and its Levantine dependencies, an eagle with closed wings had made frequent appearances,[10] and this design had been copied by the Arab kingdom. It had also appeared, at some undetermined date, on the coinage of Herod himself, who thereby committed his one and only numismatic infringement of the ban on graven images.[11] These representations on his coins are very much in the pagan, Hellenistic tradition; and in spite of the eagle's Jewish associations, it was by no means difficult for Herod's enemies to ascribe the same sinister interpretation to his eagle over the Temple. Besides the king was now very seriously ill, and there was some chance of protesting with impunity.

So now two notable and popular professors of one of the Pharisee academies, Matthias the son of Margalothus and Judas the son of Sariphaeus, began to declare in their lectures that Herod's illness was evidently the judgment of God for his various breaches of the Law. Among these infringements, they specifically mentioned the erection of the golden eagle over the Temple door. They then proceeded to indicate that no students who decided to cut the eagle down could possibly have subsequent reason to regret what they had done, since after such a deed 'the virtue acquired by them in death would seem far more advantageous than the pleasure of living'.

At this point rumours began circulating that the king was now

The eagle depicted by Herod had been a traditional design of Ptolemaic coinage. Here is is used by Ptolemy VI Philometor (181–146 BC).

dying or was actually dead, and militant students decided that the time had come to act upon the exhortations of their radical teachers. Then at mid-day, when the courts of the Temple were crowded with people, they climbed up to its roof, let themselves down on to the appropriate point by ropes, and pushed the eagle over the façade on to the ground. Then they hacked it to pieces with axes. When the commander of the neighbouring Antonia fortress heard what was happening, he hastened across with a body of soldiers and attacked the offenders. Josephus' comment on the inexperienced student demonstrators is this. 'His attack took them by surprise, because, as is usual with such crowds, they had taken this step on a foolish whim rather than with the caution of foresight, and were therefore in disorder, not having looked round before-hand for a way to help themselves.'[12]

Most of them fled, but forty stood their ground and were arrested, and their two professors were arrested with them. Teachers and students alike were taken before the king. But when he interrogated them about their behaviour, they replied defiantly that they had been acting in defence of the Law. Herod dispatched them in chains to Jericho, out of the way of possible intervention from turbulent Jerusalem crowds; and in spite of his grave illness, he arranged to be transported to Jericho himself. Assembling a people's court in the amphitheatre (or perhaps the theatre), he had himself carried in on his sick bed, and delivered a violent tirade. First of all he enlarged on his own unique services to the Temple – services which his Hasmonaean predecessors had not even begun to equal. And then, at the end, he graciously consented to spare the majority of the demonstrators, and only punish those who had been actually arrested. And so on 13 March 4 BC the two professors and the youths who actually pushed the eagle down into the court were burnt alive, and the other detainees, too, were handed over to the executioners.

The high priest of the time was regarded as partly to blame, and was removed from office. He had already, once previously, been suspended from his duties, though only for a single day. This was because of a dream: he had dreamt he was having sexual intercourse, which disqualified him, according to the Law, from officiating on that day. Now he was deposed altogether, and another high priest was appointed in his place.[13] But the new appointee was his kins-man, and a close relative also (brother or uncle) of the second Mariamme, whom Herod had recently divorced. The king was keen to employ her family as the nucleus of a new subservient Sadducee aristocracy (see Chapter 7), and did not propose to allow his divorce to stand in the way.

However, Herod's illness had now taken a very serious turn. The references to his symptoms by Josephus are horrible, including descriptions of a moist suppuration of the feet and an invasion of the genitals by worms. It is doubtful, however, whether these gloating accounts are authentic. For they sound rather too much like the classic penalties of evil-doers. In the Old Testament, the prophet Elijah had shown similar gusto in forecasting how the bowels would fall out of a murderous king of Judah, Joram. Antiochus IV, who had abolished the Temple, allegedly died of worms; and so did Herod's own grandson, Agrippa I, because he had allowed the non-Jewish community of Caesarea to hail him as a god.[14] It is therefore no use speculating whether Herod was, in fact, suffering from the unpleasant symptoms described, or, for that matter, whether his illness was cancer of the bowels, or diabetes, or cirrhosis of the liver, or arterio-sclerosis. At all events, he was in very severe pain. When it became almost unendurable, his doctors took him to the warm sulphur baths of Callirhoe (Hammam ez-Zara), near the north-eastern end of the Dead Sea.[15] But the cure did him no good; and when his doctors had him lowered into a bath of hot oil he lost consciousness. And so all that could be done was to take him back to Jericho.

Before leaving for the springs, he had roused himself to give thought to what would happen after his rapidly approaching death. For he was determined that the arrangements he himself would finally decide upon, whatever they might turn out to be, must not be over-turned by anyone else. As a first step, then, he had given orders that a gratuity should be distributed, here and now, to all the soldiers in his army, so that they would be ready, once he was dead, to carry out his commands.

Then, on his return at Jericho, he took the exceptional step of summoning all the notable Jews from every part of the country to come to him at once. When they arrived, however, he arrested the whole lot of them, employing the Jericho hippodrome as an intern-ment camp. Conditions must have been far from comfortable, but the additional story that he intended them all to be slaughtered after his death is mere fiction. It is the sort of legend regarded as appropri-ate for a tyrant; the same sort of tale had already been told about Alexander Jannaeus, and would soon be told again about Nero.[16]

While Herod was giving his last instructions to his sister Salome and her husband, a letter came from the envoys he had sent to the emperor. He had dispatched them to report the guilt of his eldest son Antipater, and now he learnt that Augustus, though he must long since have despaired of the sanity of the king's domestic arrangements, had recognised the justice of the case against Antipater. The female slave, Acme, who had forged letters on Antipater's behalf, had been put to death. As for Antipater himself, however, the emperor left it to Herod to decide whether this sinister character should be executed or merely sent into exile. But if this was a hint that lenient treatment might still, in spite of every-thing, be preferable, it fell on deaf ears.

At first, the message briefly caused Herod to feel more cheerful. But soon:

When his pains became much more intense, he felt thoroughly miser-able and refused to take any food. And he asked for an apple and a knife – for it had long been his custom to peel the fruit himself and cut it into small pieces for eating – and when he had been given the knife, he looked around with the intention of stabbing himself, and he would have done so if his cousin Achiabus had not seized his right hand before he could do so.

Achiabus then uttered a loud cry, and the sound of lamentation filled the palace, and there was great consternation as if the king had died. And Antipater, who believed that his father's life had really come to an end, began to adopt a bolder tone as though he were now wholly released from his bonds and could seize the throne for himself without a struggle. And he discussed the question of his release with the jailor, promising him great rewards both for the present and for the future, as though the time had come for him to exert himself about such matters. But the jailor not only refused to do as Antipater asked but also revealed his intentions to the king and added many embellishments of his own. When Herod, who even before this time had been far from overwhelmed by affection for his son, heard the jailor's disclosures, he cried out and beat his head although he was at the point of death.[17]

Raising himself on his elbow, and uttering a shout which seemed beyond a sick man's strength, he immediately sent off soldiers of his body-guard with orders to kill Antipater at once. They carried out his command; the corpse was buried without ceremony in the fortress of Hyrcania.

At this late moment Herod caused a turmoil among his entourage by changing his will yet again. In this fourth and last testament, which reverted once again to the idea of a divided kingdom, the offspring of the Samaritan Malthace were still to the forefront: but one of them Antipas (II), who had been the chief heir in the third will, was moved down a peg to become tetrarch of Galilee and Peraea, while his elder brother, the eighteen-year-old Archelaus (II), found himself promoted above him. For Archelaus who, like his brother, had just completed his education at Rome, now learnt that the king's objections to him had vanished – and indeed had vanished so thoroughly that he was not merely to be a tetrarch or prince but if his father, Herod, had his way he was destined to become king of Judaea. However, Archelaus' future kingdom was to be greatly diminished in size, for it was to lose not only the slice given to his brother Antipas but also the recently annexed north-eastern territories, which were to go to his half-brother Philip. In conclusion, the coastal towns of Jamnia and Azotus and the settlement of Phasaelis in the interior were to be allotted, with a large sum of money, to Herod's loyal though frequently ill-tempered sister Salome (who outlived him by fourteen years).

It is not very easy to see why Herod had changed his mind once again; and indeed the workings of his mind may not have been any longer susceptible to rational explanations. Perhaps it was just that he realised his former suspicions of Archelaus had come from a discredited source (Antipater) – and Archelaus was, after all, older than his brother Antipas who had been preferred in the immediately preceding will.

It is also possible that the emperor, when he had given Herod a free hand over Antipater, went on to say something more: to deliver a strong hint about his own views on the succession. It is

The 'Tomb of Zacharias' again shows the impact on the Jewish world of the Hellenistic taste for sepulchral monuments.

true that some years earlier Herod had partially been restored to the imperial favour. But it is not altogether likely that this rehabilitation included the formal restoration of his right to name his own heirs. This had, in any case, been unique for a client king; and it seemed difficult to justify in the case of a monarch who was involved in such lamentable domestic troubles, and was no longer able to judge them quite sanely. Yet, even so, probably Augustus' directions took the form of a hint rather than an order, for Herod's final will, after reiterating the expected lavish bequests to the emperor's family, made it clear that the imperial decision still had to be known: before the testament could be regarded as valid, the confirmation of Augustus must be awaited. And when Archelaus' enemies later contested this ultimate will, its dependence on the corroboration of the emperor was stressed by Nicolaus of Damascus to emphasise its validity.[18]

At the end of March or the beginning of April, Herod died. Thirty-six years had passed since the Romans first made him king, and he had actually ruled over Judaea for thirty-three of them.

His body, crowned and sceptred, was carried in procession for twenty-four miles to Herodium, the place he had chosen for his burial. The bier was of solid gold, studded with jewels and draped in purple. It was escorted by all Herod's surviving sons and relations. Behind them marched the army, led by spearmen, and then Thracians, Germans and Galatians; next came five hundred house slaves and freedmen, carrying spices.[19]

IV

SUMMING UP

The aftermath

Coin of Archelaus, with Greek inscription 'Herod the ethnarch.' The war-galley and cornucopiae are imitated from his father Herod.

Herod's kingdom, as he had directed in his final will, was duly divided into three parts. This was a matter of some difficulty, because Antipas questioned the latest testament which had given him second place to his brother Archelaus, and Herod's former ministers disagreed sharply before the emperor confirmed the new document. Archelaus, though supported by Herod's chief minister Ptolemy and by Nicolaus, got off to a desperately troubled start. And Augustus, even if partly or wholly responsible for his appointment to the rulership of Judaea, did not think it advisable to confirm his kingly title. Instead, while allowing the possibility of promotion in the future, he only allowed the young man to call himself a superior sort of prince (ethnarch).

Archelaus had everything against him. One of his parents was an Idumaean, and the other a Samaritan: both races were equally unpopular in Judaea. The revenue of his kingdom had been greatly diminished by its truncation. The winding up of his father's public works programme caused unemployment. And it was difficult for a youth who had been educated in Rome, and wanted to carry on with his father's Hellenising programme, to do so in a state that had been largely reduced to its Jewish elements.[1] After Archelaus had managed to carry on for ten years, the Judaeans and Samaritans jointly protested against him to Augustus. This unprecedented unity, in which the people of his mother's country joined, shows that he must indeed have been a failure. At any rate that is what the emperor decided. He was banished to Vienna (Vienne) in southern France, and his principality was annexed by Rome.

Antipas, who had been given Galilee and Peraea, was known to Josephus as a lover of the peaceful life. But it was he who granted the request of his stepdaughter Salome (III), prompted by her mother Herodias, that her reward for a successful dance should be the head of John the Baptist upon a dish.[2] When Jesus Christ was arrested – outside Galilean territory – Antipas carefully refused to allow Pontius Pilatus (the Roman prefect of Judaea) to involve him. Jesus described Antipas as a fox. But he was, in fact, the ablest of Herod's sons, and dealt well with the arduous task of controlling the Galileans. It was also an achievement to win the friendship of Augustus' successor, who turned out (after the death of his grand-

Opposite: Herod the Great's son Antipas and his wife Herodias, on a mosaic of the late thirteenth century in the Baptistery at Florence.

A servant presents the head of John the Baptist to Salome, as her stepfather
Herod Antipas and his guests look on. Sinope Gospel, sixth century.

sons) to be his immensely capable but grim stepson Tiberius
(AD 14–37). But Antipas could not maintain these good relations
with the next emperor Caligula (Gaius), who exiled him in AD 39
to Lugdunum Convenarum (S. Bertrand de Comminges).

The third princedom created after Herod's death went to Philip,
his son by his Jewish queen Cleopatra. The realm of Philip com-

prised the north-eastern territories annexed in 23 and 20 BC, including the difficult mountain territories that are now on the Syrian border. His capital Panias was enlarged and renamed Caesarea Philippi after him, and he depicted the neighbouring shrine of Panion on his coins. Philip was quiet – 'the best sort of British colonial district commissioner', says Stewart Perowne; 'instead of gadding to Rome or Beirut, like so many of his family, he lived in his own little principality'.[3]

The south-eastern corner of the old city-wall of Jerusalem, partly erected by Herod's grandson Agrippa I.

Herod's grandson Agrippa I, the son of Mariamme (I)'s son Aristobulus (IV)[4] whom the king had executed, was a versatile and colourful character who deserves a biography to himself. In the course of an adventurous career, he obtained from Caligula the succession to the combined tetrarchies of Philip and Antipas. Then Claudius revived the kingship of Judaea in his favour (AD 41). But Agrippa I died in 44, and his kingdom was reannexed by Rome. During those three years he had occupied the inheritance of Herod – the only successor Herod ever had. Agrippa I possessed his grandfather's gift for getting on with great Romans (except Tiberius, who imprisoned him for treason). And he learnt from Herod's troubles the advisability of getting on with the Jews: Pharisaic opinion looked back on Agrippa's reign as a new golden age. But he was

Bronze coin of Herod's son Philip the tetrarch with head of Tiberius and Temple of Augustus at Panias, refounded as Caesarea Philippi.

often less successful with the Greeks, and inclined to over-reach himself politically. Moreover, in marked contrast to Herod, he was a poor financial administrator.[5]

The brother of Agrippa I, who was likewise called Herod, ruled the princedom of Chalcis beneath Lebanon (Gerrha), and obtained from the Romans the right to nominate the high priest at Jerusalem. This Herod (III) died in 48, and two years later his kingdom, together with the same right, was given to Agrippa I's son Agrippa II. Subsequently Agrippa II exchanged this territory for a different tract of the same south Syrian country together with the northern and eastern parts of Herod the Great's old kingdom.[6] It was Agrippa II who said about Paul: 'The fellow could have been discharged, if he had not appealed to the emperor'.[7] When the Jews rebelled against the Romans in AD 66 – more will be said of this shortly – he took the Roman side, and in the Year of the Four Emperors (68–9) he performed the extraordinary conjuring trick of supporting each of the four in turn.[8] Agrippa II is of importance to our story because, until he died towards the end of the century, the historian Josephus always had to look over his shoulder to make sure he did not offend this very powerful Jew, or his sister Berenice who was for a long time the mistress of Titus, the Roman conqueror of Jerusalem (see Chapter 19).

And now to return to the central region itself, which had formed the principality of Herod the Great's son Archelaus. After his dismissal, Judaea had become a minor Roman province, governed by prefects who resided at Caesarea. These officials were not important senators like the ex-consuls who governed Syria, but members of a lower stage in the social hierarchy, the knights (*equites*) – and not usually particularly eminent or skilful members of the order at that. With the exception of the brief reversion to a kingdom under Agrippa I (AD 41–4), Judaea henceforward remained a Roman province.

Looking at the empire of the first century AD *as a whole,* a strong case can be made for the high (if a trifle passive and unimaginative) quality of the Roman administration. At any rate it was much better than anything the Republic had ever provided; and indeed scarcely a single territory governed by Rome could claim that anyone before the Romans had ever ruled them half as well as the Romans did. The outstanding, tragic exception was Judaea. Here things went wrong from the outset, owing to total incomprehension and resentment on both sides.[9]

These unhappy circumstances led to the rise of Jewish underground resistance movements. One of the earliest, and perhaps the most important, was the movement of the Zealots (from the Greek word *zelos,* meaning jealousy, enmity and rebellion). The Zealots were led by Judas of Galilee, son of the Ezekias whose band Herod had ferociously stamped out in that country at the very outset of his career. There was also a separate but not always distinguishable terrorist organisation, 'men of the knife' or assassins (*sicarii*). But it is particularly hard to learn the true facts about these resistance groups, since our principal source, Josephus, lets us down. Owing to his extreme distaste for this sort of thing he falls back on unsatisfactory superficial utterances about undesirable bandits and brigands.

As for those Jews who were not disposed to follow such adventurous courses, quite a number of them, faced with the glaring disadvantages of the sort of Roman administration that they were experiencing, very soon began to forget whatever reservations they had felt about Herod during his lifetime and started to look back to the times of Good King Herod. Indeed, in spite of all the ferocities of his last years, there must have been considerable veneration of his memory, because both his principal heirs, Archelaus and Antipas, very soon and very significantly took on 'Herod' as their own first name: and it is as Herod the ethnarch and Herod the tetrarch that they appear on their coinages.[10]

There had always been a branch of the Sadducees supporting their father, and, as we saw, he had gradually built round this group an aristocracy of service. When the Romans annexed Judaea, the members of this section of opinion were proud to describe themselves as Herodians. Their headquarters were in the cities of Galilee,[11] and their loyalty was centred upon their ruler Herod

Antipas: for they could see what a mess the Roman governors were making across the border in Judaea. Jesus Christ, on the other hand, encountered their hostility. And he, for his part, was inclined to bracket these Herodians, in derogatory fashion, with the moderate or right-wing section of the Pharisees, since both groups showed a marked lack of sympathy with Messianic, apocalyptic ideas, which seemed to them potentially disruptive of public security and private property.

Meanwhile, within the new Roman province of Judaea, things were going from bad to worse. During and after the governorship of Pontius Pilatus (AD 26–36) there were almost continual acts of violence and bloodshed on both sides, suspended only (for the most part) during the brief restoration of the Jewish client kingship under Agrippa I (41–4).

He and his son Agrippa II, backed by the priestly aristocracy, did their utmost to stave off the catastrophe. Yet finally, in AD 66, the First Jewish Revolt broke out; or, as Jews call it, the First Roman War. The struggle was heroic, and it involved frightful sufferings and carnage. At Masada the desperate resistance went on until 73. But in 70 Jerusalem had fallen to Titus, the son of Vespasian who had first commanded against the rebels and then became emperor (69–79). Josephus was there – but, unforgivably to Jews of all periods, he was on the wrong side, since the hopelessness of the cause had made him defect to the Romans. He was with them when they finally entered Jerusalem, and he paints an appalling picture of the hardship, carnage and Roman retribution.[12]

Titus, known as the darling of the human race, did not reveal the more attractive side of his character in his treatment of the prisoners. For at Caesarea soon afterwards

he celebrated the birthday of his brother Domitian in the grand style, reserving much of his vengeance on the Jews for this notable occasion. The number of those who perished in combats with wild beasts or in fighting each other or by being burnt alive exceeded 2,500. Yet all this seemed to the Romans, though their victims were dying a thousand different deaths, to be too light a penalty. Titus next went on to Berytus (Beirut) ... Here he made a longer stay, celebrating the birthday of his father Vespasian with a still more lavish display, both in the magnificence of the shows and in the originality of the other costly entertainments. Vast numbers of prisoners perished in the same way as before.[13]

Although the coastal plain did not suffer so badly, the highlands of Judaea for a time were almost depopulated. Towns were destroyed, and the wealthy class ruined and decimated; imperial domains were enormously magnified at the expense of large and small properties alike. As the province passed, henceforward, to a succession of governors of high rank, capable of dealing with disruption by military means, a colony of Roman ex-soldiers was established at Emmaus (Kuloniyeh) close to Jerusalem,[14] and a Roman legion was stationed in the city itself. As for the Jewish religion, the Temple and its worship were obliterated when Jerusalem fell to Titus, and the money which had been sent for its upkeep from all over the world was now redirected to the Temple of Jupiter on the Roman Capitol. The office of high priest was no more.[15]

Stairway to the 'Tombs of the Kings', necropolis of Queen Helena of Adiabene (Assyria), who migrated to Jerusalem in c. AD 45.

In a sense, Jerusalem had already ceased to be a national centre ten years after the death of Herod, when his son Archelaus had been deposed and the country became a Roman province. Yet, for all that, Jerusalem had continued to survive as a Jewish religious centre. Now, after the disastrous events in AD 70, it ceased to possess that status, and did not resume it again, on any impressive scale, for over eighteen hundred years to come.

An incidental result of this partial obliteration of Palestine in 70 was a further Dispersion. This, incidentally, assisted the spread of Christianity, which gained ground among the widely scattered Jews. As for Judaism, the fact that it survived at all after these holocausts was largely due to the synagogues and the moderate

Pharisees who controlled them. The most prominent among these men was Johanan ben Zakkai, who left Jerusalem while the city was still under siege and, like his co-religionist Josephus shortly before him, went over to the Romans. He persuaded Titus and Vespasian to allow him to found a new centre of Hebrew studies at Jamnia (Yavne).

True to the tradition of his predecessors Hillel and Shammai, who had recognised the inevitability of Herod and what he stood for, Johanan ben Zakkai sought to comfort a student who was gazing upon the ruins of the Temple. 'My son,' he said 'do not be distressed! We have another atonement as effective as this – acts of loving kindness.'[16]

Yet the Jews who remained in Judaea were still hard-working people, and recent research indicates that from the early part of the second century AD the country was beginning to recover its economic prosperity. It is strange that the next savage blow should have been struck by Hadrian (117–138), the most cosmopolitan and liberal of all emperors. But so liberal was he that he could not understand anyone who failed to reciprocate; and during the reign of his predecessor Trajan there had been serious riots, amounting to insurrection, among the Jews of the Dispersion. The first outbreak took place in Cyrene, and others followed in Cyprus, Egypt and Babylonia. During these widespread troubles it was said that a million people, first Gentiles and then Jews, lost their lives. Even if this figure was exaggerated, the casualties had truly been shattering, and Hadrian could not fail to suspect that the impetus had come from Judaea. So he ordered that ruined Jerusalem should be rebuilt as a colony of imported Roman citizens, Aelia Capitolina, and that its Jewish character should be brought to an end once and for all. Jews were forbidden to set foot in the place except on one day a year, and upon the site of the Temple was installed the worship of Jupiter and the emperor.[17]

Revolt broke out again in AD 132 – the Second Jewish Revolt or Second Roman War. Although the Pharisees, once again, were divided in their allegiance, the national Jewish leader Simon was hailed (on at least one occasion) by his sacred name of Bar Kochba, the Messianic Son of a Star, by the nonagenarian Pharisaic leader, the rabbi Akiba. The rebellion lasted three and a half years; six legions were needed to put it down. At the final terrible reckoning, the Romans claimed to have taken fifty mountain fortresses and nine hundred and eighty-five large villages, and to have killed 580,000 men. Here the figures seem reliable enough – and an incalculable additional number died of hunger, pestilence and fire. From now onwards there was to be a garrison of two legions instead of one, under a governor of the very highest rank. Innumerable Jews were sold into slavery abroad, and Judaea was denuded of its Jewish inhabitants. If any Jew, from this time on, so much as set foot in Jerusalem, he was liable to the penalty of death.

The achievement of Herod

These Jewish revolts, with their appalling loss of life, would never have taken place if Herod's policy had been allowed to prevail. In order to see what this policy was, we have to avoid paying too much attention to the sordid domestic troubles of the last decade of his life and the withdrawal of Augustus' confidence during part of the same period. A clearer view can be obtained if we look instead at his reign as a whole, and at the major achievements of its zenith.

Herod's policy, above all, was pro-Roman. He was deeply convinced that there was no possibility of complete Judaean independence, and he regarded collaboration with Rome as the price of survival and prosperity. This view, exactly opposed to the low-flash-point nationalism of his Hasmonaean foes, was the product of an accurate diagnosis and prognosis. It is incorrect to see Herod as a quisling collaborating with the national enemy when he should have been fighting against them. Such a view neglects the fact that the Romans were not only in complete control of the entire Mediterranean area, but would certainly retain this control for as far ahead as the imagination could envisage. There was no 'other side' which could prevent this. Certainly the Jews could not. There

Herod orders the Three Wise Men to find the infant destined to be Israel's King. Mosaic in the Basilica of S. Marco, Venice.

was not one chance in a million that rebellions would succeed: when they came, they achieved nothing but a gigantic and frightful toll of Jewish casualties, together with the obliteration of the Jewish national home which has not been revived until recent times. Herod was right, just as Johanan ben Zakkai and even the turncoat Josephus were right, in counselling peace with Rome as the only salvation. It is fallacious to condemn Herod on the grounds that he placed prudence and safety before honour and freedom.[1] These were not the real alternatives. In realistic terms the second alternative was not honour and freedom at all, but destruction of self, home, family and country.

This was the alternative that the Jews twice chose after Herod

Herod the Great ordering the Massacre of the Innocents at Bethlehem. Basilica of S. Stefano, Bologna.

was dead. Herod himself had made the other choice. And his solution need not be criticised on the grounds that it would have led to Jewry being engulfed. As Abraham Schalit declares: 'Its spiritual concession would have been nothing compared to the enormous advantage of the continued possession of the land of its forefathers.'[2]

To say all this is by no means to excuse the Romans for the lamentable mistakes they continually made, and the cruelties they committed, when dealing with the Jewish problem. These blunders naturally exacerbated the Jews. And they invite a second criticism of Herod which is perhaps more serious than the first: was he attempting the impossible? Those who believe this to be the case

Massacre of the Innocents depicted by Fra Angelico (c. 1387/1400–1455). Museum of S. Marco, Florence.

maintain that no one, not even a more acceptable sort of Jew capable of earning whole-hearted loyalty from the main Jewish groups, could have stemmed the rising tide of nationalism and fanaticism, the inevitable oriental reaction against alien Hellenisation. But this conclusion is more than doubtful. For example Herod's grandson Agrippa I, to whom Rome gave back his kingdom, managed to be popular, on the whole, with Jews and Romans alike. In spite of a few inevitable criticisms, most Jews did not even hold it against him that he was of Idumaean origin. True, people had by that time got used to Idumaean rule, which had been a greater shock to Jewish susceptibilities in the earlier days of Herod and his father. In any case, the task Agrippa I set himself was perfectly possible: and the policy of his grandfather Herod, though harder, had been practicable too.

But here a third criticism of Herod can be heard, and it is harder to answer than the others. He allowed it to become too clear, amid

Herod the Great's Massacre of the Innocents by Matteo di Giovanni (*c.* 1435–95). Church of S. Agostino, Siena.

his Hellenising enthusiasms, that he did not feel whole-heartedly a Jew. By revealing this he inflicted a handicap on his own conduct of affairs.[3] But that does not mean that his policy was wrong.

Herod can also be blamed for the repressions which he embarked upon so as to push this policy through. To us, who are not ruling Judaea during the first century BC, they appear inexcusably savage. To him, it seemed absolutely essential to annihilate those who were trying to sabotage the policy on which the whole future of their country depended. Those who felt his heavy hand, operating for the sake of this cause which he regarded as so urgent, ensured his future infamy. And so he became Herod the Wicked, villain of many a legend, including the Massacre of the Innocents:[4] the story is invented, though it is based, in one respect, on what is likely to be a historical fact, since Jesus Christ was probably born in one of the last years of Herod's reign[5]. The supposed day of the Massacre, 28 December, passed into the Christian calendar; and as for the Jews, they began to celebrate the day of Herod's death as a festival.[6]

Nevertheless, the Jews in other countries acted in a contrary fashion, holding festivals which did honour to his memory.[7] And even in Judaea itself, as we have seen, his political followers were still proud to call themselves Herodians. Already during his lifetime, there had been many leaders among the Sadducees and Pharisees alike who were willing to give him at least passive support, because it was so abundantly clear that Judaism, classified by the Romans as a tolerated and acceptable faith, had little to gain and everything to lose by revolution.

And the same favourable verdict could have been obtained in more humble Jewish circles too. Apart from small groups of ruined noblemen and Messianic extremists, the Jews had never had

Massacre of the Innocents: a tapestry from designs attributed to Tommaso Vincidor of Bologna, early sixteenth century. Galleria degli Arazzi, Vatican.

Massacre of the Innocents by Bonifazio Veronese (de' Pitati) (1487–1553).
Accademia di Belle Arti, Venice.

it so good. The ordinary peasants, merchants and citizenry were
prospering, and knew it,[8] and Herod's mighty public works had
given full employment and had eliminated social agitation. When
complaints against Herod burst out after his death, his friend
Nicolaus of Damascus was quick to point out that there had been
little sign of them while he was alive (see Chapter 11). This was
partly, it is true, because his intelligence service was so efficient,
but it was also due to the fact that provided one got on quietly with
one's work there was not very much to complain about.

For what Herod had brought his kingdom was peace. This state
of affairs, an extraordinarily unusual one for Judaea, lasted, with
only minor and peripheral interruptions, for the entire thirty-three
years of his reign. Moreover it was a peace free from the incursions
of Roman officials. Herod was justly able to claim that throughout
the long duration of his rule he had never been asked by Augustus
to admit Roman ex-soldier settlers, and he had kept the Roman
administrators and tax-gatherers out – an advantage his people
were better able to appreciate ten years after his death when these
functionaries came flocking in.

On the other hand there was one aspect of his pro-Roman programme which was more than just a negative question of fending off direct rule: Herod was truly eager to integrate Judaism and Jewry with the surrounding world. One of the reasons for this desire was psychological, and not particularly creditable. Even if all the tuition of Nicolaus had left him, in the words of W. W. Tarn, only 'moderately well varnished', he longed to cut a figure in that opulent, chic other world. For he had to be a match for both worlds, the Graeco-Roman and the Jewish, and in neither of them did he ever feel really at ease. Jew by religion, Idumaean and Arab by race, Greek by cultural sympathy, Roman by political allegiance, these different instincts and inclinations mingled uncomfortably in Herod's mind and heart. Yet to describe him as a man without any roots, always hankering to exchange one tradition for another, would be an injustice to the spirit that lay behind his cosmopolitanism. For he possessed the absolute conviction that the only way his country could survive was by aligning itself, as far as this could be done, with the wider world outside: an ambition that was all the more realisable because his own territory had been enlarged to include so many non-Jewish lands.

Whether Herod is entitled to the appellation 'King of Israel' is a question Israelis are actively discussing today. Some say yes, others protest that he watered down the concept of Israel far too much.[9] Whether he deserves to be called 'the Great' is another matter again. In his own time he was not so described.

Later on, his grandson and great-grandson, Agrippa I and II, both described themselves as 'Great Kings'[10], a title which by then had become a not very glorious symbol of quite minor royalty. But Herod did not call himself 'the Great'. When Josephus applies the term to him, he means 'the elder', to distinguish him from other Herods.

Nevertheless, while his judgment still remained unimpaired, he achieved as much greatness as was possible for any man of his time who was not a Roman. He devoted his many talents to making Judaea as peaceful, important and prosperous a country as it was capable of becoming in a world dominated by the western power. The eastern power, Parthia, with its inferior organisation and culture, never tempted him.[11] In many ways he resembled King David. But Herod's task was the harder of the two, because he had to pursue his aims under the shadow of another, all-powerful state.

Herod also resembled David in his catastrophic family life. This is described at enormous length by Josephus, because most of the tragedies occurred during the last part of the king's reign, when the historian's chief informant Nicolaus of Damascus was at the centre of events. It is a nauseating story. But it is also worth reading Conor Cruise O'Brien's imaginary account of how Herod might justify himself to modern critics. When compared to his disadvantage with a list of idolised twentieth-century rulers and statesmen, he reminds the audience that these modern heroes had caused many more deaths than Herod did. These deaths had not, it is true, been perpetrated within their own households. But in terms of strict ethics, was it very much better when they killed thousands of people in morally questionable wars?

> Everyone of them shed blood, as I did, for reasons of State.
> For the preservation of the State
> Which is essential to ordered human life
> And to the very existence of such an audience as yourselves.
> The people whom a statesman must kill in war or in peace
> Are those whom it is politically relevant to kill.
> In my day the people who were politically relevant
> Were dynastic people, members of the family
> Of the successful statesman.
> I loved Mariamme, Aristobulus and Alexander
> .. And had I lived in a political context such as your own
> I would not have found it either relevant or rewarding
> To put them to death.[12]

The horrors of Herod's court remain appalling. But until, during his last years, they impinged on world affairs and on Augustus, they do not very much affect our estimate of the general beneficence or otherwise of his reign. Moreover, what we know about other eastern Mediterranean courts during these centuries suggests that the sordid horrors at the court of Jerusalem were very far from unique. They are merely better known than the others, owing to the accident that Josephus' accounts have survived. There are quite a number of other late Hellenistic monarchs of whose domestic goings-on we know virtually nothing at all – except for one or two scarifying details which hint that a rich mine of authentic squalor has been lost. Nor is one entitled to adopt the superior occidental view that there was something specially eastern about all these murders within the family; a glance at the pages of Tacitus and Suetonius will recall that imperial Rome was seething with murderous domestic strife. Indeed, even the great Augustus himself may have ordered the murder of a grandson.[13] But this was a modest contribution compared to those of his imperial successors, who did their best, in Hamlet's phrase, to out-Herod Herod.

Nor, of course, are these royal domestic slaughters limited to the ancient world. A brief examination of the Italian Renaissance will rapidly correct any such impression. The Ottoman imperial house is another particularly relevant analogy – and does, it must be admitted, lend strength to the comforting view that such atrocities are oriental – because what really got Herod into all his trouble was the unfortunate fact that there was nothing to stop him from being polygamous. The result, inevitably, was a mass of warring wives and sons. And it was here that Herod quite lacked the temperamental capacity for dealing with the intrigues he had brought upon himself. Although affection for members of his family was one of his strongest characteristics – it may sound curious to say so since he killed so many of them, but it is true – this was accompanied by a hysterical readiness to suspect the worst.

This is a fertile field for the psychologist; and so is Herod's attitude to the Hasmonaeans. There was a great deal of snobbery going around about the superiority of this former royal family, a point of view which those who possessed a share of its blood never

The Massacre of the Innocents. Relief on the pulpit of the church of S. Andrea at Pistoia, by Giovanni Pisano in 1298–1301.

ceased to advertise. Herod, himself of despised ancestry, shared this standpoint thoroughly, and yet was easily and continually convinced – often, it must be admitted, with some justice – that offshoots of the Hasmonaean house were his worst enemies, and the worst enemies of the Idumaean relatives whom he so patiently supported. That was the cause of the greatest personal tragedy of his life: his marriage to the beautiful and difficult Hasmonaean Mariamme (1), whom he later condemned to death.

233

Still, Herod kept his political judgment for many years after that. It was only in his last decade that his domestic troubles affected his performance as a ruler. By then the impetuous, passionate element in his character had overcome the portentous brain-power that had kept it in check hitherto. Until that time, he had been a monarch of exceptional gifts – subtle, pertinacious, untiring; an admirable administrator, soldier, financier and diplomatist, and a person capable of exercising a charm that even the toughest Roman grandees found wholly irresistible.

Herod saw the catastrophe which would fall upon the Jews if they ceased to play the Roman game. When, later on, because of faults on both sides, Jews and Romans came to blows, the disasters that duly descended upon the Jews were frightful and irremediable. Herod had foreseen that this was likely to happen, and had done everything possible to avert it; and for this reason all the blood-letting in his harem cannot alter the conclusion that, in so far as his strange and limited circumstances permitted, he was truly Herod the Great.

Sources of information

An extremely large proportion of what we know about Herod comes from the Jewish writer Josephus – and from attempts by modern scholars to interpret his chronicles. Four works, written in Greek, were left by Josephus, and by an exceptional chance every one of them survives. They are *The Jewish War, The Jewish Antiquities, Against Apion,* and an autobiographical *Life.*

Owing to his significance to Christianity, a significance which was great but has been exaggerated,[1] Josephus used to be studied extensively in eighteenth-century Britain, in a monumental but not very reliable translation by the Reverend William Whiston (1737). Lately, however, he has been read much less, for reasons that were suggested in the Introduction. Yet he is a very remarkable historian, who gives us a mass of information, sometimes distorted but often true, about some of the most absorbing and poignant events in all history. A priest of aristocratic family with Hasmonaean connections,[2] he spent his youth trying out various brands of Jewry, and then became a Pharisee. After the Revolt, he settled in Rome, where he wrote his *Jewish War,* the Greek version (prepared by collaborators)[3] of a first edition written in Aramaic (or Hebrew?) for the Jews of Babylonia, Assyria and Arabia (AD 75–9) – in an endeavour to persuade them how pointless such rebellions are. The work includes a substantial introduction including quite an extensive life of Herod the Great. Then Josephus spent eighteen years writing *The Jewish Antiquities* (AD 93–4), a history of the Jews from the Creation to AD 66,[4] designed to magnify the Jewish race in the eyes of the Graeco-Roman world. This work, too, includes a life of Herod. The two accounts, taken in conjunction, mean that we know more about his kingdom than about any other of Rome's client states anywhere in the world, and more about Herod himself than about any other Roman client king.

Yet an extraordinarily difficult problem is raised by the fact that Josephus' two stories are by no means the same. For one thing, the earlier version is more dramatic, deriving its structure and a good many detailed touches from the Greek tragedians, whom one of Josephus' helpers had evidently read. The second description, though less readable, is more than twice the length of the first, and consequently a good deal more comprehensive. Moreover, it shows a considerable increase in the number of passages that are critical of Herod. Perhaps, in the form in which this account has come down to us, it is a second edition amended after the death of Herod's influential great-grandson King Agrippa II (*c.* 100?). For while Agrippa had been alive, it had been necessary for Josephus to defer to some extent to his susceptibilities, because he was a patron of Josephus[5] (and he may have been particularly sensitive since the historian, before changing sides during the rebellion, had actually fought against Agrippa's royal troops). There was also the sister of Agrippa II, Berenice (II), to be reckoned with. Not only had she been the mistress of Titus, but she was also the patron of a rival Jewish historian with whom Josephus was on the worst possible terms, Justus of Tiberias in Galilee.

At all events, *The Jewish Antiquities* speaks out more openly than *The Jewish War* against Herod. Josephus is proud of this new outspokenness, observing that his similar frank utterances on other occasions had annoyed certain of the king's descendants. The historian also remarks that he feels himself under an obligation to speak plainly because of his family connection with the Hasmonaeans, whom Herod had superseded. And yet perhaps this would not altogether have displeased Agrippa II and Berenice, who were descended from Herod's union with the Hasmonaean Mariamme (I).

Sometimes, however, the differences between *The Jewish War* and *The Jewish Antiquities* do not take the form of increased sharpness towards Herod; occasionally even a contrary tendency is apparent.[6] In such cases the change, we must suppose, is merely due to additional research, or to the ancient literary convention that you can say the same thing twice but you must say it in different terms.

Yet the various discrepancies between the two accounts remain puzzling. And equal perplexity is caused by Josephus' simultaneous employment of some sources that are extremely favourable to Herod and others that are extremely unfavourable to him. Nor does he always employ them in a very critical spirit, or try to accommodate them to one another: very often they appear side by side, creating a contradictory impression.

Although ancient historians do not feel called upon to specify their authorities with any degree of regularity, in this case the chief source favourable to Herod employed by Josephus can be readily identified from the historian's own allusions. It is Herod's personal friend, secretary and cultural guide Nicolaus of Damascus (see Chapter 7). The writings of Nicolaus included an account of his own life and a biography of the young Augustus, of which we possess six fragments and two large sections respectively. But his main work was his *Universal History* in 144 books, extending from the earliest times down to Herod's death. This *History* is virtually lost, and its disappearance is very unfortunate. Yet there is no doubt that Josephus employed it extensively. This reliance explains why he has so much more to say about Herod than about the immediately preceding periods: because Nicolaus' own history, too, had possessed a similar bias, seeing that he himself had fulfilled a leading role in the events of Herod's reign. And the reason why Josephus devotes such a disproportionate amount of space to the domestic intrigues of Herod's last years is the same. For those were precisely the years in which Nicolaus had played the largest part – and consequently the years he had written about in the greatest detail.[7]

Josephus mentions Nicolaus in no less than thirty-three contexts; and his debts go a long way beyond that. For example, *The Jewish War*, as we saw, is dramatic and theatrical in structure, and this feature, too, may be owed to Nicolaus, who was himself the author of at least one Greek tragedy. Besides, far more often than not, Josephus follows Nicolaus' version of events. Yet he also explicitly criticises him on occasion. He indicates, for example, that Nicolaus only said that Herod's father came from a leading family of Babylonian Jews in order to give pleasure to Herod.[8] Elsewhere, Josephus has more to say about this bias which Nicolaus so clearly displayed.

> Since he lived in Herod's realm and was one of his associates, he wrote to please him and to be of service to him, dwelling only on those things that redounded to his glory, and transforming his obviously unjust acts into the opposite or concealing them with the greatest care. For example, in his desire to give a colour of respectability to the putting to death of Mariamme and her sons, which had been so cruelly ordered by the king, Nicolaus makes false charges of licentiousness against her and of treachery against the youths. And throughout his work he has been consistent in excessively praising the king for his just acts, and zealously apologizing for his unlawful ones.[9]

But Josephus excuses this procedure on the grounds that Nicolaus' work was intended as part of Herod's education rather than as an objective historical work: 'One may fully forgive him since what he produced was not a history for others but a work meant to help the king.'

Another source which Josephus had to view with suspicion for the same reason comprised the memoirs of Herod himself. He accuses the king, for example, of giving a false account of the reasons why Hyrcanus (II) was put to death (see Chapter 6). Whether Josephus saw the memoirs of Herod himself or only knew them through Nicolaus cannot be determined with certainty, but there is no reason why he should not have seen them.[10]

A more objective authority, whom Josephus specifically quotes as a minor source,[11] was Strabo of Amasia in northern Asia Minor (Pontus). Strabo, who died some time after AD 21, is best known to us as a geographer; and in 25 BC he had personally accompanied the Roman expedition to southern Arabia, in which some of Herod's troops were engaged. Before undertaking his seventeen-book *Geography*, he had also written forty-seven books of *Historical Commentaries*. These studies, now lost, extended down to about 30 of 27 BC, and followed a pro-Roman line. But like almost all other Greek writers Strabo felt rather at a loss in dealing with Jewish history, and was unfamiliar with Hebrew literature.

Another subordinate source of Josephus may have been a certain biographer named Ptolemy,[12] not Herod's chief minister or Nicolaus' brother of that name, but perhaps a grammarian who came from Ascalon. Evidently he was not a particular admirer of Herod since he denied that Idumaeans were the same as Jews. As for Josephus' hated rival historian Justus of Tiberias, who wrote a chronicle of Jewish kings from Moses to Agrippa II (and was censured by Josephus for holding it back until after that monarch was dead), we do not know what attitude he adopted towards Herod; not necessarily, or even probably, a very hostile one, since later he and his family supported the Romans against the Jewish rebels, and, as was mentioned earlier, Agrippa's sister Berenice (II) patronised his work.

Our greatest problem still is, then, to determine where Josephus got hold of the large quantity of anti-Herodian material which he employed, not always very cleverly, to supplement or amend his pro-Herodian sources. There are two main theories about this. One of them maintains that Josephus was drawing on a savagely hostile biographer of Herod, who cannot now be identified: he must therefore just be called the Anonymous or the Jewish Anonymous.[13] Or this designation might be pluralised, for there were no doubt quite a number of Greek and Jewish writers, some of them anti-Herodian, whose works are now lost but may have been known to Josephus.

On the other hand it is clear from some of his stories that he also derived a great deal of material from word of mouth. Oral transmission, though never very reliable after more than a couple of generations, was always frequent and strong among the Jews, and obviously a lot of it was extremely critical of Herod. Almost immediately after his death this hostile tradition found expression in a work known as *The Assumption of Moses*, which lashes into Herod while adding, however, that the people fully deserved the judgment he so formidably executed upon them.[14]

Such other portions of the Jewish tradition about Josephus as have come down to us in later theological or juridical works are, for the most part, tantalisingly uninformative, though they do supplement our evidence for his reign in a number of special ways, for example (in so far as we can follow what is being said) with regard to the rebuilding of the Temple. Our Hebrew source on this subject is one of the treatises of the Mishnah – the first part of the

Talmud[15] – which set out to teach the oral Law independently of the scriptural basis which was claimed for it. These treatises in their written form date only from the second century AD, after the Mishnah had begun to be given preference over the Midrash (the earliest manner of transmitting the oral Torah, in the form of the exposition of biblical texts).[16] But the Mishnah treatises contain material that goes back to the time of Herod, and even earlier.

Fantastic portrait of Herod by Giuseppe Arcimboldo (c. 1530–93), made up of babies he allegedly massacred. Courtauld Institute of Art, London.

Notes

References are not normally given to passages in the works of Josephus except when they are quoted verbatim or some special problem arises. *Abbreviations:* Jos = Josephus; BJ = *Bellum Judaicum* (Jewish War); AJ = *Antiquitates Judaicae* (Jewish Antiquities). Translations from the Bible are from the *New English Bible* (OUP, CUP, 1970).

Chapter 1. Herod's background: Jews and Arabs

1. He was not fifteen, as Jos, *AJ,* XIV, 158; cf. XVII, 148.
2. Jos, *BJ,* I, 429f. (trans. G. A. Williamson)
3. *Psalms,* CXXXVII, 7; *Ezekiel,* XXV, 12; etc.
4. *Numbers,* XX, 18.
5. E.g., inscription of Sesmaios, for 33 years 'archon of the Sidonians of Marissa'.
6. The name Maccabaeus means 'hammer' or 'hammer-headed', referring to his military exploits.
7. *Psalms,* CXXXV, 4.
8. *Letter of Aristeas to Philocrates* (late second cent. BC).
9. *Ruth,* I, 16; *Acts,* VIII, 28.
10. Very confusingly, he is also called Antipater and Herod.
11. Justin Martyr, *Dialogue with Trypho,* 52.
12. Julius Africanus in Eusebius, *Ecclesiastical History,* I, 6.
13. Jos, *AJ,* XIV, 9 (from Babylon); Strabo, XVI, 765 (priestly house). Josephus' attribution of his statement to Nicolaus need not be discounted.
14. E.g., *Assumptio Mosis,* p 6.
15. *Song of Songs* (*Song of Solomon*), I, 14; cf IV, 13.
16. Jos, *AJ,* XIV, 121 (doubtful text); *BJ,* I, 181.
17. Jos, *AJ,* XIV, 403.
18. *Deuteronomy,* XVII, 15.

19. Babylonian Talmud, *Jebamoth,* 45 b.
20. J. W. Burgon, *Petra,* 132.
21. The first town-walls were probably of the first century BC.
22. As far as Egra (El-Wejh), port of a town in the interior with the same name (Hygras, El-Higr).
23. Diodorus Siculus, XIX, 97.
24. Many Nabataean Arabs later settled at Puteoli. The influence of Syrian Palmyra was particularly strong.
25. E.g. *Corpus Inscriptionum Semiticarum,* II, 354, etc.
26. I *Maccabees,* VIII, 22 ff.
27. *Psalms of Solomon,* II, 29–33.
28. I *Maccabees,* XV, 33f; cf Midrashim, *Genesis Rabbah* (Bereshith Rabba), I, 3.
29. II *Kings,* XVII, 24ff.
30. John, IV, 9.
31. A. H. M. Jones, *The Herods of Judaea,* p 22.
32. But the state was not made part of the province of Syria, as Ammianus, XIV, 8.
33. Jos, *AJ,* XIII, 11, 1, against Strabo, XVI, 2, 40. The title does not appear on the Hebrew inscriptions on Aristobulus' coins, and it is possible that he employed it for relations with Greeks only.
34. Since none of the five regional capitals seems to have been in Idumaea. 'Gadara' is probably not Adora in Idumaea, as has sometimes been supposed, but Gazara (Gezer) in the maritime plain.
35. *Leviticus,* XXV, 1–7; see Ch iii, n 4.

Chapter 2. Herod the King

1. John I, 46.
2. Jos, *AJ,* XIV 159f.
3. According to one theory there were two councils, a political and

a religious one, under the Hasmonaeans, presided over by the Sadducees and the 'pairs' (*Zuggoth*) respectively.

4. Though she is also described as a 'native of Jerusalem' and 'a Jewess of some standing'; Jos, *BJ*, I, 241, 432.

5. *Deuteronomy*, XXIV, I. The *Damascus Document*, IV, 20f, was opposed to divorce.

6. See Jos, *BJ*, I, 6. The anti-Hasmonaean *Enoch*, LVI, 5–8, attacks them. Nittai of Babylonian Arbela had been president of the council in the second century BC.

7. Rabbi Joseph ben Qisma, early second century AD.

8. *Leviticus*, XXI, 17ff; *cf* Tosefta, *Parah*, III, 6.

9. Jos, *BJ*, I, 285 (trans G. A. Williamson).

Chapter 3. Herod takes over his kingdom

1. Jos, *AJ*, XIV, 421–430.

2. Jos, *BJ*, I, 340f. (trans G. A. Williamson).

3. A. H. M. Jones, *The Herods of Judaea*, pp 47f.

4. *Leviticus*, XXV, 2–7.

5. Jos, *AJ*, XIV, 490f.

Chapter 4. Herod and the Jews

1. Or after Sadduk of second century BC, or *sedaqua* (righteousness), or *syndikoi* (Greek civic officials).

2. *Genesis*, XLIX, 10; *cf* Eusebius, I, 6; Babylonian Talmud, *Baba Bathra*, 3b.

3. 'Pollio and Samaias'; Jos, *AJ*, XV, 3. The view taken here is that of A. Schalit, *König Herodes*, pp 770ff, who explains that the names of Hillel the Elder (as well as his 'fellow student' Shammai) could be corrupted in the text in this way. For Shammai earlier in Galilee, *AJ*, XIV, 173. An alternative theory holds that Josephus' Pollio is corrupted from 'Abtalion', and that the other name represents Shemaiah.

4. Or 'expounders' or 'Persians' (innovators in theology). They are called Hasidim (the name of

the earlier pietists) in the *Psalms of Solomon*.

5. *Psalms*, CXIX, 97.

6. *Ecclesiasticus*, XXIV, 3–23. Portions of the original Hebrew text of this work have now been found at Masada.

7. Matthew, XV, 2.

8. Johanan ben Nappaha (mid-third cent. AD): Mishnah, *Gittin*, 60b.

9. There is evidence for them in third century BC Egypt. A piece of pottery, probably of the sixth century BC, found at Elat, refers to a 'house of meeting', which could be a precursor of the synagogue. It is uncertain what the synagogues were called in Herod's time.

10. *Cf* later Mishnah, *Baba Bathra*, 21a.

11. *Cf* Matthew, XXIII, 15.

12. These two functions are, respectively, the Halakhah (walking) and Haggadah (showing forth).

13. *Ecclesiasticus*, XXXIX, 1–3, *cf* Mishnah, *Aboth*, I, 2.

14. The designs on tombs in and near Jerusalem increasingly demonstrate these beliefs.

15. E.g., *Commentary on Nahum* (Qumran), 11f, Babylonian Talmud, *Sotah*, 22b.

16. They were said to have founded the academies named Beth Hillel and Beth Shammai. In the second century AD the Romans conferred the title of patriarch (Nasi) on descendants of Hillel, who himself, according to tradition, was the Elder Nasi. In Herod's time rabbinism was in its embryonic stages.

17. Babylonian Talmud, *Shabbath*, 31a.

18. Mishnah, *Aboth*, I, 10 (Shemaiah).

19. E.g., *The Words of the Heavenly Lights* (Qumran), 6 (M. Baillet, *Revue Biblique*, 1961, pp 195ff).

20. R. H. Charles, *The Apocrypha and Pseudepigrapha of the Old Testament in English*, II, 418.

21. Mishnah, *Aboth*, II, 7; *cf Acts*, V, 34 (if not recast).

22. Josephus also tones down apocalyptic aspects of *Daniel*.

23. *Numbers*, XXIV, 17b; *cf Manual of*

Discipline (Qumran), IX, 10f.

24. *Psalms of Solomon*, XVII.

25. *Similitudes or Parables of Enoch*, XXXVIII, 4.

26. *Canon of Sects*, CV, 9–11.

27. *War of the Sons of Light and the Sons of Darkness*, XIff (battle formation seems Roman); *Manual of Discipline*, IV, 18f; *The Triumph of Righteousness* (J. T. Milik, *Qumran Cave*, I, pp 102–5).

28. *Commentary (Exegesis) on Habakkuk*, II.

29. J. M. Allegro, *Journal of Biblical Literature* (1956), pp 182–7.

30. E.g., recently found *Blessings of Jacob*, ibid, pp 174 ff.

31. *Damascus Document*: C. Rabin, *The Zadokite Documents* (1954). Portions also found at Qumran.

32. But C. F. Fitsch, *Journal of Biblical Literature* (1955), pp 173ff believes that Herod forced them to migrate to Damascus.

33. Jos, *AJ*, XV, 373ff; *cf* p 372. Does their name mean pious men (*Hasidim*) or refer to healing or bathing (ritual purity)?

34. John Hyrcanus I, Hillel, Judas the Essene.

35. Johanan ben Zakkai (first century AD) was very interested.

36. *Life Magazine*, 22 December 1947; *Israel Exploration Journal*, I, pl 24.

37. Babylonian Talmud, *Gittin*.

38. Jos, *BJ*, II, 140.

39. Philo, *Quod Omnis Probus*, XII, 89ff.

40. There have also been many attempts to link Jesus with the Essenes.

41. *Cf* Judas ben Gedidah to a Hasmonaean: A. Schalit, *Annual of the Swedish Theological Institute*, I, 1962, pp 138f.

42. Jos, *Against Apion*, II, 165.

43. *Ecclesiasticus*, XLV, 6–14; *cf Exodus* XXVIII–XXIX.

44. On the high ground west of the Temple enclosure, linked to it by a bridge over the ravine. Later occupied by Agrippa II and Berenice (II).

45. It was probably on one of these that Roman troops saved St. Paul from being lynched (*Acts*, XXI, 35f). Here probably was the

'Pavement' at which Pilate judged Jesus (*John*, XIX, 13); though an alternative view places the site in Herod's Palace in the Upper City.

46. Or possibly Egypt: Mishnah, *Parah*, III, 5.

47. Ezekiel, XL, 46; *cf I Chronicles*, VI, 9.

48. The Joarib family that had settled at Modin (El-Medieh). Violent regimes: Tacitus, *Histories*, V, 8. Praise for their high priesthoods: *Book of Jubilees, Testaments of the Twelve Patriarchs*. Seleucid gifts; Alexander I Bala to Jonathan (d. 142), Demetrius II to Simon.

Chapter 5. Herod, Antony and Cleopatra

1. Various chronologies are proposed for these cessions: some attribute the bulk of them to 34 BC, when Antony (on paper) also made grandiose gifts of territory to the children of Cleopatra.

2. According to another view the invitation came later, when Aristobulus was high priest.

3. Jos *AJ*, XV, 42–956 (trans R. Marcus). This story of the attempted escape of Alexandra and Aristobulus in coffins bears a considerable resemblance to the tale of Johanan ben Zakkai's escape from Jerusalem in AD 70 (Midrash, *Ekah*, X, 1, 5).

Chapter 6. Success with Augustus: tragedies at home

1. Mishnah, *Sanhedrin*, II, 1.

2. Plutarch, *Antony*, 71.

3. Ibid 72.

4. The only member-town of the Decapolis west of the Jordan was Scythopolis (Beth Shean).

5. *Inscriptiones Graecae*, III, 550, 551: not attributable, as sometimes supposed, to another Herod (of Chalcis).

6. Jos, *AJ*, XV, 198.

7. Jos, *AJ*, XVI, 219.

8. *Ecclesiasticus*, XXV, 13, XXVIII, 13.

9. Jos, *AJ*, XV, 218–246.

10. Babylonian Talmud, *Kiddushin*, 76b, *Baba Bathra*, 3b.

11. Byron, *Herod's Lament for*

Mariamme.

12. Athaliah of Judah had been a blood-thirsty exception (*II Kings,* XI, 1ff). Racine wrote a tragedy about her.

13. A Baba ben Buta appears in Rabbinic legend as an adviser of Herod: J. Derenbourg, *Essai sur l'histoire et la géographie de la Palestine* (1867), I, pp 152f.

14. *Deuteronomy,* XXIV, 1; *cf* L. Epstein, *The Jewish Marriage Contract* (1954), p 128.

15. Alternative header and stretcher courses; and a graceful 'batter' (inward sloping) of the corner stones.

16. It measured fifty by sixty yards. An alternative site is claimed to be authentic by its owners, the Russian Church.

17. *Ecclesiasticus,* XLIV, 19–21.

18. Between Siloam and Temple mount (S. wall of area): survived in the Dodecapylon of Aelia Capitolina, Hadrian's Roman colony on the site of Jerusalem.

19. M. Grant, *Gladiators,* pp 55ff.

20. *I Maccabees,* I, 10; *cf II Maccabees,* IV, 17–19.

21. A tomb at Natanya, which may be Jewish, is decorated with the athlete's strigils.

22. *II Maccabees,* IV, 12.

23. *Genesis,* XVII, 10–14.

24. *I Maccabees,* I, 15.

25. *Exodus,* XX, 4; *cf Deuteronomy,* V, 8.

26. *Commentary on Habakkuk* (Qumran), VI, 3–5.

27. Jos, *AJ,* XVIII, 55–9; *BJ,* II, 169–174.

Chapter 7. Jews and non-Jews

1. Threx and Taurus. Docus (Ain Duyuk), where Simon was murdered in 134 BC, stood a little to the north on the 'Mount of Temptation'. The location of the castles of the Hasmonaeans and Herod has suggested that many of them were originally sited by Ptolemy I against the Seleucids.

2. S. Applebaum, *Zion,* XXVII, 1962, pp 3ff. Other southern forts were at Carmel, Zif and Adora.

3. But the name Volumnius, which also appears in further contexts,

may sometimes be corrupt in Josephus.

4. Though the *Letter of Aristeas to Philocrates* gives a more or less legendary account.

5. E.g., pseudo-Hecataeus of Abdera, *On the Jews,* Aristobulus of Alexandria. *Explanation of the Mosaic Laws* (if not a Christian forgery) and the Koheleth Book (A. Schalit, *König Herodes,* pp 735ff).

6. *Commentary on Hosea* (fragment; Qumran): see *Journal of Biblical Literature* (1959), pp 142–7.

7. Tosefta, *Sanhedrin,* XIII, 2; *cf* Babylonian Talmud, *Baba Kamma,* 38a.

8. *War of the Sons of Light and the Sons of Darkness,* IX, 9; XI, 9; *Psalms of Solomon,* XVII.

9. Near Canatha (Auranitis): W. Dittenberger, *Orientis Graeci Inscriptiones Selectae,* p 415. The statue is lost; the base, with the right foot, was last seen in the mid-nineteenth century.

10. *Cf* A. Tcherikover, *'Eres Yisrael* I, 1951, p 101, n 23.

11. Jos, *AJ,* XVII, 99, *BJ,* II, 21.

12. After Herod's death this man, Ptolemy, sided with Antipas, unlike the chief minister of the same name who sided with Archelaus; *cf* Chapter 17.

13. Jacoby, *Fragmente der Griechischen Historiker,* IIA, fragment 135.

14. Plutarch, *Quaestiones Convivales,* VIII, 4.

Chapter 8. Generosity and splendour

1. Babylonian Talmud, *Sanhedrin,* 82a.

2. Implied by Pliny the elder, *Natural History,* V, 70.

3. An alternative view holds that the entire country was divided into five *merides.*

4. Jos, *AJ,* XV, 311.

5. Ibid. XVI, 154.

6. *Isaiah,* LXI, 1, 3.

7. *Ecclesiasticus,* IV, 1, 4.

8. Ibid XIII, 23.

9. Their name *Haberim* (associates) implies their organisation in associations in conjunction with the poor.

10. *John*, VII, 49.
11. Jesus, the son of Phabis (Phiabi).
12. Babylonian Talmud, *Pesahim,* 57a.
13. S. Perowne, *The Life and Times of Herod the Great,* pp 118f. For the Pharos see M. Grant, *The Ancient Mediterranean,* p 215.
14. Between Wadi Qilt and Tulul Abu-el-Alayig. These buildings could date from Herod's son Archelaus.
15. On the east bank of the Wadi Shagg ed-Debi, a northern tributary of the Wadi Qilt.
16. S. Perowne, op cit, p 121. For the date-palms see Athenaeus, XIV, 22, and Pliny the elder, *Natural History*, XIII, 45.
17. Both these palaces were destroyed in the troubles after his death. Betharamphtha was then refounded as Livias.
18. On 7 July 1969, 27 bodies of men, women and children were buried by the Israeli army with full military honours as martyrs.
19. Y. Yadin, *Masada*, p 132.
20. The painted panels here and at Herodian Sebaste, Jericho, Caesarea and Herodium – imitating stone and marble – resemble, with a time-lag, the 'First Style' at Pompeii. There were probably two main Herodian stages at Masada, perhaps with the earthquake of 31 BC between them.
21. Y. Yadin, op cit p 72.

Chapter 9. Expansion beyond the Jordan
1. The son was Ptolemy (*c.* 85– 40 BC), the father Mennaeus.
2. The extent of his concession from Augustus is disputed. His father was Lysanias (*c.* 40–36).
3. *Deuteronomy* XXXII, 14; *Psalms,* XXII, 12.
4. Jos, *AJ*, XV, 346–8
5. Strabo, XVI, 780.
6. The Himyarites had eclipsed the Sabaeans (capital Sirwah). See D. B. Doe, *Southern Arabia* (1970).
7. Before or after the expedition Syllaeus' kingdom gained control of Dedan, the capital of Lihyan state.

8. Jos, *AJ*, XVI, 220ff, seems to place these events too late, as W. Otto sees. Syllaeus is still young, and Salome was widowed in 28–7 BC.
9. This is probably how Jos, *BJ*, I, 474 should be interpreted.
10. *Cf* R. Syme, *Journal of Roman Studies* (1961), p 30, note.
11. Strabo XV, 719.
12. G. Adam Smith, *The Historical Geography of the Holy Land,* Fontana ed (1966), pp 304f.
13. A coin of Elagabalus (AD 218–22) show Pan's statue in its arched enclosure.
14. Ptolemy V Epiphanes was defeated at Panion by the Seleucid Antiochus III.

Chapter 10. The Temple
1. Mishnah, *Middoth:* this stresses the religious aspects (ignoring the exterior buildings), while Jos, *AJ*, 410ff emphasises the architectural beauty.
2. *Matthew*, IV, 5.
3. One viaduct led to the Hasmonaean palace Akra ('Wilson's Arch' – several arches of later date – barrel vault reachable via subterranean structures) and the other was at the south-west corner ('Robinson's Arch', remains built into wall).
4. *Matthew*, IV, 5.
5. Perhaps it, too, was originally double, like most other gates.
6. Jos, *AJ*, XV, 416.
7. E.g., Arak-al-Amir and Si'a, which is scarcely Greek except for some inscriptions and the influence of the Corinthian column.
8. Tombs of 'Absalom' and 'Zacharias'; *cf* Tomb of Hamrath at Suwaida (Hauran), early first century BC. Herod's mausoleum in Jerusalem (Nikophorieh, opposite the palace) was probably somewhat similar.
9. According to one interpretation this was the Corinthian (later Nicanor) Gate.
10. *Luke*, II, 22.
11. It is uncertain if this was the

Beautiful Gate.

12. *II Samuel*, XXIV, 24; on the hill-top nearest the Jebusite city; where the wind would carry away the chaff.

13. S. Perowne, *The Life and Times of Herod the Great,* p 141.

14. From the spring Arrub (five miles south of the ancient reservoir of Solomon's Pools). It was fifteen miles long.

15. *II Chronicles,* III, 4.

16. Jos, *BJ,* V, 223.

17. Aristobulus (II) in 63 BC.

18. *Psalms,* LXXX, 8ff.

19. M. Grant, *The Roman Forum,* pp. 168f.

20. *Israel Exploration Journal,* VI, 1956, pp 127f.

21. *Thymiaterion:* sometimes wrongly described as a helmet.

22. *Matthew,* XXVII, 51. According to another view there was a wall between the two chambers, with a low door and a curtain right across the wall.

23. *John,* XI, 30.

24. Bamidbar-rabba 14.

25. Jos, *AJ,* XVII, 161.

Chapter 11. How Herod paid for it all

1. There were 1½ million acres of fertile soil according to pseudo-Hecataeus of Abdera, *On the Jews.*

2. Mishnah, *Kelim,* XVII, 4. Pomegranates are also represented in synagogues at Hammath (Galilee) and Dura Europos.

3. *Ecclesiasticus,* XXVII, 2.

4. Knudtzon, *Die el Amarna Tafeln,* p 1347, no 256.

5. Babylonian Talmud, *Megillah,* 6a.

6. The system in the north-east territories annexed in 23 and 20 BC (and in Samaritis as well) may have been different.

7. Ten years after Herod's death (not apparently in 4 BC, as Luke II, 2 on 'Cyrenius'), P. Sulpicius Quirinius introduced a new census, probably on a different and more thorough basis.

8. *Cf Admonitions of Enoch,* CIII.

9. Not, as sometimes suggested, imperial Roman domain bestowed upon him in usufruct.

10. Though he reduced the proportion of lead in the coinage to give it a more attractive appearance.

11. Babylonian Talmud, *Kiddushin,* II, 4. Some of Herod's smallest coins may be the 'small' prutah mentioned in the Jerusalem Talmud, *Sotah.*

Chapter 12. Marcus Agrippa and the Jews outside Judaea

1. Augustus' stepsons Tiberius and Drusus elder held major commands in the west.

2. T. Rice-Holmes, *The Architect of the Roman Empire,* II, p 52.

3. *Leviticus,* XXII, 25, *cf* Mishnah, *Shekalim,* VII, 6.

4. Philo Judaeus, *Embassy to Gaius,* XXXVII, 295ff.

5. Jos, *AJ,* XVI, 22.

6. *Sibylline Oracles,* III, 271.

7. Cicero, *In Defence of Flaccus,* XXVIII, 66.

8. Jos, *AJ,* XVI, 174ff.

9. Manetho of Sebennytus, *Aegyptiaca (c.* 280 BC), had voiced this dislike of the Jews.

10. Tacitus, *Histories,* V, 4.

11. On the shekel see *New English Bible,* O.T., pp 1165f.

12. Mishnah, *Shekalim,* II, 5.

13. Our estimate of the wealth of the Temple depends on whether the Copper Scroll found at Qumran (of disputable date) is speaking accurately or figuratively of its great treasure: *cf* G. Vermes, *The Dead Sea Scrolls in English,* 1970 ed, p 251.

Chapter 13. Changed plans for the succession

1. I.e. from Temenus, son of Heracles. Through her father she claimed descent from Darius I the Great of Persia.

2. Jos, *BJ,* 478ff (trans G. A. Williamson).

3. Jos, *AJ,* XVI, 200.

4. *Deuteronomy,* XXI, 15f.

5. *Inscriptiones Graecae,* III, 551.

6. Jos, *AJ,* XVI, 133.

7. Jos, *AJ,* XVI, 8ff, 66f records two reconciliations with the sons. Probably this is correct, and the two accounts are not a doublet.

Chapter 14. The second Arab war

1. Jos, *AJ*, XVI, 283. The name of the imperial agent (procurator) is given as Volumnius: see Chapter 7, note 3.
2. Jos, *AJ*, XVI, 289.
3. Aretas IV, whose name (in its Greek form) was originally Aeneas, proceeded to reign for forty-nine years (9 BC – AD 40). He placed the heads of his sister-wives on his coins. Aretas founded or refounded Oboda (Avdat) in honour of his predecessor, who was deified and buried there. Petra, Khirbet-et-Tannur and Egra owe much to his reign, which was a period of major artistic development. In 1 BC Augustus' grandson Gaius planned but did not carry out an Arabian expedition. Later, Palmyra took away much north Arabian trade.
4. Herod's bodyguard was alleged to be an assassin in Syllaeus' pay.

Chapter 15. The downfall of Herod's sons

1. He controlled the Eleutherolaconians, and Cythera was his personal possession. Nevertheless, he always appears as a city magistrate on his coins. See G. W. Bowersock, *Journal of Roman Studies* (1961), pp 112–118.
2. Macrobius, *Saturnalia* II, 4, 11.
3. Jos, *AJ*, XVI, 353.
4. Ulatha: not Huleh but Holath Antioch of the Talmud, C. Kraeling, *Journal of Biblical Literature* (1932), pp 133ff.
5. Tyre, too, was given an assembly hall and Byblus a city wall.
6. A. H. M. Jones, *The Herods of Judaea*, pp 133f. For the name of the imperial agent (procurator) Volumnius, see Chapter 7, note 3.
7. F. Jacoby, *Fragmente der Griechischen Historiker*, IIA, fragment 136.
8. Jos, *AJ*, XVI, 318.
9. The marriages now planned (though they did not materialise) were the following: Antipater (instead of his half-brother Herod

[II]) would now marry one of the daughters of his deceased half-brother Aristobulus (IV) (Antipater's first wife was the daughter of Antigonus); and Antipater's son (instead of Aristobulus' son Herod [III], later of Chalcis) would marry a daughter of the king's brother Pheroras.
10. Herod (II), son of Mariamme (II).
11. Jos, *AJ*, XVII, 69–70 (trans R. Marcus). Antipater's Samaritan agent bore the same name as himself (Antipater [III]).
12. Jos, *BJ*, I, 627–8 (trans G. A. Williamson).
13. *Cf* Jacoby, loc cit.
14. Antipas' brother Archelaus and half-brother Philip were somewhat illogically passed over owing to insinuations by the now discredited Antipater. Another half-brother, Herod (II), who had figured in the previous document, was also dropped (p 202), perhaps because there was enough power in his mother's high-priestly family already. See Genealogical Table.

Chapter 16. Repression of the Jews: the last days of Herod

1. Though he is unlikely to have ordered them himself, as Philo Judaeus, *Embassy to Gaius*, XXIII, 157.
2. E.g., W. Dittenberger, *Orientis Graeci Inscriptiones Selectae*, II, 532 (Gangra: to Augustus and his sons and kinsmen).
3. Roxana and Salome (III), both apparently married later to her sons (*AJ*, XVII, 322). See Genealogical Table.
4. *Isaiah*, LVI, 3.
5. *Cf* A. Schalit, *König Herodes*, pp 450 ff. The claim is denounced by a certain Jonathan in the Slavonic version of Jos, *BJ*, I, 364–70 (Loeb No 2): on this see Chapter 19 note 1. *Cf* No 22. King Agrippa II.
6. *Numbers*, XXIV, 17. But the six-pointed star (or shield) of David, though found at a Capernaum synagogue and on a Hebrew seal, is not biblical or

rabbinical, but was adopted in the seventeenth century.

7. *I Kings*, VII, 25, 36.
8. *Deuteronomy*, XXXII, 11; *The Rest of the Words of Baruch (Paralipomena Ieremiae)*, VII, 18, 58; *Yalquth Shimoni, Jithro* 19, folio 84b, 276.
9. E.g., Jewish steles in the Crimea (Cimmerian Bosphorus).
10. E.g., on a coin of Ascalon in honour of Cleopatra; also occasionally the Seleucids, e.g. Achaeus (221–214 BC).
11. Later, the palace of Herod's son Antipas at Tiberias had statues of animals, and they were even seen at Jerusalem itself, according to Rabbi Eleazer the son of Zadok. Kings Agrippa I, Agrippa II and Herod (III) of Chalcis (see Chapter 15) all placed their own heads on their coins, though not at Jerusalem.
12. Jos, *AJ*, XVII, 157 (trans R. Marcus).
13. Joazar, replacing Matthias. For the cause of his earlier suspension, *cf Horayoth*, 12b; Babylonian Talmud, *Yoma*, 12b; Jerusalem Talmud, *Yoma*, I, 1.
14. *II Chronicles*, XXI, 15, 18f; Jason of Cyrene; *Acts* XII, 23.
15. S. Perowne, *The Life and Times of Herod the Great*, pp. 172ff, describes Callirhoe.
16. Tosefta, *Megillat Taanith*, 25; Suetonius, *Nero*, XXXVI, 1.
17. Jos, *AJ*, XVII, 183–7 (trans R. Marcus).
18. Ibid, p 244.
19. Jos, *BJ*, I, 670–3.

Chapter 17. The aftermath

1. Nicolaus advised him not to oppose the detachment of the Greek cities from his principality.
2. *Matthew*, XIV, 6ff, *Mark*, VI, 17ff (but only Josephus enables us to identify her name). But Herodias had previously been the wife not of Antipas' half-brother Philip, as stated in the Gospels, but of another half-brother Herod (II) (or 'Herod-Philip'): see Genealogical Table. Antipas had previously been married to a daughter of King Aretas IV of

Arabia.
3. S. Perowne, *The Later Herods*, p 20.
4. One of the sons of his brother Alexander (III), who had been executed at the same time, briefly (some time between AD 6 and 12) became Tigranes IV of Armenia, and was executed in 36. Tigranes' nephew, who disastrously became Tigranes V of the same country (c. AD 60–2: M. Grant, *Nero*, pp 119, 126), had a son Alexander (V), who was given a Cilician princedom (Cetis) by Vespasian (AD 72): his sons held high office under Trajan. See Genealogical Table.
5. Under Nero (AD 57) his son Aristobulus (V) (d AD 92) moved from a princedom at north Syrian Chalcis (ad Belum in Chalcidene, near Beroea = Aleppo) to Lesser Armenia.
6. AD 53 Abilene, Arca, Batanea, Trachonitis; 61 Peraea and part of Galilee; 70 further extension. He was called Marcus Julius Agrippa.
7. *Acts*, XXVI, 32. Verse 28, on Paul, was mistranslated in the Authorised Version.
8. Galba, Otho, Vitellius, Vespasian (AD 69–79).
9. A. Momigliano, *Cambridge Ancient History*, x, pp 850f.
10. Thus the Gospels call both Herod and Antipas 'Herod'. *Acts*, XII, 1, 23 add further to the confusion by calling Agrippa I 'Herod'. Agrippa II (*Acts*, XXV, XXVI) should likewise not be described as 'Herod'.
11. Especially Sepphoris (temporarily called 'Autocratoris' = of the emperor) and the new city of Tiberias. Possibly the name of the Herodians goes back to the time of Herod.
12. Jos, *BJ*, VI, 420, 429ff.
13. Ibid VII, 37–40 (trans G. A. Williamson).
14. Three miles from the city, i.e. not the Emmaus (later Nicopolis, now Anwas) twenty miles away. It is uncertain which, if either, of these places is the Emmaus where Luke (XXIV, 13) records that Jesus appeared to the disciples

after the Resurrection.

15. The Jewish council, which had assisted the high priest since Herod's death (it is uncertain to what extent this was the later Sanhedrin), had been dissolved in 66, but was later restored at Sepphoris and Tiberias in Galilee.

16. *Aboth de' Rabbi Nathan,* 4.

17. Circumcision was forbidden: E. M. Smallwood, *Latomus* (1959), p 334; (1961), p 93.

Chapter 18. The achievement of Herod

1. Many of the severest judgments go back to H. Grätz, *Geschichte der Juden,* III, 1, (5th ed 1906), pp 178ff. *Cf,* with modern conditions in mind, Y.F. Baers, *Zion,* XXVII, 1962, p 125 n 17.

2. A. Schalit, *The Crucible of Christianity,* ed. A. Toynbee, p 74. For a thoroughgoing whitewash of Herod's policy see J. Vickers, *The History of Herod* (1901).

3. To that extent, alone, there is something in the view of S. Grayzel, *A History of the Jews* (Mentor ed 1968), p 101, that Herod was to blame for the disasters which lay ahead, because he sympathised too little with the Jews.

4. The Massacre (*Matthew,* II, 1–8), the folklore version of history's judgment on a great but evil potentate, offers analogies with the Midrash of Moses' rescue from the slaughter of Hebrew children in Egypt, and is paralleled by similar stories referring to the births of Augustus and Nero (Suetonius, *Augustus,* 94–3; *Nero,* 36): compare also later tales of child-martyrdoms in Thomas of Monmouth and Matthew Paris. A number of events reported during the last years of Herod's life could have contributed to the growth of the legend: e.g., the violent deaths of the supporters of Alexander (III) and Aristobulus (IV) (the fourth-century pagan polymath Macrobius, telling how Herod killed children in Syria under the age of two years, says

that the king's own son was one of the victims), the execution of the Messianic Pharisees, and the alleged order to massacre all the Jewish notables just before Herod's death.

5. The belief that the Nativity should be dated to AD 1 only came into existence in the sixth century AD, when a monk from south Russia living in Italy, Dionysius Exiguus, made a miscalculation. Jesus was probably born in 6, 5 or 4 BC, though some prefer 7 or 11. The suggestion of AD 6 has not been widely accepted. For the latest discussions of the evidence see M. Craveri, *The Life of Jesus* (1969), pp 44f, 58ff; E. M. Smallwood, *Greece and Rome* (April 1970), pp 85f, 89f. A recent theory that Herod died as late as 1 BC is unlikely to be accepted.

6. J. Derenbourg, *Essai sur l'histoire et la géographie de la Palestine* (1867), 1, 146f.

7. E.g., Persius, *Satires,* V, 180: his birthday or accession. A festival in his honour was kept by one of the Jewish communities in Rome.

8. Against R. Learsi, *Israel* (Meridian ed, 1966), p 149: 'Herod won nothing from the people he ruled but hatred and contempt.'

9. A. Schalit, *König Herodes,* p 675, supports this view, against M. Stern, *Journal of Jewish Studies* (1960), XI, pp 57f.

10. E.g., coin of Agrippa I, Berytus inscription of Agrippa II; *cf* Eucratides (second century BC) and other Indo-Greek monarchs, and Antiochus IV of Commagene.

11. The alleged assertion of Herod's son Alexander (III) that his father was plotting with Parthia against Rome (Jos, *AJ,* XVI, 253) was obviously mistaken. The report gets the name of the Parthian king wrong.

12. Conor Cruise O'Brien, *The Observer,* 21 Dec. 1969 (from his play *King Herod Explains*).

13. Agrippa Postumus: *cf* E. Hohl, *Hermes* (1935), LXX, pp 350 ff, R. Syme, *The Roman Revolution,* p 439.

Chapter 19. Sources of information

1. The value of Josephus' alleged references to Christianity is very dubious owing to the suspect status of the Slavonic version in which they appear, M. Grant, *The Ancient Historians,* pp 400, 449, note 56.
2. Jos, *AJ,* XVI, 187.
3. Jos, *Against Apion,* I, 50.
4. He calls it *Jewish Archaeology,* echoing the *Roman Archaeology* of Dionysius of Halicarnassus.
5. Jos, *Life,* 362–6.
6. E.g., *AJ,* XIV, 163–7 is actually more favourable to the Idumaean house than *BJ,* I, 208–9.
7. *Cf* G.W. Bowersock, *Augustus and the Greek World,* p 135.
8. Jos, *AJ,* XIV, 9.
9. Ibid XVI, 184–6, trans R. Marcus.
10. Ibid XV, 174 is no evidence to the contrary; *cf* H.J.H. Shutt, *Studies in Josephus* (1961), p 85.
11. In his account of Antony's execution of Antigonus, *AJ,* XV. 9. Strabo may have derived this account from Timagenes of Alexandria. Quintus Dellius could be another source of Josephus.
12. Ammonius, *De Adfinium Vocabulorum Differentia, sv* Idoumaioi.
13. J. Destinon, *Die Quellen des Flavius Josephus* (1882): W. Otto in Pauly-Wissowa-Kroll, *Realencyclopädie,* Suppl. Band 11, columns 6ff.
14. R. J. Charles, *The Apocrypha and Pseudepigrapha of the Old Testament in English,* II, 418.
15. The second part (the completion of the Mishnah) is the Gamara, comprising the Jerusalem or Palestine Talmud (which received its final shape in the late fourth or early fifth century) and the superior Babylonian Talmud (sixth century).
16. Both Talmuds assume that the editor of the Mishnah was 'Rabbi', i.e. Judah the Patriarch (born *c.* AD 135, became Patriarch *c.* 165), though it is much disputed if he himself had reduced it to writing. Systematisation had probably begun with the Rabbi Akiba (*c.*AD 50–135).

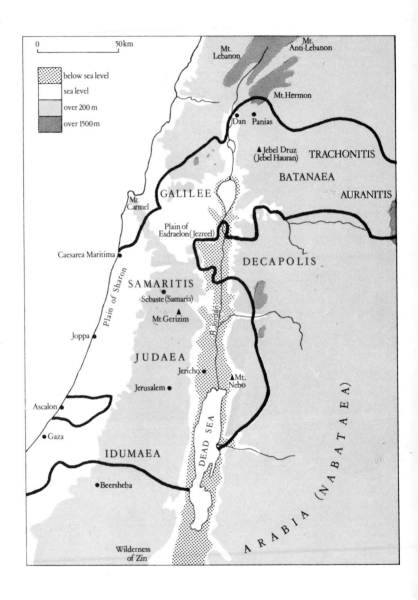

0   50km

below sea level

sea level

over 200 m

over 1500m

Mt.
Lebanon

Mt.
Anti-Lebanon

Mt.Hermon

Dan   Panias

▲ Jebel Druz
(Jebel Hauran)   TRACHONITIS

BATANAEA

GALILEE   AURANITIS

Mt.
Carmel

Plain of
Esdraelon(Jezreel)

Caesarea Maritima

DECAPOLIS

Plain of Sharon

SAMARITIS

Sebaste (Samaria)

▲
Mt.Gerizim

Joppa

R. Jordan

JUDAEA

Jericho

▲Mt.
Nebo

Jerusalem

Ascalon

Gaza

DEAD SEA

IDUMAEA

ARABIA (NABATAEA)

Beersheba

Wilderness
of Zin

2 Modern Israel showing frontiers
before 1967 (dotted area) and
territory occupied in 1967 (striped
area)

3 The kingdoms of Israel (*c.* 937–721
BC) and Judah (*c.* 937–597 BC)

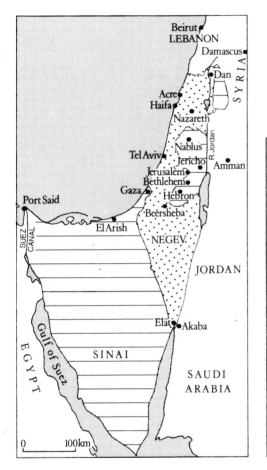

4 Judaea under the Hasmonaeans
   (Maccabees)

5 Judaea after Pompey's settlement
   (63 BC) (the shaded portion is all
   that was left to the ethnarch
   Hyrcanus)

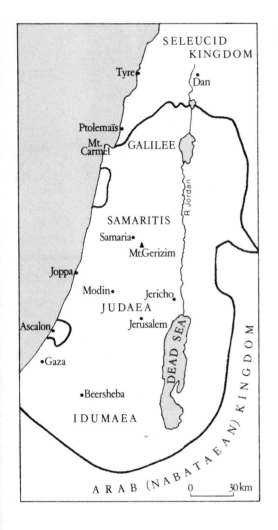

SELEUCID
KINGDOM

Tyre

Dan

Ptolemaïs

Mt.
Carmel

GALILEE

R. Jordan

SAMARITIS

Samaria

Mt.Gerizim

Joppa

Modin

Jericho

JUDAEA

Ascalon

Jerusalem

DEAD SEA

KINGDOM

Gaza

Beersheba

IDUMAEA

ARAB (NABATAEAN)

0   30km

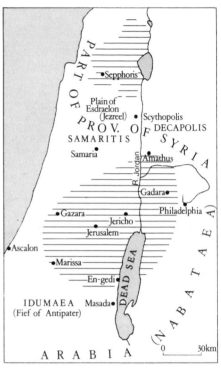

PART OF

Sepphoris

Plain of
Esdraelon
(Jezreel)

Scythopolis

PROV. OF

DECAPOLIS

SAMARITIS

SYRIA

Samaria

R. Jordan

Amathus

Gadara

Gazara

Philadelphia

Jericho

Jerusalem

Ascalon

Marissa

En-gedi

DEAD SEA

(NABATAEA)

IDUMAEA
(Fief of Antipater)

Masada

ARABIA

0   30km

6 Rome's Syrian frontier and beyond in the time of Herod the Great (client kingdoms of Rome shaded)

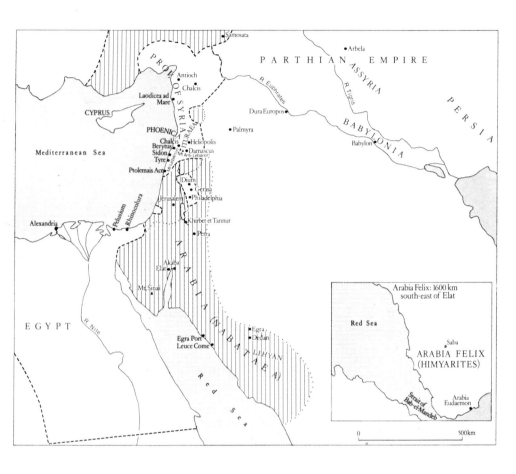

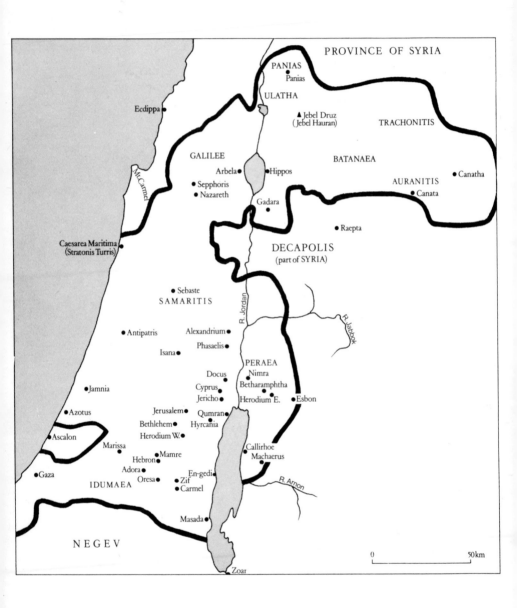

PROVINCE OF SYRIA

PANIAS
• Panias

ULATHA

Ecdippa •

▲ Jebel Druz
(Jebel Hauran)

TRACHONITIS

GALILEE

BATANAEA

Arbela • • Hippos

AURANITIS

• Sepphoris
• Nazareth

Gadara •

• Canatha

• Canata

• Raepta

Caesarea Maritima •
(Stratonis Turris)

Mt. Carmel

DECAPOLIS
(part of SYRIA)

• Sebaste
SAMARITIS

R. Jordan

R. Jabbok

• Antipatris

Alexandrium •

Phasaelis •

Isana •

Docus

PERAEA

Nimra

Cyprus • • Betharamphtha

• Jamnia

Jericho • Herodium E. • • Esbon

Jerusalem • Qumran •

• Azotus

Bethlehem • Hyrcania

Herodium W. •

• Ascalon

Marissa •

Mamre •

Hebron •

Callirhoe

Machaerus •

Adora •

• Gaza

Oresa •

En-gedi •
• Zif

R. Arnon

IDUMAEA

• Carmel

Masada •

NEGEV

0   50km

Zoar

8 Israel in the reign of Solomon
(furthest extent of territory under
Solomon's political and commercial control)

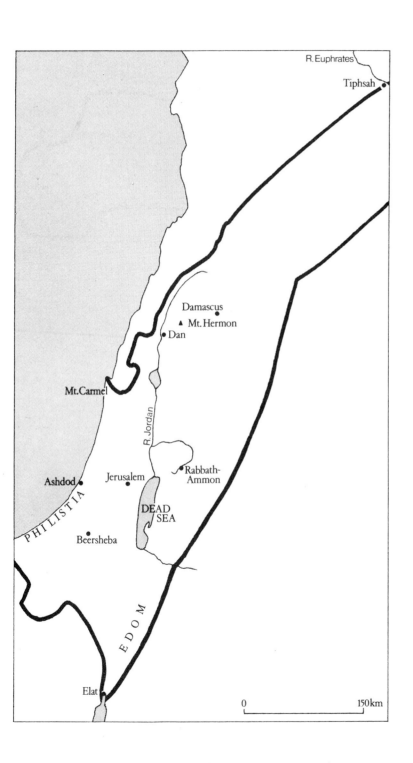

R.Euphrates

Tiphsah

Damascus

▲ Mt.Hermon

● Dan

Mt.Carmel

R.Jordan

Rabbath-
Ammon

Ashdod ●   Jerusalem

DEAD
SEA

PHILISTIA

Beersheba

EDOM

Elat

0   150km

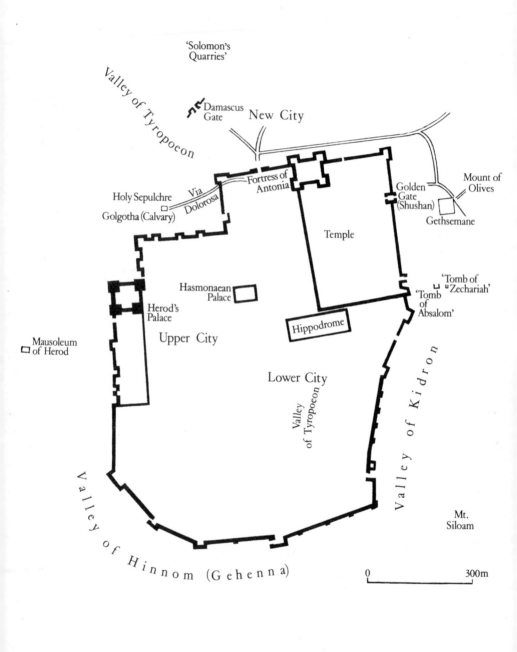

'Solomon's
Quarries'

Valley of Tyropoeon

Damascus
Gate   New City

Fortress of
Antonia

Holy Sepulchre   *Via
Dolorosa*

Golgotha (Calvary)

Golden
Gate
(Shushan)

Mount of
Olives

Gethsemane

Temple

'Tomb of
Zechariah'

Hasmonaean
Palace

'Tomb
of
Absalom'

Herod's
Palace

Mausoleum
of Herod

Upper City

Hippodrome

Lower City

*Valley
of Tyropoeon*

Valley of Kidron

Mt.
Siloam

*Valley
o f H i n n o m (G e h e n n a)*

0   300m

256

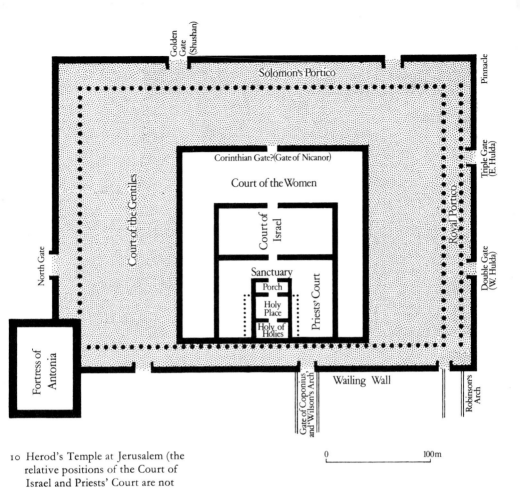

Golden Gate (Shushan)

Pinnacle

Solomon's Portico

Court of the Gentiles

Corinthian Gate? (Gate of Nicanor)

Court of the Women

Court of Israel

Triple Gate (E. Hulda)

Royal Portico

North Gate

Sanctuary

Porch

Holy Place

Holy of Holies

Priests' Court

Double Gate (W. Hulda)

Fortress of Antonia

Gate of Coponius and Wilson's Arch

Wailing Wall

Robinson's Arch

0   100m

10 Herod's Temple at Jerusalem (the
    relative positions of the Court of
    Israel and Priests' Court are not
    clearly known)

quileia

ILLYRICUM

R. Danube

CIMMERIAN BOSPHORUS

LY

Beneventum

Brundusium

Tarentum

MACEDONIA

THRACE

Byzantium

Sinope

PROV. BITHYNIA-PONTUS

PAPHLAGONIA

Amasia

PONTUS

ARMENIA MINOR

KINGDOM OF ARMENIA

Philippi

Ilium

Gangra

Pharsalus

ACHAIA

Nicopolis

Actium

Athens

Mytilene

ASIA

Caesarea

PROV. GALATIA

CAPPADOCIA

Samosata

COMMAGENE

PARTHIAN EMPIRE

Olympia

Corinth

Chios

Samos

Ephesus

Tarsus

Sparta

Cos

Celenderis

Elaeussa Sebaste

R. Euphrates

R. Tigris

Cythera

Rhodes

0   500km

11 Italy, Greece and Asia Minor
    (client kingdoms of Rome shaded)

257

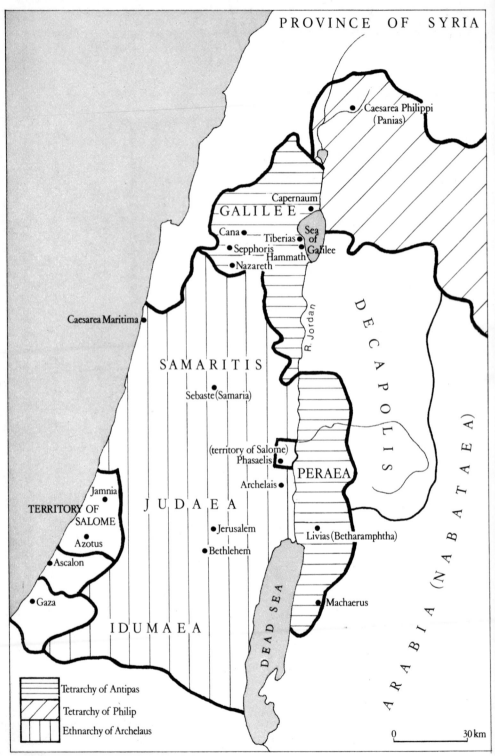

PROVINCE OF SYRIA

Caesarea Philippi
(Panias)

Capernaum

GALILEE

Cana
Tiberias
Sepphoris
Hammath
Nazareth

Sea
of
Galilee

DECAPOLIS

Caesarea Maritima

SAMARITIS

R. Jordan

Sebaste (Samaria)

(territory of Salome)
Phasaelis
PERAEA

Archelais

ARABIA (NABATAEA)

Jamnia

JUDAEA

TERRITORY OF
SALOME

Azotus

Jerusalem

Livias (Betharamphtha)

Ascalon

Bethlehem

DEAD SEA

Gaza

Machaerus

IDUMAEA

Tetrarchy of Antipas

Tetrarchy of Philip

Ethnarchy of Archelaus

0   30 km

12 Judaea under Herod's sons

Chronological table

103–76 BC	Reign of King·Alexander Jannaeus: Herod's grandfather Antipas becomes governor of Idumaea
76–67	Reign of Queen Alexandra Salome: Herod's father Antipater supports the high priest Hyrcanus II
73	Birth of Herod
	Herod sent to Arabian capital Petra during Judaean civil war
63	Pompey captures Jerusalem and makes Hyrcanus II ethnarch (prince), and Antipater chief minister
57	Gabinius divides Judaea into five administrative districts
49	Civil War breaks out between Pompey and Caesar
48	Murder of Pompey after battle of Pharsalus
47	Hyrcanus II and Antipater help Caesar in Egypt: their offices confirmed. Herod becomes governor of Galilee; puts down rebellion of Ezekias; is menaced by state council at Jerusalem; is granted Syrian command and possession of Samaritis
c. 47	Herod's marriage to Doris
44	Murder of Caesar; Herod appointed by Cassius to collect taxes in Galilee and then given other duties in Syria and Judaea
43	Murder of Antipater by Malichus; murder of Malichus
42	Herod defeats Antigonus (nephew of Hyrcanus II); Herod betrothed to Mariamme (I), divorces Doris; Brutus and Cassius commit suicide after their defeat by Antony and Octavian at Philippi
41	Herod made tetrarch (prince) of Galilee by Antony
40	Parthian invasion of Syria and Judaea: Antigonus made king. Death of Herod's brother Phasael and deportation of Hyrcanus II; Herod escapes to Egypt, goes to Rome and is appointed king with enlarged territory.
39	Herod returns to Judaea and fights Antigonus. Reconstruction of Alexandrium is begun by Herod's brother Pheroras
38	Herod joins Antony at Samosata. Victories at Sepphoris, Arbela and Isana
37	Herod's marriage to Mariamme (I); Herod captures Jerusalem, appoints Ananel high priest, receives Hyrcanus II back from exile, and begins construction of Antonia. Coastal territory and Jericho groves are ceded to Cleopatra
37 or 36	Aristobulus (III) replaces Ananel as high priest
36	Murder of Aristobulus (III)
35	Herod summoned by Antony to Laodicea
34	Cession of Gaza to Cleopatra, who visits Herod
c. 33	Revolt by sister of Antigonus at Hyrcania
32–1	First Arab War
31	Earthquake
30	Octavian defeats Antony and Cleopatra at Actium; execution of Hyrcanus II; Herod visits Octavian at Rhodes and accompanies him to Egypt. Suicides of Antony and Cleopatra
29	Execution of Mariamme (I)
28	Execution of Mariamme's mother Alexandra

28 or 27	Execution of Costobarus and the sons of Babas; games instituted to celebrate Actium
27	Construction of Sebaste (Samaria) begun: named after Octavian who is now Augustus (Sebastos)
c. 27	Herod's marriage to Malthace the Samaritan
25	Contingent of Herod's troops joins Roman expedition to south-west Arabia; famine and measures of relief
c. 25	Breakdown of proposed marriage between Herod's sister Salome (II) and the Arab chief minister Syllaeus
23	Construction of palace begun; Herod's marriage to Mariamme (II): her father Simon made high priest; Augustus grants Herod territories of Trachonitis, Batanaea and Auranitis (south-west Syria)
22	Construction of Caesarea Maritima begun
22–1	Herod with Marcus Agrippa at Mytilene; Herod's sons Alexander (III) and Aristobulus (IV) go to Rome
20	Augustus in Syria: grants Ulatha, Panias and Syrian appointments to Herod, and rejects complaints of Gadara. Herod's brother Pheroras is made tetrarch of Peraea (Transjordan)
19	Reconstruction of the Temple begun
18	Celebrations on completion of Temple Sanctuary
17	Herod's second visit to Rome: brings back his sons
c. 17	Pharisees and Essenes excused from oath to Herod
15	Marcus Agrippa tours Judaea
14	Herod in Asia Minor with Marcus Agrippa: gifts to cities and assistance to Jews of the Dispersion
13	Herod's eldest son Antipater (II) goes to Rome with Marcus Agrippa, taking Herod's first will in favour of Antipater
12	Death of Marcus Agrippa; Herod and his sons meet Augustus at Aquileia. Herod granted half the revenue of the copper mines of Cyprus. Revolt of Trachonitis, aided by Arabs
10	Dedication of the Temple
10 or 9	Dedication of Caesarea Maritima. Second Arab War: loss of favour of Augustus
9	Mediation of Archelaus of Cappadocia in Herod's domestic affairs
8	Nicolaus of Damascus reconciles Augustus with Herod. Herod sends his sons Archelaus (II), Antipas (II) and Philip to Rome
c. 7	Ostensible mediation of Eurycles of Sparta in Herod's domestic affairs
7	Trial of Herod's sons Alexander (III) and Aristobulus (IV) at Berytus, followed by their execution
7 or 6	Pharisees refuse oath to Augustus and Herod
5	Antipater goes to Rome with Herod's second will in favour of himself and his half-brother Herod (II). Death of Pheroras; return, trial and arrest of Antipater; Herod's third will in favour of his son Antipas (II)

c. 5	Probable date of birth of Jesus Christ at Bethlehem
4	Student demonstrations crushed; trials at Jericho. Execution of Antipater; Herod's fourth and last will in favour of his sons Archelaus (II), Antipas (II) and Philip; death of Herod
4 BC–AD 6	Archelaus ethnarch of Judaea
4 BC–AD 39	Antipas tetrarch of Galilee and Peraea
4 BC–AD 34	Philip tetrarch of Panias, Batanaea etc
AD 6–41	Judaea a Roman province
c. 33	Crucifixion of Jesus Christ
41–4	Agrippa I king of Judaea
44	Judaea becomes a Roman province again
60	St Paul sent from Caesarea to Rome
66	Outbreak of First Jewish Revolt (First Roman War)
70	Titus captures Jerusalem
73	Fall of Masada
79	*The Jewish War* of Josephus
93–4	*Jewish Antiquities* of Josephus
115–17	Revolts of Jews of the Dispersion
132	Outbreak of Second Jewish Revolt (Second Roman War)
135	Jerusalem destroyed and rebuilt as Aelia Capitolina; Jews forbidden to enter the city

Genealogical tables

THE EARLIER HASMONAEANS

(*MACCABEES*)

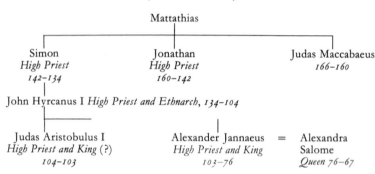

Mattathias

Simon	Jonathan	Judas Maccabaeus
High Priest	*High Priest*	*166–160*
142–134	*160–142*	

John Hyrcanus I *High Priest and Ethnarch, 134–104*

Judas Aristobulus I	Alexander Jannaeus	=	Alexandra
High Priest and King (?)	*High Priest and King*		Salome
104–103	*103–76*		*Queen 76–67*

THE LATER HASMONAEANS

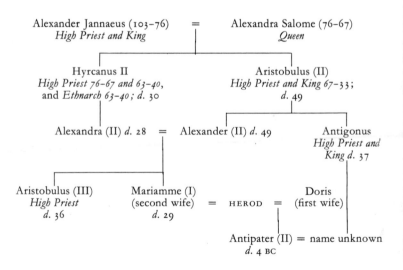

Alexander Jannaeus (103–76)	=	Alexandra Salome (76–67)
High Priest and King		*Queen*

Hyrcanus II	Aristobulus (II)
High Priest 76–67 and 63–40,	*High Priest and King 67–33;*
and Ethnarch 63–40; d. 30	*d. 49*

Alexandra (II) *d.* 28 = Alexander (II) *d.* 49   Antigonus
High Priest and King d. 37

Aristobulus (III)	Mariamme (I)			Doris
High Priest	(second wife)	=	HEROD	= (first wife)
d. 36	*d.* 29			

Antipater (II) = name unknown
d. 4 BC

THE IDUMAEAN HOUSE

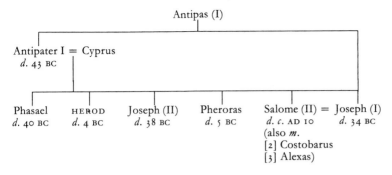

Antipas (I)

Antipater I = Cyprus
d. 43 BC

Phasael	HEROD	Joseph (II)	Pheroras	Salome (II) = Joseph (I)
d. 40 BC	*d.* 4 BC	*d.* 38 BC	*d.* 5 BC	*d. c.* AD 10 *d.* 34 BC

(also *m.*
[2] Costobarus
[3] Alexas)

THE CHILDREN OF HEROD

HEROD = a. Doris, b. Mariamme (I) *d.* 29 BC, c. Malthace *d.* 4 BC, d. Mariamme (II), e. Cleopatra, f. Pallas, g. Phaedra, h. Elpis, i. a daughter of his sister Salome (II), j. a daughter of one of his brothers

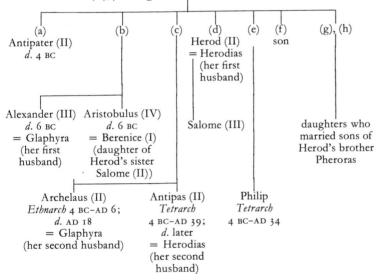

(a)
Antipater (II)
d. 4 BC

(b)

(c)

(d)
Herod (II)
= Herodias
(her first
husband)

(e)

(f)
son

(g), (h)

Alexander (III)
d. 6 BC
= Glaphyra
(her first
husband)

Aristobulus (IV)
d. 6 BC
= Berenice (I)
(daughter of
Herod's sister
Salome (II))

Salome (III)

daughters who
married sons of
Herod's brother
Pheroras

Archelaus (II)
Ethnarch 4 BC–AD 6;
d. AD 18
= Glaphyra
(her second husband)

Antipas (II)
Tetrarch
4 BC–AD 39;
d. later
= Herodias
(her second
husband)

Philip
Tetrarch
4 BC–AD 34

THE DESCENDANTS OF HEROD AND
THE FIRST MARIAMME

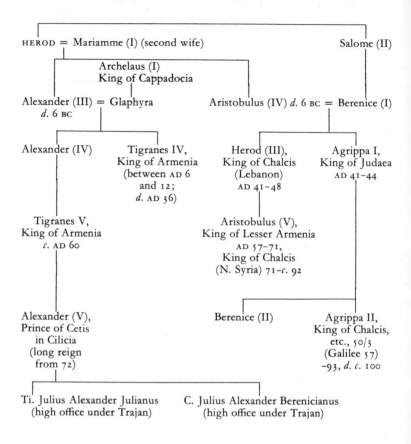

HEROD = Mariamme (I) (second wife)   Salome (II)

Archelaus (I)
King of Cappadocia

Alexander (III) = Glaphyra   Aristobulus (IV) *d.* 6 BC = Berenice (I)
d. 6 BC

Alexander (IV)   Tigranes IV,   Herod (III),   Agrippa I,
            King of Armenia   King of Chalcis   King of Judaea
            (between AD 6   (Lebanon)   AD 41–44
               and 12;   AD 41–48
               d. AD 36)

Tigranes V,   Aristobulus (V),
King of Armenia   King of Lesser Armenia
c. AD 60   AD 57–71,
                 King of Chalcis
                 (N. Syria) 71–*c.* 92

Alexander (V),   Berenice (II)   Agrippa II,
Prince of Cetis   King of Chalcis,
   in Cilicia   etc., 50/3
   (long reign   (Galilee 57)
    from 72)   –93, *d. c.* 100

Ti. Julius Alexander Julianus   C. Julius Alexander Berenicianus
(high office under Trajan)   (high office under Trajan)

Notes for further reading

F.-M. ABEL. *Géographie de la Palestine,* 2nd ed, Vols I and II. Paris 1949.

F.-M. ABEL. *Histoire de la Palestine depuis la conquête d' Alexandre jusqu'a l'invasion arabe.* Paris 1952.

M. AVI-YONAH. *Historical Geography of Palestine* (in Hebrew), 3rd ed Jerusalem 1962.

M. AVI-YONAH. *The Holy Land.* Baker Book House, Grand Rapids, Michigan 1966.

M. AVI-YONAH, ed *A History of the Holy Land.* Weidenfeld and Nicolson 1969.

S.W. BARON, *Social and Religious History of the Jews.* Vols I and II. Columbia University Press, New York 1952.

E.R. BEVAN. 'The Jews', Chapter IX of *Cambridge Ancient History,* Vol. IX. Cambridge University Press 1932.

J. BRIGHT. *A History of Israel.* London 1960.

A. BUECHLER. *Types of Jewish Palestinian Piety from 70 BCE to 70 CE.* Oxford University Press 1926.

H. DANBY. *The Mishnah* (English translation). Oxford University Press 1933.

G. DIX. *Greek and Jew.* London 1953.

I. EPSTEIN. *Judaism.* London, Penguin 1959.

I. EPSTEIN, ed *The Babylonian Talmud in English,* Vols 1–36. Soncino Press 1935–53.

L.H. FELDMAN. *Studies in Judaica: Scholarship on Philo-Josephus 1937–1962.*

W. FORSTER. *Palestinian Judaism in New Testament Times.* Edinburgh and London, Oliver and Boyd 1964 (German ed 1959).

N. GLUECK. *Deities and Dolphins.* Cassell, 1966 (about Nabataean Arabia).

S. GRAYZEL. *A History of the Jews.* New York, Mentor 1968 (first ed 1947).

C. GUIGNEBERT. *The Jewish World at the Time of Jesus Christ.* Routledge 1939.

M. HADAS. *Hellenistic Culture: Fusion and Diffusion.* New York, Columbia University Press 1959.

G.E. HILL. *Catalogue of Greek Coins in the British Museum: Palestine.* London, 1914.

F.J. HOLLIS. *The Archaeology of Herod's Temple: with a Commentary on the Tractate Middoth.* London 1934.

A.H.M. JONES. *The Herods of Judaea.* Oxford, Clarendon Press 2nd ed 1967 (first ed 1938).

JOSEPHUS (ed Loeb). II (*Jewish War,* Books I–III) (trans H. St J. Thackeray, 1927); VII (*Jewish Antiquities,* Books XII—XIV (trans R. Marcus, 1943); VIII (*Jewish Antiquities,* Books XV–XVII (trans R. Marcus and A. Wikgren, 1963); Heinemann, London and Harvard University Press, Cambridge, Massachusetts.

JOSEPHUS. *The Jewish War* (trans. G.A. Williamson). London, Penguin 1959.

JOSEPHUS (ed M.I. Finley). *The Jewish War and Other Selections.* New York, Washington Square Press, 1965.

K.M. KENYON. *Jerusalem.* Thames and Hudson 1967.

J. KLAUSNER. *The Messianic Idea in Israel* (in Hebrew), 3rd ed Tel Aviv 1950.

S. KLEIN. *Das Land Galiläa,* 2nd ed Jerusalem 1967.

R. LEARSI. *Israel* (Part II). Cleveland and New York, World Publishing Company 1966 (first ed 1949).

S. LIEBERMAN. *Hellenism in Jewish Palestine.* New York 1950.

J. MEYSHAN. 'The Coins of the Herodian Dynasty', in *Essays in Jewish Numismatics.* Jerusalem 1968.

J. MEYSHAN. *The Dating and Meaning of Ancient Jewish Coins and Symbols.* Jerusalem 1958.

A. MOMIGLIANO. 'Herod of Judaea', Chapter XI of *Cambridge Ancient History,* vol X. Cambridge University Press 1934.

A. MOMIGLIANO. *Ricerche sull' organizzazione della Giudea sotto il dominio romano.* Amsterdam, Hakkert 1967 (first ed, *Annali della Scuola Normale Superiore di Pisa,* N.S. III, Bologna 1934).

G. F. MOORE. *Judaism in the First Centuries of the Christian Era.* 3 vols. Harvard University Press, Cambridge, Mass. 1927–30.

New English Bible (with Apocrypha). Oxford University Press and Cambridge University Press 1970.

M. NOTH. *The History of Israel.* London, 1960 (5th German ed, Göttingen 1963).

W. O. E. OESTERLEY, Vol. II of W. O. E. Oesterley and T. H. Robinson. *A History of Israel.* Oxford, Clarendon Press 1932.

W. OTTO. 'Herodes' (No. 22) in Pauly-Wissowa-Kroll, *Realencyclopädie der klassischen Altertumswissenschaft,* Supplement-Band II, columns 1–158. Stuttgart 1913.

J. PARKES. *The Foundations of Judaism and Christianity,* 2nd ed. Valentine Mitchell 1960.

S. PEROWNE. *The Later Herods.* Hodder and Stoughton 1958.

S. PEROWNE. *The Life and Times of Herod the Great.* Hodder and Stoughton 1956.

C. F. PFEIFFER. *Between the Testaments.* Grand Rapids, Michigan, Baker Book House 1959.

M. RADIN. *The Jews among the Greeks and Romans.* Jewish Publication Society, Philadelphia 1915.

A. REIFENBERG. *Ancient Jewish Coins.* Jerusalem 1947.

D. S. RUSSELL. *The Jews from Alexander to Herod.* Oxford University Press 1967.

A. SCHALIT. *König Herodes.* Berlin, 1969 (Hebrew ed, Jerusalem 1960).

E. SCHÜRER. *History of the Jewish People in the Time of Jesus Christ.* Abridged ed by N. N. Glatzer, New York 1961 (German ed, Vol I, 4th ed, Leipzig 1901).

R. J. H. SHUTT. *Studies in Josephus.* London, SPCK 1961.

V. TCHERIKOVER. *Hellenistic Civilisation and the Jews.* Jewish Publication Society, Philadelphia 1959 (Hebrew ed, Tel Aviv 1931).

H. ST J. THACKERAY. *Josephus: The Man and the Historian.* New ed, New York, Ktav Publishing House 1967 (1st ed 1929).

G. VERMES. *The Dead Sea Scrolls in English.* 3rd ed London, Penguin 1968 (short bibliography, p 253).

L. H. VINCENT and F.–M. ABEL. *Jerusalem.* 2 vols. Paris 1912–26.

L. H. VINCENT and A. M. STEVE. *Jérusalem de l' Ancien Testament.* 2 vols. Paris 1954.

B. Z. WACHOLDER. *Nicolaus of Damascus.* Berkeley and Los Angeles, California University Press 1962.

C. WATZINGER. *Denkmäler Palästinas.* Leipzig 1935.

G. A. WILLIAMSON. *The World of Josephus.* Secker and Warburg 1964.

H. WILLRICH. *Das Haus des Herodes zwischen Jerusalem und Rom.* Heidelberg 1929.

Y. YADIN. *Masada* (translated from Hebrew). Weidenfeld and Nicolson 1966.

Index

Aaron, 50, 67, 73, 76
Aboud, see Obodas
Abraham, 20, 101–4, 159
'Absalom', 159, 244
'Abtalion', 241
Ace, Acre, see Ptolemais
Achaeus, 247
Achiabus, 99, 115, 211f
Acme, 203, 211
Actium, 87f, 90, 95, 103, 118, 139, 145, 195
Aden, see Eudaemon
Adiabene, see Assyria
Adora, 240, 243
Aelia Capitolina, see Jerusalem
Aelius Gallus, see Gallus
Aeneas, see Aretas IV
Aesop, 80
Afek, see Antipatris
Agrippa I, 23, 210, 219–22, 227f., 231, 247f.
Agrippa II (Marcus Julius Agrippa), 220, 222, 231, 236, 238, 242, 247f.
Agrippa, Marcus Vipsanius, 30, 88, 118, 120, 126f., 130, 144f., 164, 175–80, 182, 185
Ahab, 106, 108
Ahuramazda, 56
Ain Duyuk, see Docus
Ajlun, 190
Akaba, 14
Akiba ben Joseph, Rabbi, 224, 249
Akko, see Ptolemais
Akra, 73, 99, 126, 244
Alexander (I) Jannaeus, 21f., 22, 26, 30, 33, 46, 54, 112, 115, 147, 211
Alexander (II) (son of Aristobulus [II]), 30, 33ff., 42
Alexander (III) (son of Herod the Great and Mariamme [I]), 145, 184–9, 195–200, 232, 237, 247f.
Alexander Bala, 242
Alexander the Great, 21, 26ff., 48, 106
Alexandra (I) Salome (queen), 21, 26, 52, 65, 99
Alexandra (II) (mother-in-law of Herod the Great), 42, 44, 76f., 82–5, 90, 92, 98f., 101, 242
Alexandria, 35, 48, 84, 127, 180
Alexandrium, 54, 92, 98, 110, 176, 199
Alexas (I) (of Laodicea), 95

Alexas (II) (brother-in-law of Herod the Great), 143, 211
Amasia (Amasya), 237
Amman, see Philadelphia
Ananel (Hananel), 76f., 80, 82, 124f.
Andromachus, 117
Antigonus (Mattathias), 30, 33, 42, 46–54, 56–9, 61, 73, 137, 162, 187, 246, 249
Antioch (Antakya), 35, 59, 95, 98, 136, 146, 188, 197f.
Antiochus I (Commagene), 55
Antiochus IV (Commagene), 248
Antiochus IV Epiphanes (Seleucid), 150, 160, 210
Antipas (I) (grandfather of Herod the Great), 21f.
Antipas (II), Herod (son of Herod the Great), 112, 200, 203, 212, 216, 218f., 221f., 243, 247
Antipater (I) (father of Herod the Great), 18, 22f., 26ff., 30, 33–6, 38–41, 44, 62, 81, 173
Antipater (II) (son of Herod the Great), 145, 184–7, 195, 199–203, 206, 211f., 246
Antipatris (Capharsaba, Afek), 170
Antonia (fortress), 73ff., 85, 99, 110, 113f., 126f., 151, 153, 209
Antonius, Marcus (Mark Antony), 11, 14, 44, 48ff., 54ff., 59f., 73, 75, 77f., 82–8, 90, 92, 94f., 118, 179, 184, 242, 249
Aphrodite, 128
Apion, 235
Apollo, 22
Aquileia, 186f., 189
Arabia Felix, see Arabs (S. Arabian)
Arabs (Ituraean, Lebanon), 92, 137, 144, 146ff.
Arabs (Nabataean), 14, 20, 23–8, 30, 33, 41, 47f., 54, 59, 78f., 85–8, 90, 92, 101, 103, 111, 114f., 117f., 138–44, 147, 173f., 189–94, 196, 246
Arabs (S. Arabian), 52, 140ff., 167, 208, 231, 238, 244, 246
Aramaic, 23f., 64, 116, 150, 235
Aramain, see Platana
Araunah, 160
Arbela in Babylonia, 241
Arbela in Galilee (Arbel), 54
Archelaus (I) Sisinnes (king of

Cappadocia), 184, 187ff., 195ff., 199
Archelaus (II), Herod (son of Herod the Great), 200, 212, 214, 216, 220f., 243f., 246
Aretas (Harith) II, 26
Aretas III Philhellen, 26f., 33
Aretas IV Philopatris (Aeneas), 191–4, 246f.
Aristobulus I (Judas, Jehuda), 33, 37, 240
Aristobulus II, 26, 28, 30, 33ff., 81, 245
Aristobulus (III), Jonathan (brother-in-law of Herod the Great), 50f., 76, 80ff., 90, 98, 125, 130, 242
Aristobulus (IV) (son of Herod the Great and Mariamme [I]), 145, 184–7, 195–200, 219, 232, 237, 246, 248
Armenia, 128, 146, 247
Armenia Minor (lesser Armenia), 247
Arnon, River, 112
Arous (Haris), 117
Ascalon (Ashkelon), 22f., 31, 35, 78, 96, 136, 166f., 174, 178, 188, 238, 247
Ashdod, see Azotus
Asia Minor (Asia, Bithynia, Cilicia, Ionia, Pontus), 13, 31, 35, 40, 48f., 54f., 60, 97, 115, 120, 145, 178, 180f., 184, 200, 237, 247
Assumption of Moses, 66, 238
Assyria (Adiabene), 31, 106, 157, 223, 235
Atargatis (Tanit), 128, 139
Athens, 11, 97
Atratinus, Lucius Sempronius, 50
Augustus (Octavian), 11, 14f., 30, 44, 48ff., 60, 85–8, 90, 92, 94–8, 106f., 109, 117f., 126f., 130, 137, 139, 141–9, 164, 168ff., 173ff., 177f., 180, 184–8, 190–8, 201, 203ff., 211–14, 216, 220, 225, 230, 232, 236, 244, 246, 248
Aujeh, River, 170
Auranitis (Hauran), 88, 137f., 144, 189, 244
Avdat, see Oboda
Azotus (Ashdod), 96, 122, 212

Baalbek, see Heliopolis

Baalshamin, 117, 138
Bab-el-Mandeb, Straits of, 141f.
Baba ben Buta, 243
Babas, sons of, 101
Babylon, Babylonia, 20, 23, 48, 65f.,
    72, 76, 90, 114, 124, 150, 162, 190,
    224, 235, 237, 241, 249
Bagoas, 205
Bannus, 72
Banyas, see Panias
Bar Kochba, Simon, see Simon
Baris, see Bira
Bashan, 96, 138
Batanea, 137f., 190
Beersheba, 147
Beirut, see Berytus
Bekaa, 137
Bel, 153
Ben Gurion, David, 66
Ben Sira, 63, 98, 123
Ben Zakkai, Johanan, see Johanan
Beneventum, 145
Berenice (I) (niece of Herod the
    Great), 185
Berenice (II) (great-grand-daughter
    of Herod the Great), 220, 236,
    238, 242
Berytus (Beirut), 197f., 219, 222, 248
Beth Shean, 242
Beth Shearim, 63, 114
Betharamphtha (Beth-Haram), 132,
    244
Bethlehem, 12, 20, 114, 161, 226
Bira (Baris), 73
Black Sea, 180
Boethus, 125
Bosphorus, see Cimmerian Bospho-
    rus (Crimea)
Brundusium (Brindisi), 49
Brutus, Quintus Caepio (Marcus
    Junius), 40, 44
Burg-el-Isaneh, see Isana
Byblus, 246
Byzantium, 134, 178

Caesar, Gaius Julius (dictator), 11,
    18, 34ff., 40, 49, 97, 168
Caesar, Sextus Julius, 40
Caesar Augustus, see Augustus
Caesarea Maritima (Stratonis Tur-
    ris), 114, 167–70, 174, 176, 178,
    182, 190f., 198f., 201, 210, 221f.,
    244
Caesarea Philippi, see Panias
Caligula, see Gaius
Callirhoe, 211
Canatha (Qanawat), 88, 138, 243
Candlestick, Seven-Branched, see
    Menorah
Capernaum, 246
Capharsaba, see Antipatris
Cappadocia, 60, 184, 187, 195ff.
Carmel (Idumaea), 243

Carmel, Mount, 31
Carus, 206
Cassius Longinus, Gaius, 40f., 44
Catullus, Marcus Valerias, ·8
Celenderis (Gilindere), 200
Chalcis beneath Lebanon (Gerrha),
    137, 220
Chalcis in Chalcidene, 247
Chios, 178f.
Christ, see Jesus
Christians, 11f., 22, 63, 65, 123, 223,
    229
Chronicles, Book of, 162
Cicero, Marcus Tullius, 18, 30, 180
Cilicia, see Asia Minor
Cimmerian Bosphorus (Crimea),
    178, 247
Claudius, 219
Cleopatra (wife of Herod the Great),
    200, 218
Cleopatra VII (queen of Egypt), 14,
    16, 34f., 47–50, 77–86, 90, 94f.,
    97f., 100, 115, 118, 137, 139, 147,
    166, 242, 247
Commagene, 55, 248
Commandment, second (forbidding
    statues, etc.), 19, 106, 117, 138,
    157f., 206ff., 247
Constantinople, see Byzantium
Coponius, 156
Coriolanus, Cnaeus Marcius, 39
Cos, 180
Costobarus, 82f., 100f., 115, 142
Council, Herod's, 92, 120, 200
Council, Jewish (Synedrion, San-
    hedrin), 38f., 61, 120, 240f., 248
Crassus, Marcus Licinius, 34, 46,
    146
Cyprus (fortress), 110, 130
Cyprus (island), 173, 224
Cyprus (mother of Herod the Great),
    23, 41, 83, 92, 110
Cyrene, 224

Damascus, 26, 28, 30, 39, 116ff.,
    137f., 144, 242
Dan, 147
Daniel, 67, 241
David, 58, 61, 66f., 69, 101, 127, 129,
    159f., 205ff., 231, 246
Dead Sea, 16, 23f., 47, 54, 65, 70,
    78, 85f., 92, 110–13, 116, 119, 125,
    132, 147, 211
Dead Sea Scrolls, see Qumran
Decapolis (Transjordan), 31, 96f.,
    147, 166, 242
Dedan, 244
Dellius, Quintus, 80, 249
Demetrius II, 242
Deuteronomy, 20, 23, 43, 207
Dionysius Exiguus, 248
'Dispersion' (Jews outside Judaea),
    13, 66, 180–3, 223f.

Dium (Tell-el-Ashari), 87
Docas (Ain Duyuk, near Jericho),
    243
Dome of the Rock, see Omar Mosque
Domitian, 222
Doris, 43, 109, 145, 184–7, 200f.
Druz (Jebel), Druses, 138, 144
Drusus senior (Nero Drusus), 169,
    245
Dura Europos, 245
Dusares, 193

Ecclesiasticus, 63f., 98, 123, 166
Ecdippa (Haziv, Ez-Zib), 46
Ed-Deir, 193
Edom, 20, 26, 101, 170; see also
    Idumaea
Egra (two towns), 240, 246
Egypt, 13f., 18, 26, 30, 35f., 47–50,
    59, 77, 79f., 84, 86, 88, 90, 95, 97,
    101f., 115ff., 121f., 128, 140f., 147,
    162, 165, 168, 171ff., 180, 202, 208,
    224, 241, 248
Eilat, see Elat
El-Aqsa, Mosque, 154
El-Arish, see Rhinocolura
El-Harithiyye, 114
El-Higr, see Egra
El-Hubbeisa, see Herodium
El-Mashnaka, see Machaerus
El-Medieh, see Modin
El-Wejh, see Egra
Elagabalas, 244
Elat (Eilat), 14, 23f., 26, 241
Eleazer ben Zadok, 247
Elijah, 210
Emmaus (Kuloniyeh), 223
En-Gedi, 23
En-Nakra, 138
Ephesus, 178
Er-Rame, see Betharamphtha
Er-Ras, 103
Esbon (Heshbon), 114, 116
Esdraelon, see Jezreel
Essenes, 71f., 125, 204, 242
Ethiopia, 21
Eudaemon (Aden), 140f.
Euphrates, River, 46, 84
Eurycles, Gaius Julius, 195
Ez-Zara, Hammam, see Callirhoe
Ez-Zib, see Ecdippa
Ezekias (Hezekiah), 38, 221
Ezekiel, 73

Fandaqumia, Five Villages, see Pente
    Komai
Fureidis, Jebel, see Herodium (West)
Fusail, see Phasaelis

Gaba, 114
Gabinius, Aulus, 34, 44, 106
Gadara, 97, 148f., 166, 174
Gaius (Caligula), 218f., 246

Gaius Caesar (grandson of Augustus), 164, 217f., 246
Galatians, 60, 97, 115, 214
Galilee (Galil), 18f., 31, 36–40, 44, 46, 52ff., 56, 61, 114, 117, 121, 132, 136, 148, 166, 174, 212, 216, 221, 236, 241, 245
Galilee, Sea of (Lake Gennesaret, Tiberias), 37, 96, 137, 147
Gallus, Aelius, 141
Gamara, 249
Gaulanitis (Golan), 14, 40, 88, 137f.
Gaza, 14, 23, 26, 31, 52, 78, 82, 85, 149, 166f.
Gazara (Gezer), 240
Gazith, 38
Geba (Gibeah), 166
Gehenna, *see* Hinnom
Gemellus, 117
Gennesaret, Lake, *see* Galilee, Sea of
Gerasa (Jerash), 127, 153
Gerizim, Mount, 31
Germans, 115, 202, 214
Gerrha, *see* Chalcis beneath Lebanon
Gibeah, *see* Geba
Gilead, 78, 138, 147
Gilindere, *see* Celenderis
Glaphyra (daughter of Archelaus [I] Sisennes), 184f., 187
Glaphyra (mother of Archelaus [I] Sisennes), 184
Golan Heights, *see* Gaulanitis
Greece, Greeks, 13f., 22, 26, 31, 97, 103f., 108f., 115–21, 148f., 174, 179, 227f., 231, 235, 237

Haberim, *see* Pharisees
Hadrian, 224, 243
Haifa, 168
Hammam-ez-Zara, *see* Callirhoe
Hammath, 245
Hananel, *see* Ananel
Hanina ben Dosa, Rabbi, 65
Haram-al-Sherif, *see* Temple
Haran, *see* Carrhae
Haris, *see* Arous
Harissah, *see* Oresa
Harith, *see* Aretas
Hasmonaeans (Maccabees), 21, 30f., 34, 38, 40, 42f., 46, 48, 51f., 54, 57, 59, 62, 65ff., 69, 71, 73, 75f., 82, 85, 90, 92, 96–101, 103f., 109, 114ff., 121, 125f., 145, 147, 151, 160, 162, 165, 173, 180, 184, 187, 199f., 206, 210, 225, 233, 235f., 243
Hauran, *see* Auranitis
Haziv, *see* Ecdippa
Hebron, 20, 47, 101f.
Helena of Adiabene (Assyria), 157, 223
Heliopolis (Baalbek), 137

Heracles (Hercules), 56, 245
Hermon, Mount, 54, 147
Herod (II) (Herod Philip, son of Herod the Great), 200, 202, 246f.
Herod (III) (Chalcis beneath Lebanon), 220, 242, 246f.
Herod Agrippa I, II, *see* Agrippa
Herod Antipas, *see* Antipas (II)
Herod Archelaus, *see* Archelaus (II)
Herodians, 221f., 229, 247
Herodias, 216, 247
Herodium (East) (El-Hubbeisa), 113, 147
Herodium (West) (Jebel Fureidis), 46, 113f., 176, 214, 244
Heshbon, *see* Esbon
Hezekiah, *see* Ezekias
Hillel the Elder, 18, 64ff., 116, 174, 206, 224, 241
Himyarites, 140, 244
Hinnom (Gehenna) Valley, 125, 127
Hippicus, 127f.
Hippos (Susita), 96, 148
Hispania, *see* Spain
Horshah, *see* Oresa
Huldah Gates, 154
Huleh, *see* Ulatha
Hygras, *see* Egra
Hyrcania, 85, 110, 113, 176, 212
Hyrcanus I, *see* John Hyrcanus
Hyrcanus II (Jehonathan, Jonathan), 26ff., 30, 33f., 36, 38–44, 46, 48, 50f., 57, 62, 72f., 76, 90, 92, 98, 115, 120, 237

Idumaea, 18, 20–3, 26, 37f., 40f., 47f., 50ff., 54, 62, 82f., 92, 94, 99ff., 103, 115, 117, 121, 128, 132, 136, 143, 147ff., 167, 173, 185, 190f., 200, 216, 227f., 231, 238, 249
Ilium (Troy), 118, 180
India, 140f., 146, 173
Innocents, Massacre of the, *see* Massacre
Ionia, *see* Asia Minor
Irenaeus, 117
Isaac, 101, 159
Isaiah, Book of, 123, 205
Isana, 57
Ituraea, *see* Arabs

Jabbok, River, 54
Jacob, 21, 101
Jaffa, *see* Joppa
Jamnia (Yavne), 31, 96, 122, 212, 224
Jannaeus, Alexander, *see* Alexander Jannaeus
Jason, 179, 201
Jeba, *see* Geba
Jebel Druz, *see* Druz
Jebel Fureidis, *see* Herodium (West)

Jebel Hauran, *see* Auranitis
Jebusites, 160, 245
Jehonathan, *see* Alexander Jannaeus, Aristobulus (III)
Jehuda, *see* Aristobulus (I)
Jerash, *see* Gerasa
Jeremiah, 207
Jericho, 54, 56, 67, 78, 81, 85, 96, 110f., 113, 130, 132, 166, 173, 196, 210f., 244,
Jerusalem, 11, 14, 18, 20, 28, 31, 34, 36, 38–44, 46, 52, 54, 57–9, 62, 64, 71, 73, 83, 85, 96, 101, 103ff., 110–15, 125–8, 130, 132, 142, 148, 150–64, 166f., 172f., 176, 180f., 187, 201f., 206, 210, 219f., 222ff., 232, 242f., 247
Jesus Christ, 12, 16, 18, 37f., 65, 79, 153f., 157f., 161f., 164, 171, 216, 229, 242, 248
Jezreel (Esdraelon), 31f., 36, 106, 114
Joazar, 247
Johanan ben Nappaha, 241
Johanan ben Zakkai, 224, 226, 241
John Hyrcanus I, 21, 31, 37, 85, 106, 206
John Hyrcanus II, *see* Hyrcanus II
John the Baptist, 70, 112, 216
Jonah, 116
Jonathan (Hasmonaean High Priest), 242
Jonathan, *see* Alexander Jannaeus, Aristobulus (III)
Joppa (Jaffa, Yafa), 31, 36, 52, 78, 122, 127, 130, 166f.
Joram, 210
Jordan, River, 14, 26, 31, 54, 87f., 97, 113, 132, 137, 147, 242
Joseph (husband of Mary), 158
Joseph (I) (uncle of Herod the Great), 83f., 92, 100
Joseph (II) (brother of Herod the Great), 47, 54, 56, 142
Josephus, 13, 19, 28f., 39, 46, 50, 54, 59, 62ff., 66, 71f., 75, 83, 98f., 117f., 120, 122f., 127, 130, 138, 152, 157, 170, 181f., 185, 209f., 216, 220, 222, 226, 231f., 235–8, 249
Judah (kingdom), 20, 150, 210, 243
Judas Aristobulus I, *see* Aristobulus
Judas Maccabaeus, 21, 28, 38, 151, 178f.
Judas (son of Sariphaeus), 209f.
Judas the Galilean, 38, 221
Judas the Patriarch ('Rabbi'), 249
Julia (daughter of Augustus), 145, 175f., 180
Julia Augusta, *see* Livia
Julius Caesar, *see* Caesar
Jupiter, 50, 223; *see also* Zeus
Jupiter Dusares, *see* Dusares

Jupiter, *see also* Zeus
Justus of Tiberias, 236, 238

Kefar Harissah, Horshah, *see* Oresa
Khirbet-et-Tannur, 139, 246
Khirbet Mird, *see* Hyrcania
Khirbet Qumran, *see* Qumran
Kidron Valley, 125, 154, 158f.
Koza, 83
Kuloniyeh, *see* Emmaus

Laodicea (Lattakia), 41, 82f., 92
Law, *see* Torah
Leah, 101
Lebanon, 20, 38, 46, 78, 128, 137, 146, 220; *see also* Arabs (Ituraean), Phoenicia
Leja, 138
Lentulus Spinther, Publius Cornelius, 40
Lepidus, Marcus Aemilius, 44, 85
Lesbos, 144, 178, 182
Lesser Armenia, *see* Armenia Minor
Levites, 67, 76
Lihyan, 244
Livia (Julia Augusta), 143, 191, 203
Livias, *see* Betharamphtha
Lucretius, 18
Lugdunum Convenarum (S. Bertrand de Comminges), 218
Luke, 245

Maccabees, *see* Hasmonaeans
Macedonia, 44, 106
Machares, 55
Macpelah, 101
Macrobius, 248
Magi (Wise Men), 12, 225
Malichus (Malik) (rebel in Judaea), 41
Malchus or Malichus (king of Nabataean Arabs), 47f., 86, 88, 90, 92, 139
Malthace, 109, 124, 145, 184, 200, 203, 212
Mamre, 102f.
Manetho, 245
Manual of Discipline, 70, 241f.
Marcellus, Marcus Claudius, 144f.
Mariamme (Mariamne) (I), 42f., 50, 57, 76, 80, 83ff., 92, 94, 98f., 109, 120, 123, 127, 145, 184f., 219, 232f., 236f.
Mariamme (II), 123ff., 127f., 145, 184, 202, 210, 246
Marissa (Maresha), 20, 48, 128, 240
Mark Antony, *see* Antonius, Marcus
Mary (mother of Jesus), 158
Masada, 47, 54, 92, 94, 110f., 132–6, 166, 222, 241, 244
Mashiah, *see* Messiah
Massacre of the Innocents, 12, 15, 226–30, 239, 248

Mattathias, *see* Antigonus, Matthew, Matthias
Matthew, 12, 154
Matthias (son of Margalothus), 209f.
Meleager, 97
Menaemus (Menahem), 71
Menorah (Seven-Branched Candlestick), 63, 162f.
Mesopotamia, 31; *see also* Babylon
Messalla Corvinus, Marcus Valerius, 50
Messiah, Messianic beliefs, 16, 46, 66–70, 205, 222, 224, 229, 248
Midrash, 239, 248
Miletus, 191
Mishnah, 238f., 249
Mithridates VI the Great (Pontus), 28
Mkaur, *see* Machaerus
Moab, 21, 111, 119, 139, 147
Modin (El-Medieh), 178, 242
Mohammedans, *see* Moslems
Moriah, Mount, 150, 159
Moses, 20, 63f., 76, 165, 238, 248
Moses, Assumption of, *see* *Assumption of Moses*
Moslems, 58, 102, 129; *see also* El-Aqsa, Omar, Ottoman Turks
Musa, River, 26
Mytilene, *see* Lesbos

Nabataea, *see* Arabs (Nabataean)
Nablus, *see* Neapolis
Nacebus (Naguib), 190
Natanya, 243
Nathanael, 38
Nativity, *see* Jesus Christ
Nazareth, 37f.
Neapolis (Shechem, Nablus), 32, 57
Nebuchadnezzar, 150, 180
Negev, 20, 47, 111
Nehemiah, 31
Neptune, 175
Nero, 211, 248
Nero Drusus, *see* Drusus senior
Nicolaus of Damascus, 14, 19, 23, 117f., 120, 130, 137, 146, 164, 173, 180, 182, 192, 198, 201, 203, 214, 216, 230ff., 236ff., 247
Nicopolis (Epirus), 103
Nimrud, Mount, 55
Nittai, 241
Numbers, Book of, 67

Oboda (Avdat), 24, 193, 246
Obodas II, 33
Obodas III, 139, 191ff.
Octavian, *see* Augustus
Olives, Mount of, 79, 150
Olympic Games, 186
Omar Mosque, 159
Omri, 106, 108
Ophel, Hill of, 206f.

Oresa, 47, 111
Ottoman Turks, 232

Pacorus, 44, 48, 55
Palmyra, 153, 246
Pan, 147, 244
Panias (Caesarea Philippi), 147, 219f.
Panion, 147, 244
Pannychis, 188
Pappus, 56
Parthia, 16, 28, 44, 46, 50, 52ff., 72f., 82, 97, 113, 128, 133, 137, 146, 181, 231, 248
Paul, 170, 220, 242
Pegae, *see* Antipatris
Peloponnese, 195
Pelusium, 34, 48, 85
Pentateuch, 116
Pente Komai (Five Villages), 109
Peraea (Transjordan), 111f., 116, 121, 132, 136, 147f., 166f., 206, 212, 216
Persia, 26, 116, 150, 204
Petah Tikvah, 170
Peter, 170
Petra, 24ff., 47, 54, 192f., 246
Pharisees, 16, 62–6, 123ff., 204ff., 222, 224, 229, 243, 248
Pharsalus, 35
Phasael, 27, 36, 38f., 41f., 44, 46ff., 58, 71, 115, 127–30, 170
Phasaelis, 170, 212
Pheroras (and wife), 54, 92, 144, 148, 185, 187, 189, 199–202, 204ff., 246
Philadelphia (Amman), 14, 88
Philip (disciple of Jesus), 38
Philip (son of Herod the Great), 200, 212, 218f., 246f.
Philip, Herod, *see* Herod (II)
Philippi, 44
Philistines, 21f., 96
Philo Judaeus, 71, 103, 176
Philodemus, 97
Phoenicia, 20, 22, 41, 46, 53, 78, 95, 136f., 174, 198
Phraates IV, 146
Pilatus, Pontius, 105, 170f., 216, 222, 242
Piraeus, 168
Platana (Aramain), 198
'Pollio', 241
Pollio, Gaius Asinius, 145
Pollio, Publius Vedius, 145
Pompeii, 130, 244
Pompeius Magnus, Cnaeus (Pompey the Great), 11, 18, 26, 28, 30ff., 34ff., 40, 47f., 106, 111, 137, 162, 167, 180
Pontius Pilatus, *see* Pilatus
Pontus, *see* Asia Minor
Psalms, 21, 63
Psalms of Solomon, 68

Ptolemais Ace (Acre, Akko), 53, 57, 95, 167
Ptolemies, *see* Egypt, and Ptolemy I, II, V, VI
Ptolemy of Ascalon, 238
Ptolemy of Damascus (brother of Nicolaus), 118, 243
Ptolemy (chief minister of Herod the Great), 117, 120, 216, 243
Ptolemy I Soter, 28, 243
Ptolemy II Philadelphus, 167
Ptolemy V Epiphanes, 244
Ptolemy VI Philometor, 209

Qanawat, *see* Canatha
Qilt, Wadi, 111, 130, 244
Qubbet-es-Sakhra, 159
Quirinius, Publius Sulpicius, 245
Qumran (Dead Sea Scrolls), 11, 16, 65, 67–72, 105, 116, 241f., 245
'Rabbi', *see* Judah the Patriarch
Raepta, 190
Raphaim, 103
Ras-al-Ain, *see* Antipatris
Rebecca, 101
Rebellions, Jewish, *see* Revolt
Red Sea, 26, 59
Revolt, First Jewish (First Roman War), 13, 133, 220, 222f., 234–7
Revolt, Second Jewish (Second Roman War), 13, 224
Rhinocolura (El-Arish), 31, 47
Rhodes, 49f., 90, 94f., 98, 118, 179
Roman Wars, First and Second, *see* Revolt
Ruth, 21

Sabaeans, 244
Sabbion, 81
Sadducees, 61–4, 125, 210, 221, 229, 241
Safa, 138
Saida, *see* Sidon
S. Bertrand de Comminges, *see* Lugdunum Convenarum
Salome (I) Alexandra, queen, *see* Alexandra
Salome (II) (sister of Herod the Great), 83f., 92, 98, 100f., 142ff., 185, 187, 189, 199, 201, 203, 205, 211, 244
Salome (III) (grand-daughter of Herod the Great), 112, 216, 218, 246
Salonae (Split, Spalato), 75
Samaria (Sebaste), 31f., 54, 57, 99, 106–10, 114, 117, 166, 168f., 176, 199, 244
Samaritis (Shomron), 31f., 40, 52, 92, 106, 110, 117, 121, 148, 168, 200, 202f., 212, 216, 245
Sameas, *see* Shammai

Samos, 178, 180
Samosata (Samsat), 55f.
Sanhedrin, *see* Council (Jewish)
Sarah, 101
Saramalla, 46
Sargon, 106
Sartaba, *see* Alexandrium
Saturninus, Gaius Sentius, 189, 198
Scaurus, Marcus Aemilius, 26, 33
Scribes (Sopherim), 64
Scrolls, Dead Sea, *see* Qumran
Scythopolis (Bethshean), 242
Sdot Yam, 169
Sea of Galilee, *see* Galilee
Sebaste, *see* Elaeussa, Samaria
Seeia, *see* Si'a
Selçuk, *see* Ephesus
Seleucids, 20, 28, 34, 48, 76f., 104, 116f., 121, 147, 150, 160, 165, 204, 243, 247
Seleucus, 21, 28
Sentius Saturninus, Gaius, *see* Saturninus
Sepphoris (Zippori), 54, 132, 247f.
Septuagint, 116
Sesmaios, 240
Sextus Caesar, *see* Caesar
Shadow of Death, Valley of the, *see* Qilt, Wadi
Shammai the Elder, 18, 64f., 206, 224, 241
Sharon, 106
Shechem, 32
Shemaiah, 241
Shomron, *see* Samaritis
Shullay, *see* Syllaeus
Si'a (Si', Seeia) (Temple of Zeus Baalshamin), 117, 138, 244
Sidon (Saida), 78, 198, 240
Silo, Poppaedius, 54
Simon (builder of the Temple), 150
Simon (I) Maccabaeus, 30f., 242f.
Simon (II) (father-in-law of Herod the Great), 124, 202
Simon Bar-Kochba, 224
Sinai, 20, 26, 63
Sinope (Sinop), 178, 218
Sirwah, *see* Sabaeans
Sohaemus, 92, 94, 98
Solomon, 14, 23, 30, 61, 68, 104, 147, 150, 152ff., 156ff., 160, 162, 164, 166, 206f., 245
Sopherim, *see* Scribes
Sosius, Gaius, 56–9
Spain, 28
Sparta, 95
Split, Spalato, *see* Salonae
Strabo, 237f., 249
Stratonis Turris, *see* Caesarea Maritima
Suetonius, 232
Sur, *see* Tyre
Susita, *see* Hippos

Syllaeus, 139, 141–4, 147, 189–92, 244, 246
Synedrion, *see* Council (Jewish)
Syria, 13, 20, 23, 26ff., 30–5, 38, 40f., 44, 46, 48, 50, 52ff., 58ff., 76f., 82ff., 86f., 90, 96, 106, 117, 122, 136f., 146f., 168, 170, 174, 188–91, 197f., 208, 219ff., 248

Tacitus, 97, 181, 232
Talmud, 161, 166, 239, 249; *see also* Gamara, Mishnah
Tanit, *see* Atargatis
Tarentum (Taranto), 200
Taurus, 243
Tekoa, 113
Tell-el-Akabe, 111
Tell-el-Ashari, *see* Dium
Temple, The (Jerusalem), 38, 58, 61, 64, 73, 75, 100, 103f., 126f., 150–64, 173, 176f., 181, 187, 204, 206–10, 223, 238, 242
Thessaly, 35
Thracians, 115, 214
Threx, 243
Tiberias, 236, 238, 247f.
Tiberias, Lake, *see* Galilee, Sea of
Tiberius, 143, 146, 171, 218, 220, 245
Tigranes IV, 247
Tigranes V, 247
Timagenes, 249
Tiro, 199
Titius, Marcus, 188
Titus, 162f., 220, 222ff., 236
Tobiads, 116
Torah (Five Books of the Law: Genesis, Exodus, Leviticus, Numbers, Deuteronomy), 43, 62–7, 72, 80, 96, 101, 116, 121, 123, 152, 161, 167, 182, 205, 207, 209f.; *see also* Commandment, Second
Trachonitis, 137f., 189ff.
Trajan, 224
Transjordan, *see* Arabs (Nabataean), Decapolis, Peraea
Troy, *see* Ilium
Turks, *see* Ottoman Turks
Tyre (Sur), 41, 44, 78, 166, 198, 246
Tyropoeon (Cheesemakers') Valley, 153

Ulatha (Holath Antioch), 246
Ulatha (Huleh), 147

Valley of the Shadow of Death, *see* Qilt, Wadi
Varus, Publius Quinctilius, 201ff.
Ventidius, Publius, 54
Vespasian, 222, 224, 247
Vienna (Vienne), 216
Vipsanius Agrippa, Marcus, *see* Agrippa

Virgil, 66
Volumnius, 115, 243, 246

Wadi Qilt, *see* Qilt
War of the Sons of Light and the Sons of Darkness, 72, 242
'Wilson's Arch', 155, 244
Wise Men, Three, *see* Magi

Yafo, *see* Joppa
Yavne, *see* Jamnia
Yemen, *see* Arabs (S. Arabian)

'Zacharias', 213, 244
Zacynthus (Zante), 59
Zadok, 61, 76
Zealots, 221

Zenodorus, 137, 144, 146ff.
Zerubbabel, 150, 152
Zeus, 117, 160
Zeus, *see also* Baalshamin, Dusares, Jupiter
Zif, 243
Zippori, *see* Sepphoris
Zuggoth, 64, 241